Success

Revision Guide

Science SATs

Levels 3-6

Brian Arnold, Hannah Kingston and Emma Poole

Contents

Biology

Chemistry

Chemistry

Physics

Life processes and cells

Cells are the building blocks of life. All living things are made up of cells. A living thing is called an organism. Plants and animals are organisms.

Is it alive?

To be alive you must have the following characteristics:
Movement (plant leaves move towards the Sun).
Respiration (releasing energy from food).
Sensitivity (responding to changes in the environment).
Growth (to adult size).
Reproduction (producing offspring).
Excretion (getting rid of waste products, such as carbon dioxide).
Nutrition (eating).

- Remember these using **MRS GREN**; or you could make up your own way of remembering.

Animal and plant cells

- The cells that make up plants and animals can be seen using a microscope and staining them so they show up more clearly.
- You need to know the differences between them.

They both have:	Only plant cells have:
Nucleus	Cell wall
Cytoplasm	Vacuole
Cell membrane	Chloroplasts

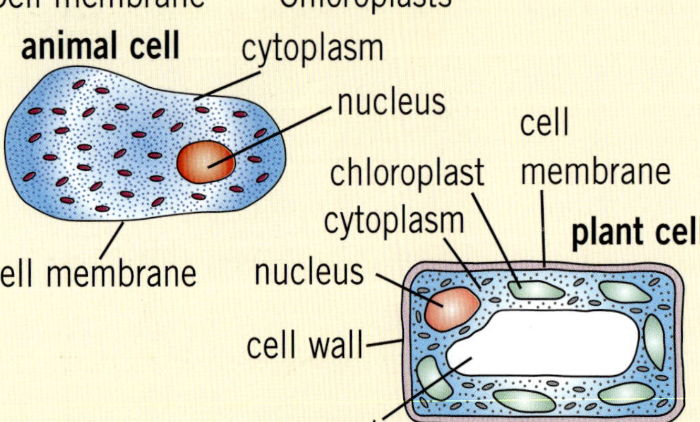

Nucleus – controls the cell. It controls everything the cell does. The nucleus also contains **all the information** needed to produce a new living organism.
Cytoplasm – where **chemical reactions** take place.
Cell membrane – holds the cell together and controls what passes **in and out** of the cell.
Cell wall – made of **cellulose**, which gives a plant cell **strength and support**.
Vacuole – contains a weak solution of salts and sugar called **cell sap**.
Chloroplasts – contain a green substance called **chlorophyll**. This absorbs the Sun's energy so that the plant can **make its own food by photosynthesis**.

Make sure you know the similarities, and in particular the differences, between an animal and a plant cell.

Cells, tissues, organs, organ system

- **A group of similar cells working together form a tissue**.
- An **organ** is made up of different tissues working together.
- Organs working together make **organ systems**.
- Cells group together to form tissues and organs until all the cells make up an organism.

Special cells

Some cells can change their shape in order to carry out a particular job. It's a bit like a factory where each person has their own job. It's more efficient this way. One cell can't do everything.

Specialised animal cells

- A **sperm cell** has a **tail** which enables it to swim towards the egg.

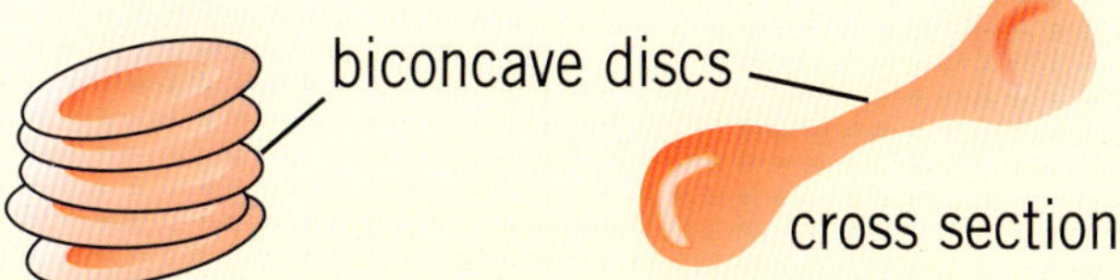

- **Red blood cells** carry oxygen around the body. **They have no nucleus**.

biconcave discs

cross section

- **Nerve cells** are shaped like wires to conduct messages around the body.
- **Egg cells** or **ova** are much larger than sperm. The nucleus contains chromosomes from the mother. In the cytoplasm is yolk, which provides a food store for the developing organism if fertilised.

cell membrane

nucleus

Specialised plant cells

- Root hair cells are **long and thin**, to absorb water and minerals from the soil. They increase the surface area of the roots.

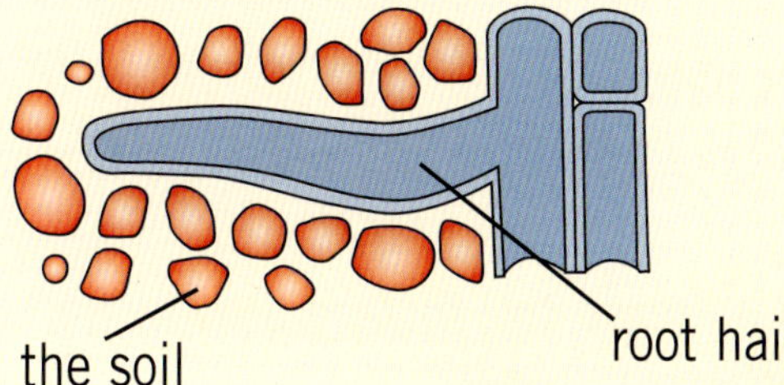

- **Palisade cells** have **lots of chloroplasts**. They are near the surface of the leaf so they can absorb sunlight for photosynthesis.

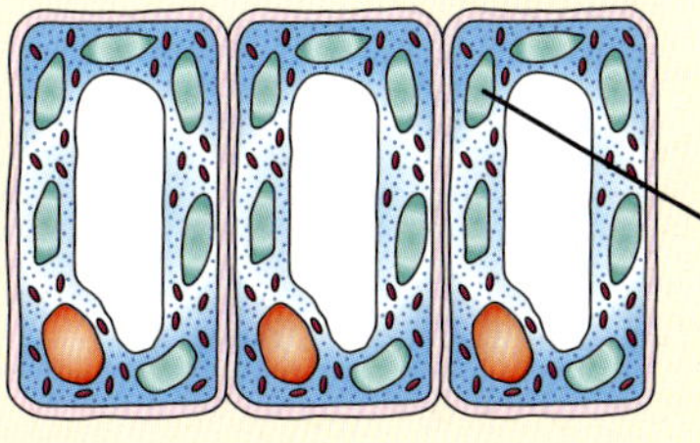

Learn the examples of specialised plant and animal cells. Note that they all have a nucleus, cell membrane and a cytoplasm.

KEY TERMS

- nucleus
- cytoplasm
- cell membrane
- cell wall
- vacuole
- chloroplasts

1. Name three differences between a plant and an animal cell.
2. What does the cell membrane do?
3. What does the cell wall do?
4. What is a specialised cell?
5. A group of similar cells carrying out the same job are called a _______?

Organ systems

Plant organs

- A plant's basic structure is divided up into **five parts**.
- Different parts of a plant have adapted to do a particular job or function.
- The plant carries out all the **seven life processes**, although some are not quite so obvious.
- Every cell in the plant will carry out **respiration**.

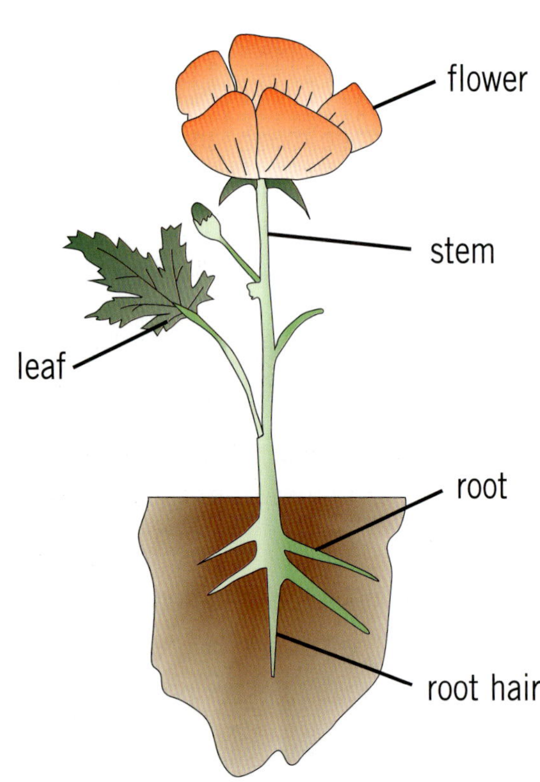

1. The flower

This contains the male and female sex organs. These make seeds.
The flower is usually brightly coloured to attract insects for pollination.

2. The stem

This holds the plant **upright**.
It contains hollow tubes called **xylem and phloem**.
Xylem tubes **carry water and dissolved minerals** from the root to the leaves.
Phloem carries glucose made by the leaf in photosynthesis up and down the plant.

3. The root

This anchors the plant in the soil.
It also takes up **water and minerals** from the soil.

4. The root hairs

Root hairs take up water and minerals from the soil.
Root hairs increase the surface area of the root for more efficient absorption.

Learn the five parts of a flowering plant and what they are for.

5. The leaf

- **The leaf is the organ of photosynthesis**. It makes all the food for the plant.
- The top layer of the leaf contains the palisade cells. This is where most photosynthesis takes place.
- The palisade cells contain lots of **chloroplasts**. The chloroplasts contain a pigment called **chlorophyll**. Chlorophyll absorbs sunlight for photosynthesis.
- On the lower surface of the leaf are tiny holes called **stomata**.
- The stomata open and close to let carbon dioxide in and water vapour and oxygen out.

Human organ systems

- The **seven life processes** are carried out by different systems in the human body.
- Three of the **nine organ systems** in the body are detailed below.
- The following are covered in detail on other pages in this book:

1) The skeletal system
2) The muscle system
3) The respiratory system
4) The digestive system
5) The circulatory system
6) The reproductive system.

Be able to name the nine organ systems of the body and say briefly what they do.

Nervous system

- We have **five sense organs**.
- They are the **nose** (smell), **eyes** (sight), **ears** (sound), **tongue** (taste) and **skin** (touch).
- All the sense organs contain nerves that detect changes in our surroundings.
- The nerves send signals to the brain and spinal cord. Together they make up the central nervous system.
- The brain and spinal cord respond by sending signals back to instruct our muscles what to do.

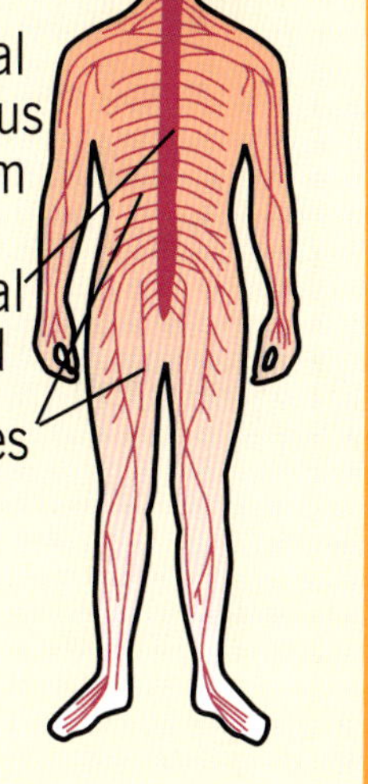

Excretory system

- The main organs of excretion are the kidneys.
- Cells produce waste products which go into the blood. Some of them are poisonous.
- The kidneys filter and 'clean' the blood by removing these waste products.
- The poisonous waste is turned into **urine** and stored in the bladder until ready to be released.

kidney
bladder

Endocrine system

- The endocrine system produces **hormones** in parts of the body called **glands**.
- The glands release the hormones into the **bloodstream**.
- Hormones travel a lot slower than nerve messages but their effects are usually longer lasting.
- Hormones control things like **menstruation** in women as well as the changes that occur to our bodies during puberty.

KEY TERMS

Make sure you understand these terms before moving on!

- xylem
- phloem
- root hairs
- hormones

QUICK TEST

1. What is the job of the leaf?
2. What is the name of the human organ system that produces hormones?
3. Which organ in the body controls the amount of urine you produce?
4. What do the palisade cells contain a lot of?
5. What are the tubes called that transport water and minerals to the leaf?

Nutrition and food tests

The nutrition groups are:

- **Carbohydrates, proteins, fat, vitamins and minerals, fibre and water.**
- **A balanced diet is made up of all of the above nutrients.**
- **There are chemical tests for carbohydrates, proteins and fats.**

proteins
fats
fibre

water
vitamins and
minerals
carbohydrates

A balanced diet

Carbohydrates

- **Carbohydrates** consist of starch and different types of sugar e.g. glucose (the sugar our bodies use for respiration).
- **We need carbohydrates to give us energy**.
- Starch is actually made up of smaller glucose molecules joined together. These are foods that contain a lot of carbohydrate:

Cereal

Chemical test for starch

- Add two drops of yellow/brown **iodine solution** to food solution.
- Solution will turn blue/black if starch is present.

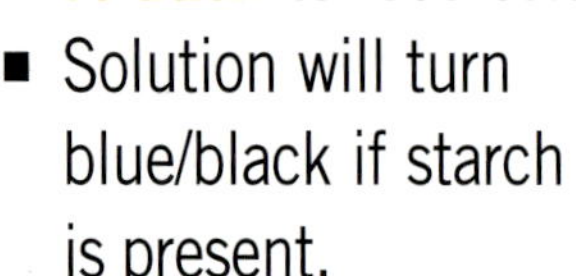

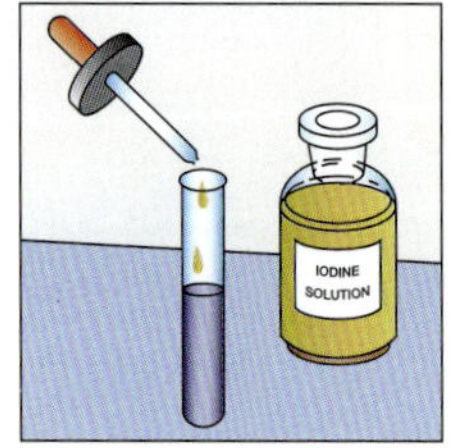

Chemical test for glucose

- Add a few drops of **Benedict's solution** to food solution.
- Heat in a water bath until it boils.
- If glucose is present, an orange/red precipitate will form.

BENEDICT'S SOLUTION

Learn the food tests for starch, glucose, protein and fats.

Fats

- **Fats** are made from fatty acids and glycerol.
- **We need fats for a store of energy, to make cell membranes and for warmth (insulation).**

These are foods containing a lot of fat:

Chemical test for fat

- Add $2\,cm^3$ of **ethanol** to the food solution in a test tube and shake.
- Add $2\,cm^3$ of **water** to the test-tube and shake again.
- Fat is present if the solution turns **cloudy white**.

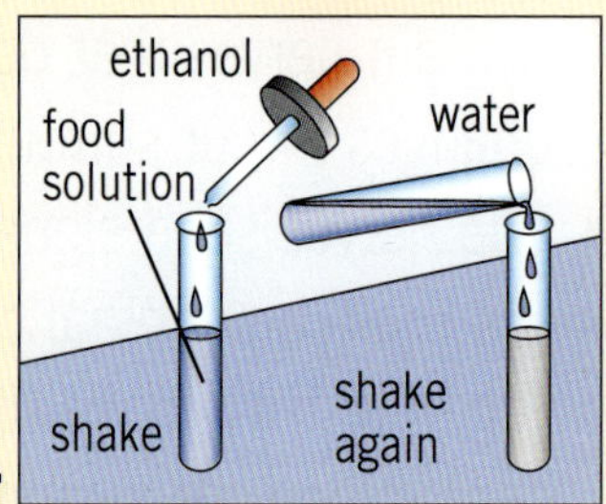

Water

Water makes up approximately 65% of your body weight. Food and drink contain water. Water is important because:

- Our blood plasma is mainly water.
- Chemical reactions in our cells take place in water.
- Waste products are removed from our bodies in water e.g. urine and sweat.

Don't forget to learn examples of food belonging to each food group.

Vitamins and minerals

We only need these in small amounts, but they are essential for good health.

Many vitamins and minerals are found in fruit, vegetables and cereals.

Deficiency diseases are caused by a lack of vitamins and minerals.

Vitamin C keeps the skin strong and supple; without it the skin cracks and the gums bleed (called scurvy).

Vitamin D helps the bones harden in children; without it the bones stay soft (a disease called rickets).

We need the mineral **iron** for making haemoglobin and the mineral **calcium** for healthy bones and teeth.

Fibre

- Fibre, or roughage, comes from plants.
- Fibre is not actually digested; it just keeps food moving smoothly through your system.
- Fibre provides something for your gut muscles to push against. It is a bit like squeezing toothpaste through a tube.
- It prevents constipation.

These are two foods containing a lot of fibre:

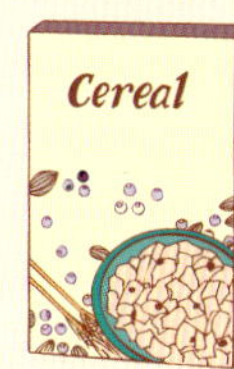

Cereal

KEY TERMS

Make sure you understand these terms before moving on!

- carbohydrates
- iodine solution
- Benedict's solution
- fats
- proteins
- copper sulphate
- sodium hydroxide

Protein

- Key parts of your body cells are mostly made of protein.
- **Proteins** are made up of lots of amino acids.
- **We need protein to repair and replace damaged cells or to make new cells during growth.**

These foods contain a lot of protein:

Chemical test for protein (the Biuret test)

- Add some weak **copper sulphate** to the food solution.
- Carefully add drops of **sodium hydroxide** to the solution.
- If protein is present, the solution gradually turns purple.

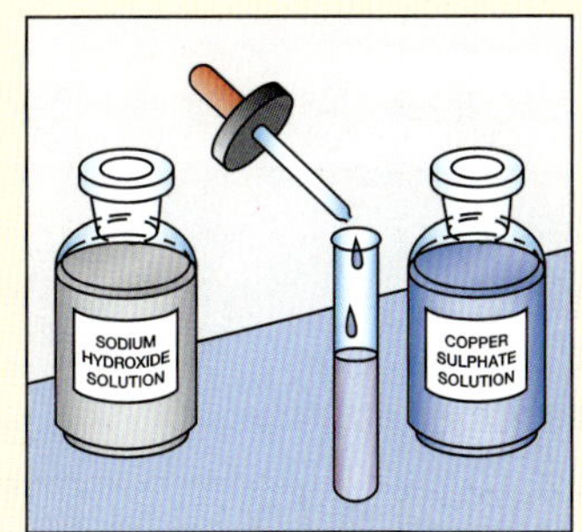

QUICK TEST

1. What do we use carbohydrates for?
2. What is the chemical test for starch?
3. What is the chemical test for glucose?
4. Why do our bodies need fat?
5. Why is protein important to our cells?
6. What is the chemical test for protein?
7. Why is fibre important?

The digestive system

- **The digestive system is really one long tube called the gut. If it were unravelled it would be about nine metres long!**
- **Digestion begins with the teeth and ends at the anus.**

Teeth begin digestion

There are four kinds of teeth, each have a role in **breaking up your food**:

premolars grind and chew your food

incisors bite your food

molars chew up your food

canines tear your food

Enzymes speed things up

- Starch, protein and fats are **large**, **insoluble food** molecules.
- **Enzymes** break down the food molecules into smaller molecules which can be absorbed through the wall of the intestine.
- **Enzymes are specific**. There are **three main enzymes** in your system.

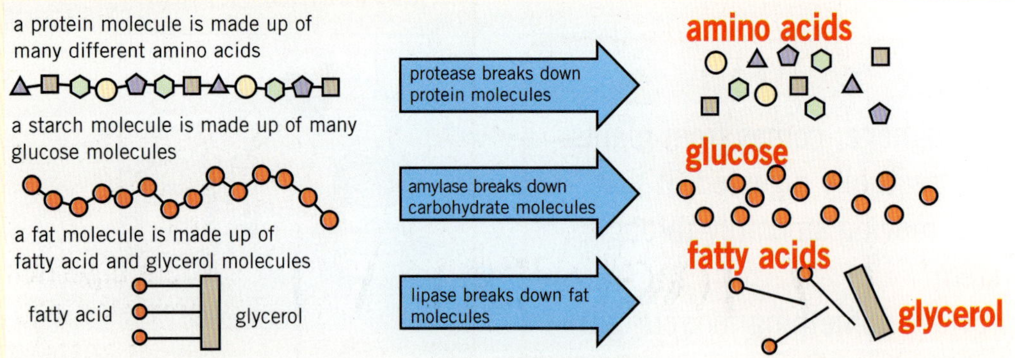

- Food is now small enough to be absorbed through the small intestine wall and into the bloodstream to be carried to the cells.

The model gut

Experiment

- You can prove that a carbohydrase called amylase breaks down starch into sugar by setting up the experiment shown.
- After leaving the test tube for 10 minutes in a water bath (maintained at 37°C), test the water for starch and for glucose.
- Visking tubing acts like a model gut; it has tiny holes in it that will only allow small molecules through.

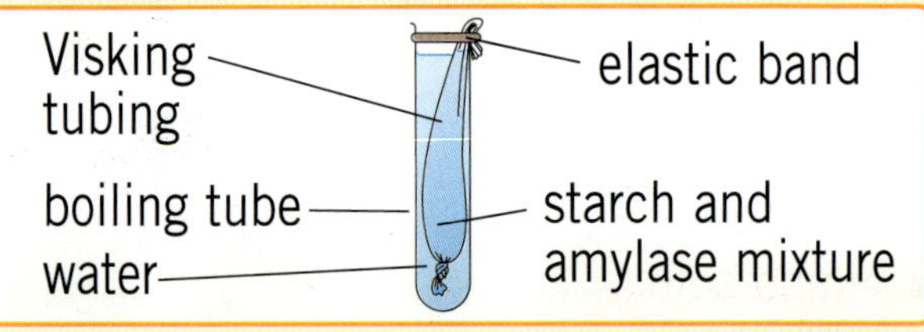

Results

- The water should test negative for starch (yellow) and positive for sugar (orange).
- The results show that the starch has been broken down into glucose.

Digestion

- Digestion is the breaking down of **large, insoluble** food molecules into **small, soluble** molecules so that they can be absorbed into the bloodstream.
- The large, insoluble molecules are starch, protein and fat.
- This action is speeded up (catalysed) by **enzymes**.

1 **Mouth** contains teeth that begin digestion by breaking up food

2 **Salivary glands** secrete amylase which is a carbohydrase enzyme. Mucus lubricates the food as it passes down the oesophagus

3 **Oesophagus** sometimes called the gullet

4 **Stomach** has muscular walls which churn up the food and mix it with **gastric juices** that the stomach produces. The gastric juices contain protease enzymes and hydrochloric acid

Pancreas produces **carbohydrase**, protease and lipase enzymes

5 **Small intestine** also produces all three types of enzymes. This is where **digestion** is **completed** and dissolved food is **absorbed** into the bloodstream

6 **Liver** produces bile which **neutralises stomach acid** so that the enzymes in the small intestine can work properly. It also breaks fats into small droplets. This is called emulsification. Emulsification increases the surface area of the fat making it easier for lipase to act

7 **Large intestine** receives any food that has not been absorbed into the blood. Excess water and salts are removed from the food. The remaining solid food is turned into **faeces**

8 **Rectum** where the faeces are stored before they leave the body via the **anus**

Note: Food does not pass through the **pancreas**, **liver** and **gall bladder**.

- enzymes
- amino acids
- glucose
- fatty acids
- glycerol
- emulsification
- carbohydrase enzyme
- protease
- lipase enzymes

1. Name the four types of teeth.
2. What does starch get digested into?
3. What does protein get digested into?
4. What do fats get digested into?
5. Where in the digestive system does the food get absorbed into the bloodstream?

The heart

- **The heart has its own blood supply called coronary arteries.**

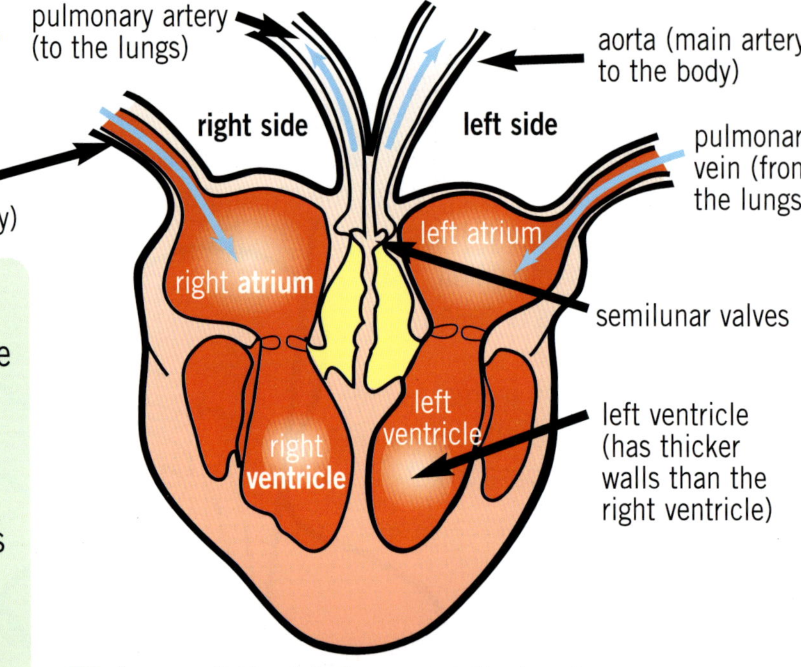

Four key points to remember...

1. Arteries carry blood away from the heart.
2. Veins carry blood back into the heart.
3. The left side of the heart receives oxygenated blood.
4. The right side of the heart receives deoxygenated blood.

Learn all the labels around the heart as you may be asked to fill in the missing labels on a diagram.

Veins

- **Veins** carry **deoxygenated** blood.
- The **pulmonary vein** is the only vein to carry **oxygenated blood**. This is because it has just been to the lungs. Find it on the diagram of the heart.
- Veins carry the blood **back to the heart** from the body at low pressure.
- They have **valves** to prevent the blood flowing backwards.

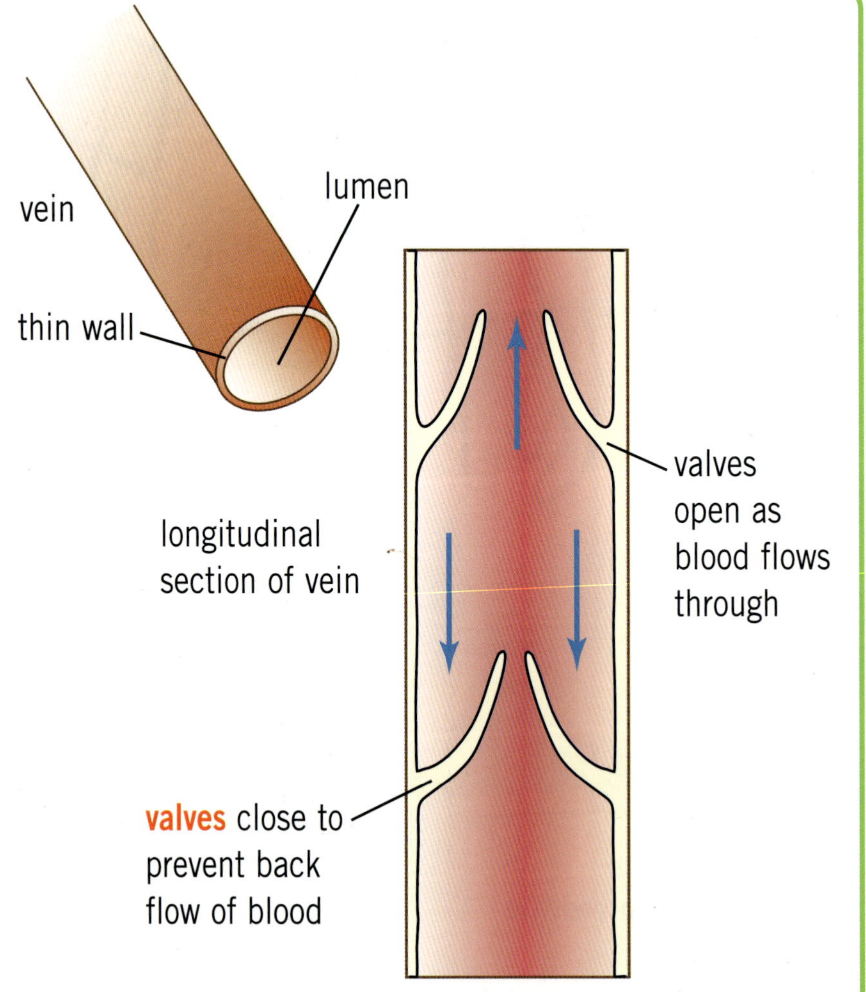

Learn the differences between arteries, veins and capillaries.

The heart

- The heart is a double pump.
- It has four chambers, the top two are the left and right **atria** and the bottom two are the left and right **ventricles**.
- The right side pumps blood to the lungs to be **oxygenated**.
- The left side pumps blood around the body and it becomes **deoxygenated** as it drops off oxygen to the cells.

Arteries

- **Arteries** carry **oxygenated** blood.
- The **pulmonary artery** is the only artery to carry **deoxygenated blood**. This is because it is going to the lungs to pick up oxygen. Find it on the diagram.
- Arteries carry blood **away** from the heart towards the body at **high pressure**.
- They have very **thick**, **elastic walls** to withstand the high pressure.
- The high pressure in the arteries causes a **pulse** that can be felt especially in the wrist and neck.
- Arteries narrow down into capillaries.

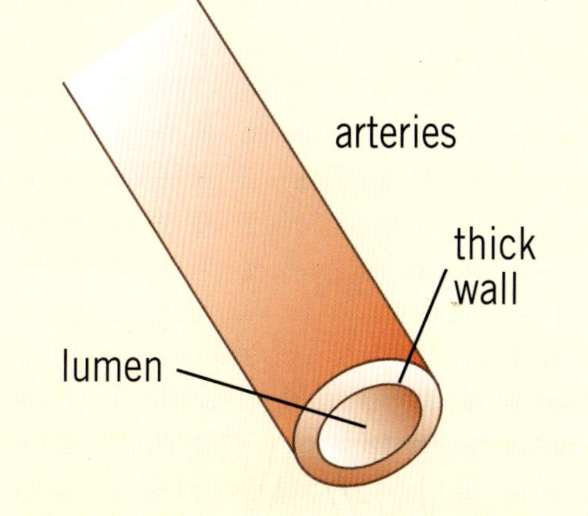

KEY TERMS

Make sure you understand these terms before moving on!

- veins
- capillaries
- atria
- valves
- arteries
- ventricles

Capillaries

- **Capillaries** are only **one cell thick** and have very thin walls, to allow oxygen and nutrients to diffuse out of them.
- They are the site of exchange between the blood and the cells of the body.

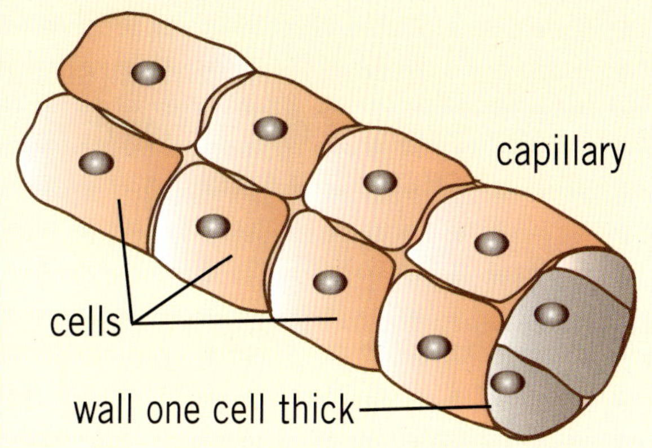

Coronary heart disease

- The coronary arteries supply the heart with oxygen and nutrients.
- Excess cholesterol, alcohol, stress and smoking all contribute to blocking these arteries.
- Excess cholesterol can 'fur' up the arteries and block blood flow. This can result in a heart attack.

QUICK TEST

1. Which blood vessels carry blood away from the heart?
2. Which blood vessels carry blood back to the heart?
3. Which side of the heart receives oxygenated blood?
4. Why do capillaries have very thin walls?
5. What is the purpose of the valves?

Blood and circulation

The 'River of Life' consists of red blood cells, white blood cells and platelets suspended in a fluid called plasma.

- **The *circulatory system* transports substances around the body to where they are needed and removes waste products.**
- **The heart is a pump that pushes the blood around the circulatory system.**

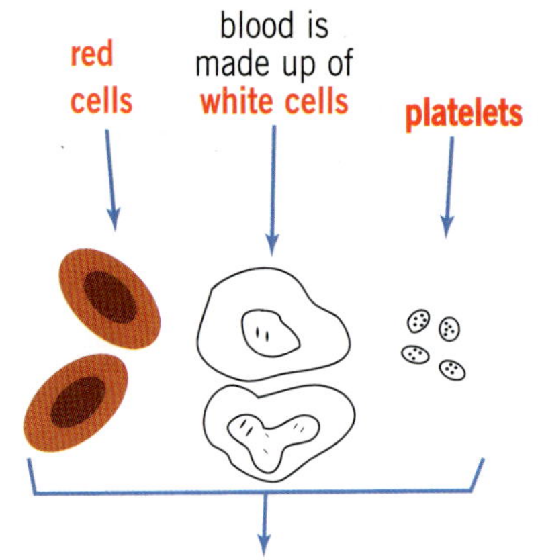

White blood cells

- **Their main function is to defend against disease.**
- They are larger than red blood cells and have a nucleus.

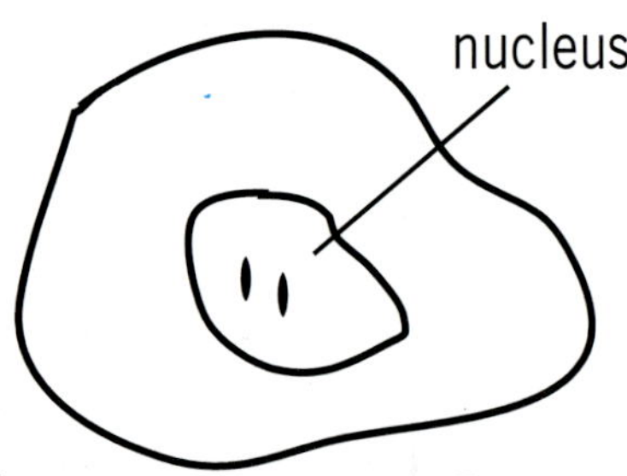

Learn the functions of the four parts of the blood.

Red blood cells

- **Their function is to carry oxygen to all the cells of the body.**
- They contain a substance called **haemoglobin**.
- They have **no nucleus** (more room for oxygen).
- The red blood cell is shaped to absorb as much oxygen as possible.
- They are very small and flexible so they can squeeze through the small capillaries and supply the cells with oxygen.

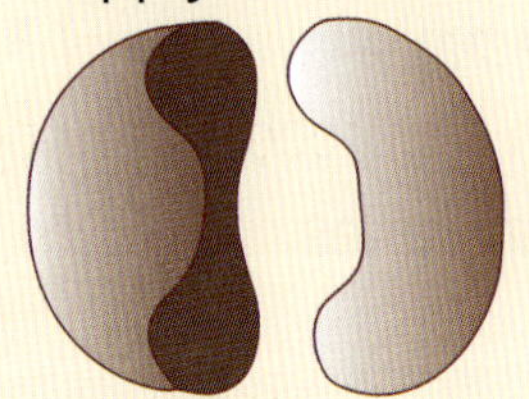

This diagram shows a red blood cell that has been sectioned to show its characteristic shape.

Platelets

- Platelets are fragments of cells.
- **Their function is to clot the blood** so you do not bleed to death if you cut yourself.

Plasma

- Plasma is a yellow fluid.
- It consists of mainly water, but has many substances dissolved in it. These include **soluble food**, **salts**, **carbon dioxide**, **urea**, **hormones**, **antibodies** and **plasma proteins**.
- **Its function is to transport these substances around the body.**

Exchange of substances

- The blood flows in the blood vessels around the circulatory system.
- 1 The arteries narrow down into capillaries and bring oxygen and dissolved food to all the cells of the body.
- 2 The cells can only exchange substances in the capillary networks of the body.
- 3 The capillaries then join up to form veins that take the blood back to the heart.
- At the cells: oxygen and food diffuse into the cells from the capillaries and waste and carbon dioxide diffuse out of the cells into the capillaries.

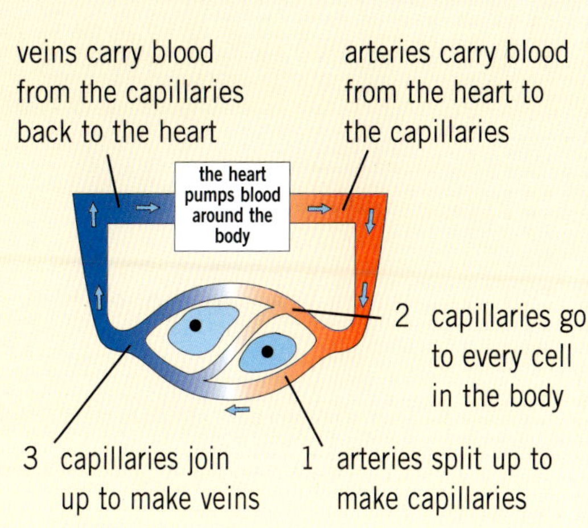

Circulation

- **We have a double circulation system**. The blood passes through the heart twice on one circuit of the body.
- The heart has two sides that act as two separate pumps.
- The **left side** of the heart has a much **thicker**, **walled ventricle** as this side has to pump blood at high pressure all around the body.
- Follow the passage of blood as it leaves the heart on the left side.
  1. The main artery of the heart, the aorta, takes **oxygenated blood** to the capillaries in the body.
  2. The blood delivers oxygen and food to the body cells and collects waste and carbon dioxide.
  3. The **deoxygenated blood** travels back to the right side of the heart in the main vein, the **vena cava**.
  4. The blood then leaves the heart in the pulmonary artery to collect oxygen from the lungs.
  5. The pulmonary vein brings oxygenated blood back to the heart and the cycle begins again.

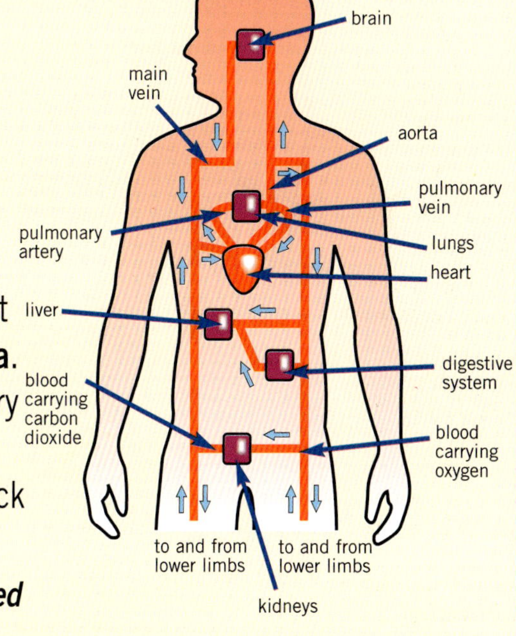

Oxygenated means the blood has oxygen, deoxygenated means the blood has given up its oxygen to the cells.

- circulatory system
- white cells
- plasma
- oxygenated blood
- red cells
- platelets
- haemoglobin
- deoxygenated blood

QUICK TEST

1. What four main things does blood contain?
2. Which type of blood cell has no nucleus?
3. Why does the blood go to the lungs?
4. Why is the circulation system called a double circulation system?

Movement

The skeleton

- The skeleton is made of bones that are strong and rigid.
- Bones are shaped like tubes; the hollow part in the middle is filled with **bone marrow**.
- The skeleton of many animals, including humans, has three important roles to play:
  1. **Support** – without the skeleton we would fall to the floor.
  2. **Protection** – the skeleton protects our organs. The skull protects the brain and the ribs protect the heart and lungs.
  3. **Movement** – many parts of the skeleton are jointed so that movement can take place. Movements are made by muscles. Muscles are attached to the skeleton by **tendons**.

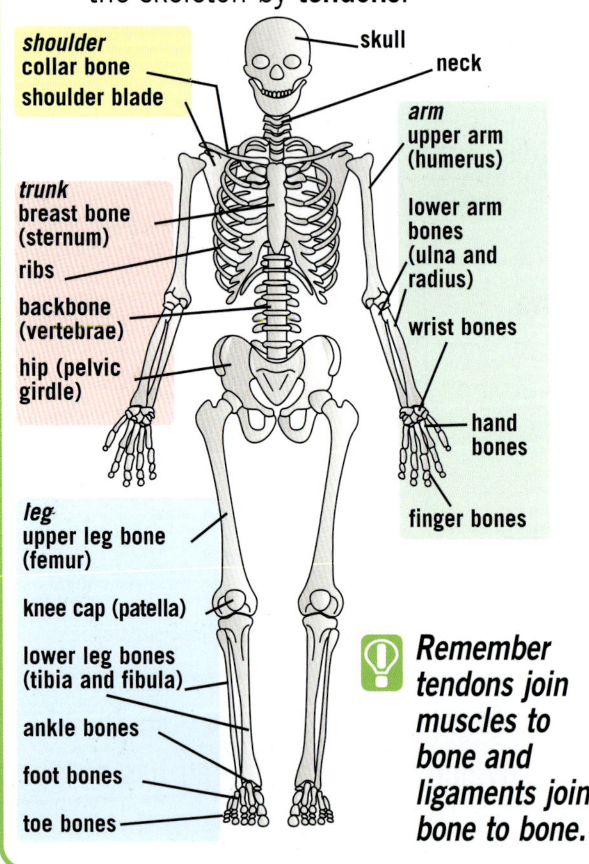

Remember tendons join muscles to bone and ligaments join bone to bone.

Joints

Joints occur when two bones meet. They allow movement.

The bones are held together by strong fibres called ligaments.

There are several different types of joint:

1. **Hinge** – e.g. knee joint, elbow joint, wrist joint.
2. **Ball and socket** – e.g. hip joint, shoulder joint.
3. **Partly movable** – e.g. the spine.
4. **Fixed** – e.g. the skull.

Ball and socket and hinge joints are also known as **synovial joints**.

The ends of the bone in these joints have a layer of **smooth cartilage**.

Cartilage acts as a **shock absorber** that prevents the wearing away of the surfaces.

The cartilage is covered by synovial fluid.

Synovial fluid helps **reduce friction** at the joint.

Reflex actions

- Often the messages from the sense organs are sent very quickly to the brain, or even just to the spinal cord, and back again.
- For example, if you touch something hot you automatically, without thinking, move your hand away.
- **This is called a reflex action** and often protects you from harm.

Control of movement

In order for muscles to move parts of your body they have to be told what to do. Your body is controlled by the central nervous system (the brain and spinal cord). The **central nervous system** is linked to the rest of the body by **nerves**. Signals travel along these nerves to the central nervous system and back to the muscle to tell it what to do.

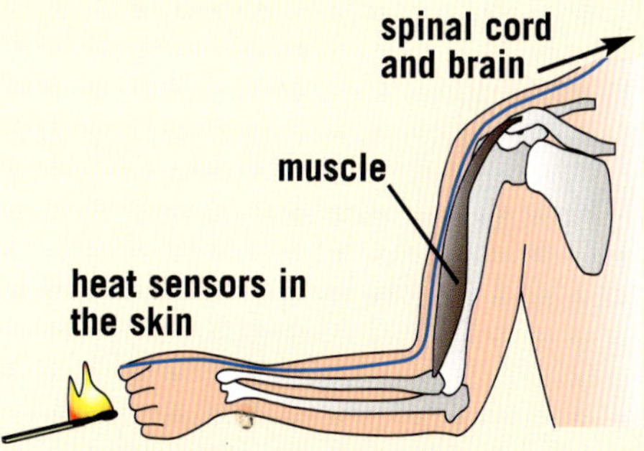

We have sense organs that detect changes to our environment and send messages to the brain.

Our **sense organs** are:	They respond to:
■ eyes	■ light
■ nose	■ chemicals in the air
■ ears	■ sound
■ tongue	■ chemicals in food
■ skin	■ touch, pressure, heat and pain

- Our skin covers the whole of our body, so it is in contact with the outside environment. It has many **sensors**.
- The skin also has a fat layer for insulation; in hairy animals the hair also traps air for extra insulation.

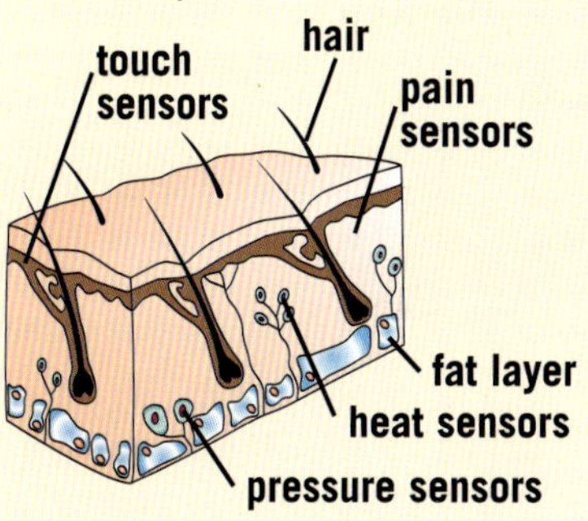

Muscles

- The muscles provide the force needed to move the bones at joints.
- Muscles can only pull; they cannot push.
- When a muscle pulls it gets shorter and fatter: it **contracts**.
- When a muscle is not contracting it relaxes and returns to its normal size.
- Muscles all over the body work in pairs; while one contracts the other relaxes.
- These are called **antagonistic pairs** because they work in opposite directions to produce movement.
- Muscles are attached to bones by **tendons**.
- An example of an antagonistic muscle pair is the **triceps** and **biceps** of the arms.

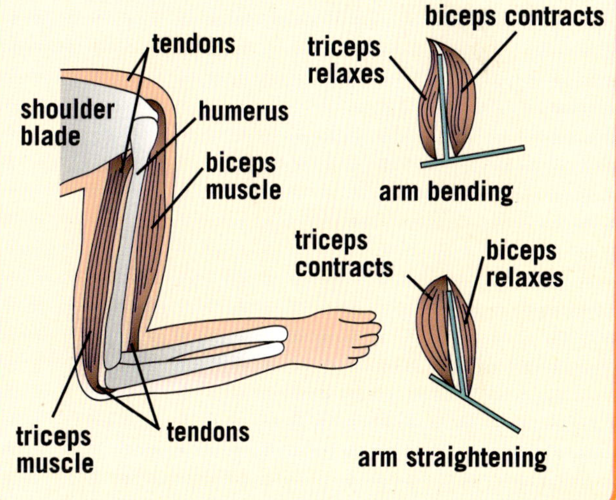

KEY TERMS

- ligaments
- synovial fluid
- antagonistic pairs
- cartilage
- reflex action
- tendons

QUICK TEST

1. What is your skeleton for?
2. Where do joints occur?
3. What is synovial fluid for?
4. What are antagonistic muscles?
5. What are tendons?
6. What are ligaments?

The lungs and breathing

- **The lungs are two big air sacs in your upper body.**
- **Their job is to supply oxygen to your cells when you breathe in and get rid of the waste product carbon dioxide when you breathe out.**
- **This is called gas exchange.**

Breathing in

- Ribs move up and out pulled by the intercostal muscles.
- The diaphragm gets pulled down.
- The volume increases, and pressure decreases, causing air to rush into the lungs.

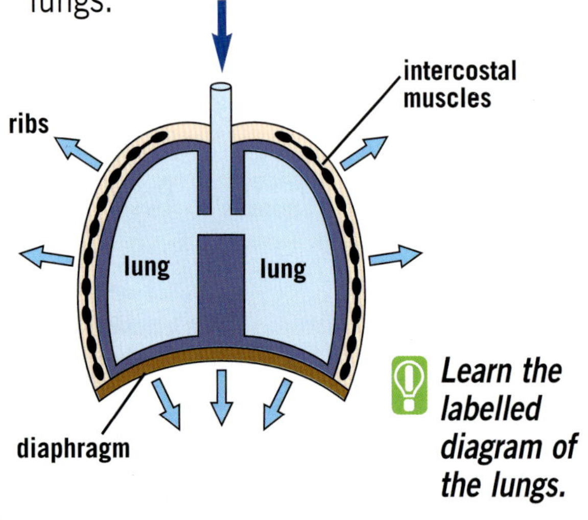

Learn the labelled diagram of the lungs.

Breathing out

- The intercostal muscles relax and the ribs move down and in.
- The diaphragm also relaxes and moves up.
- The volume decreases, pressure increases and air is forced out of the lungs.

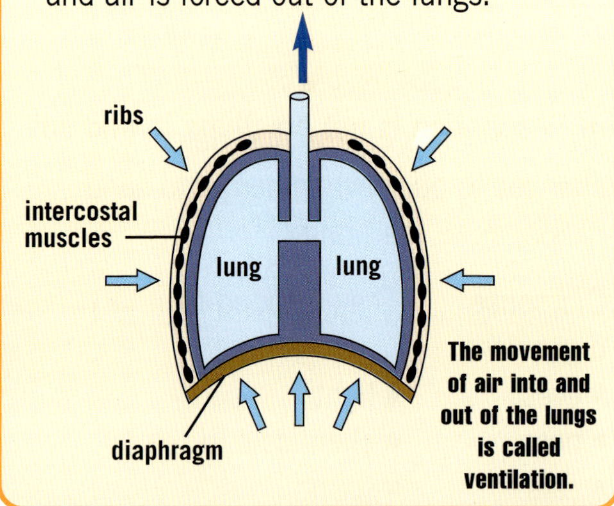

The movement of air into and out of the lungs is called ventilation.

Alveoli and gas exchange

- The **alveoli** are well suited to their job of gas exchange.
- There are millions of alveoli, so they present a **large surface area**; they are in **very close contact** with lots of blood capillaries.
- Their surface lining is moist, so that the gases can dissolve before they diffuse across the **thin membrane**.
- At the lungs, oxygen diffuses into the blood and carbon dioxide diffuses into the alveoli.

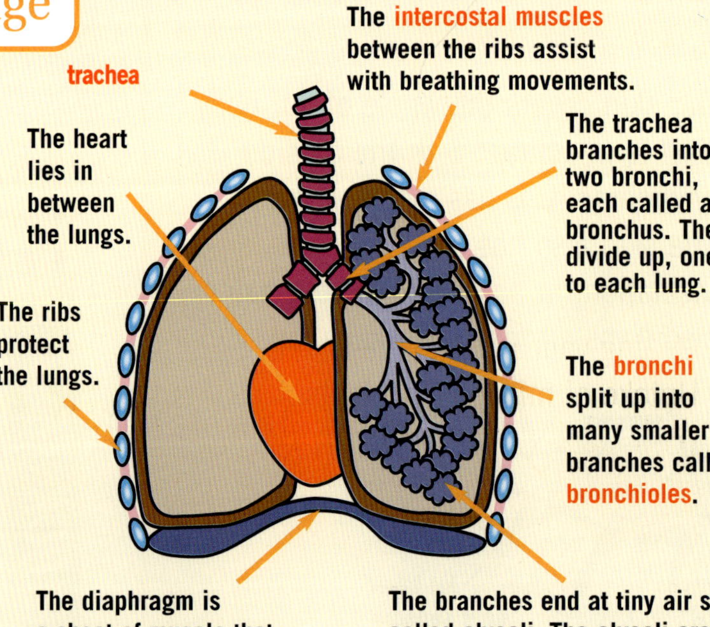

Composition of gases

In inhaled air	In exhaled air
Oxygen – 21%	Oxygen – 16%
Carbon dioxide – 0.04%	Carbon dioxide – 4%
Nitrogen – 79%	Nitrogen – 79%
Water vapour – a little	Water vapour – a lot

Note

- Notice that we breathe out oxygen and carbon dioxide as well as breathing them both in.
- It is important to note that we breathe in more oxygen and breathe out **more** carbon dioxide.
- There are other differences: the air we breathe out is warmer and contains more water vapour than the air we breathe in. It also has fewer dust particles.

Respiration

- Breathing is necessary for **respiration**.
- **Respiration is not breathing in and out.**
- Respiration is a chemical reaction that **breaks down glucose from food to release energy using oxygen**.
- Every living cell in every living organism uses respiration to make **energy**, all of the time.
- **Carbon dioxide and water are waste products** removed from the body in the lungs, skin and kidneys.
- Respiration takes place inside the **cytoplasm** of cells.

The word equation is:

glucose + oxygen ⟶ carbon dioxide + water + **energy**

 ***Learn the word equation for respiration.***

KEY TERMS

Make sure you understand these terms before moving on!

- alveoli
- trachea
- intercostal muscles
- bronchi
- bronchioles
- respiration

Uses of energy produced

The energy produced during respiration is used for:

1. Making your muscles work.
2. Uptake of minerals in plants.
3. Chemical reactions.
4. Growth and repair of cells.
5. Maintaining body temperature in warm-blooded animals.

QUICK TEST

1. Where does gas exchange take place?
2. Why are the alveoli so good at gas exchange?
3. Give a definition of respiration.
4. Where does respiration take place?
5. What are the waste products of respiration?

The menstrual cycle

- **Adolescence is a time in people's lives when the body changes from a child to an adult. Emotions also change.**
- **Puberty is the first stage of adolescence, most changes occur at this time.**
- **Puberty usually begins at the age of 10–14 in girls and a little later in boys. Not everybody starts puberty at the same time.**

Puberty

Physical changes that take place during **puberty** include:

Boys

- Testes start to produce sperm and a hormone called **testosterone**.
- Penis grows larger.
- Body hair appears on the face, chest, armpits and around the penis.
- Voice gets deeper.
- Skin produces more oil that blocks pores and causes spots.

Girls

- Ovaries start to release eggs and produce a hormone called **oestrogen**.
- **Menstruation** begins.
- Breasts grow larger.
- Body hair grows under the arms and around the vagina.
- Skin produces more oil that blocks pores and causes spots.

Emotional changes

- Boys and girls also go through **emotional changes** caused by changing levels of hormones.
- Behaviour changes occur such as **irritability** and **mood swings** and they develop an interest in the opposite sex.

The human reproductive system

- During puberty, males produce **sperm** and females start to release **eggs**.
- Sperm is made in the testes.
- During sexual intercourse the penis becomes erect and sperm is then ejaculated into the vagina.
- The sperm swim up towards the Fallopian tube.
- An egg is released once a month by **alternate ovaries** and moves down the Fallopian tube.
- In the Fallopian tube the egg may meet a sperm and be fertilised.
- If the egg is not fertilised then it will pass out of the vagina during **menstruation**.

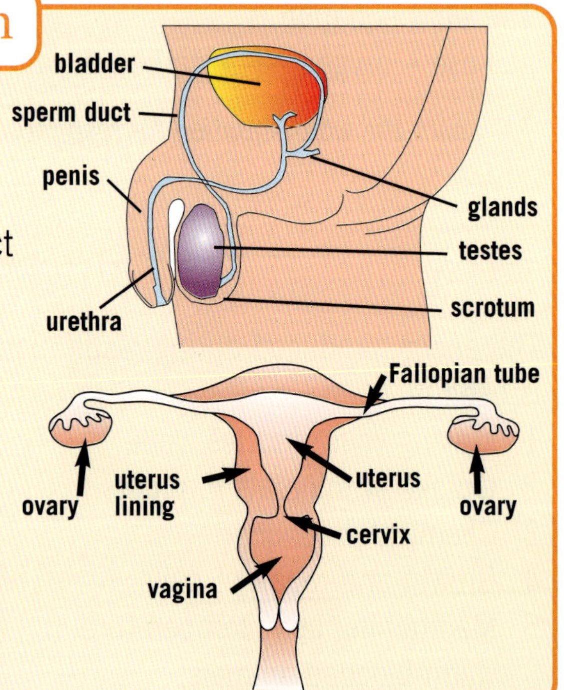

The menstrual cycle

- A sequence of events occurs each month in females called the menstrual cycle.
- The menstrual cycle lasts approximately **28 days.**
- The menstrual cycle involves preparing the uterus to receive a fertilised egg.
- If fertilisation doesn't happen then the egg and the lining of the uterus break down and leave the body through the vagina during menstruation.
- This is also known as having a **period** or a menstrual bleed and lasts between **four** and **seven** days.

The stages of the menstrual cycle

Day 1–5: A menstrual bleed (a period) occurs and the lining of the uterus breaks down.

Day 5–14: The uterus lining builds up again and becomes thicker with lots of blood vessels. This is to prepare for implantation (see page 22).

Day 14: The ovary releases an egg, a process called ovulation.

Day 14–28: The uterus lining is maintained in case a fertilised egg arrives. If no fertilisation occurs then the cycle begins again.

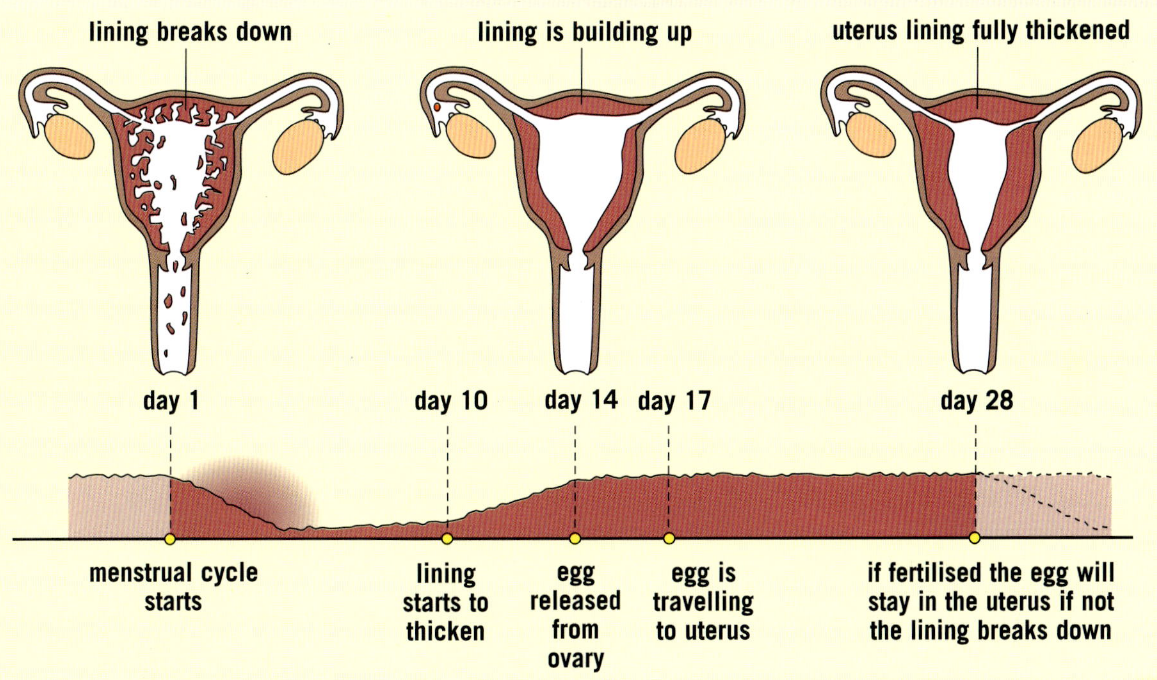

Learn the diagrams well enough so that you will be able to label them in the exam.

KEY TERMS

- puberty
- oestrogen
- eggs
- testosterone
- sperm
- menstruation

QUICK TEST

1. Where is sperm made?
2. Where are the eggs made?
3. How often does menstruation take place?
4. What is ovulation?
5. How long does a period usually last?
6. What are the two hormones produced during puberty?

Reproduction

- **Human reproduction involves the joining together of a male sperm and a female egg in a process called fertilisation.**
- **The fertilised egg implants itself into the uterus lining and begins its development into a baby.**
- **A human pregnancy lasts approximately nine months (40 weeks).**

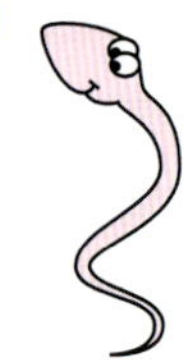

Fertilisation

- As part of the female menstrual cycle an egg is released at around the middle of the cycle, called **ovulation**.
- When a man and a woman have **sexual intercourse** sperm from the penis of the man passes into the vagina of the woman.
- The sperm swim up to the uterus and into the Fallopian tubes to meet an egg.
- Many sperm die along the way. Only one sperm is able to break through the cell membrane of the egg and fertilise it.
- **Fertilisation is the fusing together of the sperm nucleus and the egg nucleus.**
- Fertilisation takes place in the **fallopian tube**.

nucleus
sperm
head
tail
sperm enters egg

Learn the definition of fertilisation.

After fertilisation

- The fertilised egg passes down the Fallopian tube.
- The ball of cells becomes an **embryo** and embeds itself into the uterus lining. This is called **implantation**.
- At about nine weeks the embryo is called a **foetus**.

Development and protection

- The **placenta** is an organ that grows early in the pregnancy. It acts as a barrier preventing harmful substances reaching the foetus.
- The foetus is attached to the placenta by the umbilical cord.
- The foetus is provided with food and oxygen by the **umbilical cord**.
- The blood of the foetus and the mother do not mix but they pass close together to allow exchange of food, oxygen and waste.
- The baby is protected inside the uterus by a sac filled with a watery liquid called the **amniotic fluid**.
- The fluid acts as a shock absorber against minor bumps.

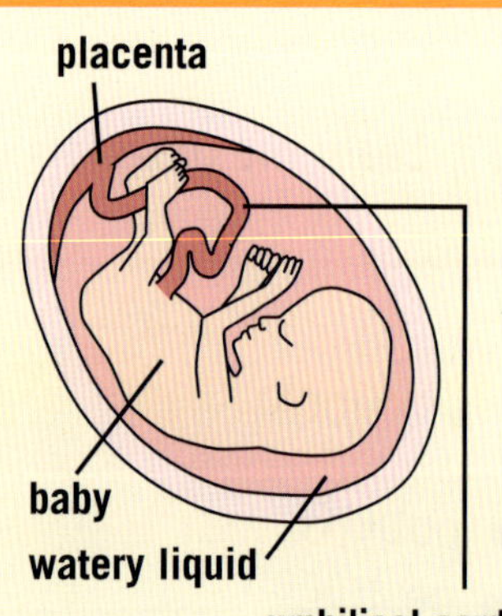

The way a baby is protected and provided with food and oxygen until birth is a common exam question.

Birth and after

- After nine months of pregnancy the baby is ready to be born through the vagina.
- The baby normally turns so that its head is down towards the **cervix**.
- Muscles in the wall of the uterus begin to contract and the cervix widens.
- The baby's head passes through the cervix into the vagina.
- The fluid sac bursts and the watery liquid runs out.
- Contractions push the baby out of the vagina.
- More contractions push the placenta out. This is called the **afterbirth**.
- The umbilical cord is cut and the baby has to breathe for itself.

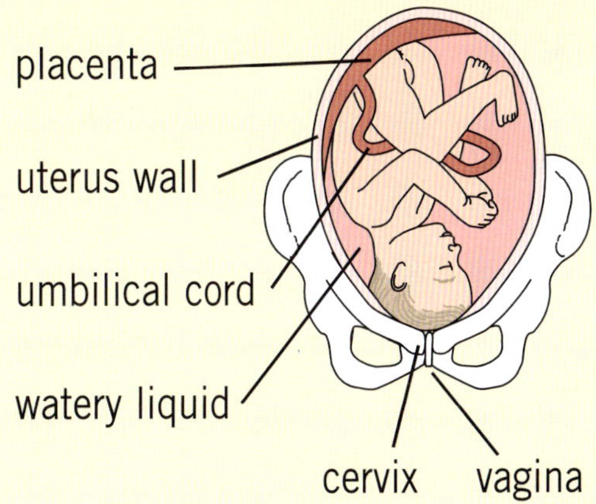

Twins

- Identical twins are formed if the fertilised egg divides into two, and each part develops into a baby.
- Non-identical twins are formed when two eggs are released from the ovary and both are fertilised.

KEY TERMS

Make sure you understand these terms before moving on!

- ovulation
- fertilisation
- fallopian tube
- embryo
- implantation
- placenta
- umbilical cord

QUICK TEST

1. What is a fertilised egg called?
2. What is implantation?
3. Where does fertilisation take place?
4. What is fertilisation?
5. How is the foetus supplied with oxygen and food while in the uterus?
6. How long does a human pregnancy usually last?

Drugs

- Smoking and solvents damage health.
- Alcohol and drugs can also be dangerous.
- To keep healthy you need to eat a balanced diet, take regular exercise and avoid health risks.

Drugs – why are they dangerous?

- **Drugs are powerful chemicals; they alter the way the body works, often without you realising it.**
- There are useful drugs such as penicillin, an antibiotic, but even these can be dangerous if misused.
- **Some drugs affect the brain and nervous system**, which in turn affect activities such as driving, as well as behaviour.
- Drugs affect people in many different ways; you can never be sure what will happen to you.
- Drugs fall into four main groups:

Sedatives

- These drugs **slow down the brain** and make you feel sleepy.
- They seriously alter reaction times and give you poor judgement of speed and distances.
- Tranquillisers and sleeping pills are often given to people suffering from anxiety and stress.
- Barbiturates, which are powerful sedatives, are used as anaesthetics in hospitals.

Painkillers

- These drugs suppress the pain sensors in the brain.
- Aspirin, heroin and morphine are examples.
- Heroin can be injected, which can increase the risk of contracting HIV; it is also highly addictive.

Hallucinogens

- These drugs make you see or hear things that don't exist. These imaginings are called hallucinations.
- Hallucinations can lead to fatal accidents.
- Examples are ecstasy, LSD and cannabis.
- Ecstasy can give the user feelings of extreme energy. This extra energy can lead to a danger of overheating and dehydration.

Stimulants

- These drugs speed up the brain and nervous system and make you more alert and awake.
- Overuse results in high energy levels, changes in personality and hallucinations.
- Dependence on these drugs is high and withdrawal causes serious depression.
- Examples include amphetamines, cocaine and the less harmful caffeine in tea and coffee.

Concentrate on the health problems for the exam, but the social aspects are still important.

Alcohol

- Alcohol is a legal drug and socially acceptable but it can still cause a lot of harm.
- Alcohol causes people to lose control and slur their words. In this state accidents are more likely to happen.
- Alcohol is a **depressant** and reduces the activity of the brain and nervous system.
- It is absorbed through the gut and taken to the brain in the blood.
- Alcohol damages brain cells causing irreversible brain damage.
- **Alcohol can destroy parts of the liver and cause a disease called cirrhosis.**

Solvents

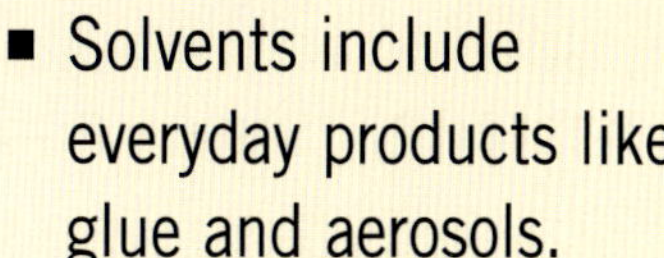

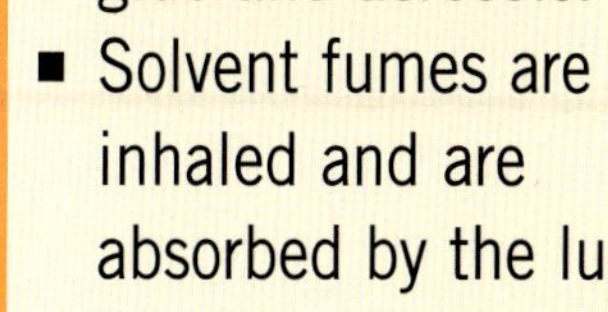

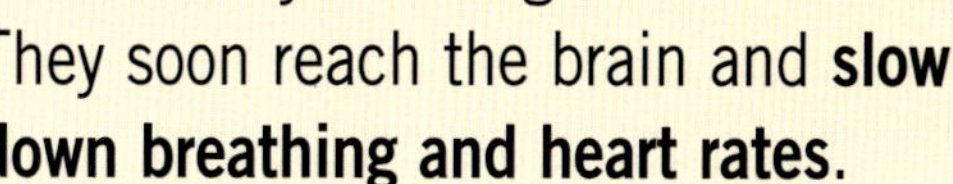

- Solvents include everyday products like glue and aerosols.
- Solvent fumes are inhaled and are absorbed by the lungs. They soon reach the brain and **slow down breathing and heart rates**.
- Solvents also damage the **kidneys and liver**.
- Repeated inhalation can cause loss of control and unconsciousness.
- Many first-time inhalers die from heart failure or suffocation.

Smoking

- Tobacco smoking is linked to many health problems, for example **emphysema**, **bronchitis**, **heart and blood vessel problems and lung cancer**.
- It contains many harmful chemicals: **nicotine** is an addictive substance and a mild stimulant; **tar** is known to contain carcinogens that contribute to cancer; and **carbon monoxide** prevents the red blood cells from carrying oxygen.

Smoking and lung disease

- Tar contained in tobacco smoke can cause cancer of the lung cells. It can also irritate air passages and make them narrower, causing a 'smoker's cough'.
- Bronchitis is aggravated by smoking. Smoke irritates the air passages making them inflamed. The cilia stop beating, so mucus collects in the lungs along with dirt and bacteria.
- Emphysema occurs when the chemicals in tobacco smoke weaken the alveoli walls. The lung tissue can become damaged and make breathing difficult.

KEY TERMS

Make sure you understand these terms before moving on!

- sedatives
- painkillers
- hallucinogens
- stimulants
- cirrhosis
- nicotine

QUICK TEST

1. Which parts of the body are affected by alcohol?
2. What are stimulants?
3. Name three chemicals contained in tobacco.
4. What diseases is smoking linked to?
5. Which disease of the liver is caused by drinking excess alcohol?

Fighting disease

- Microbes are bacteria, viruses and fungi.
- Not all microbes cause disease; some are useful.
- Microbes that get inside you and make you feel ill are called germs.

Bacteria

- **Bacteria** are living organisms.
- Bacteria reproduce rapidly.
- Bacteria can produce poisons, called **toxins**. For example, food poisoning is caused by bacteria releasing toxins.
- Other diseases caused by bacteria include tetanus, whooping cough and tuberculosis.
- Most bacteria are killed by antibiotics.

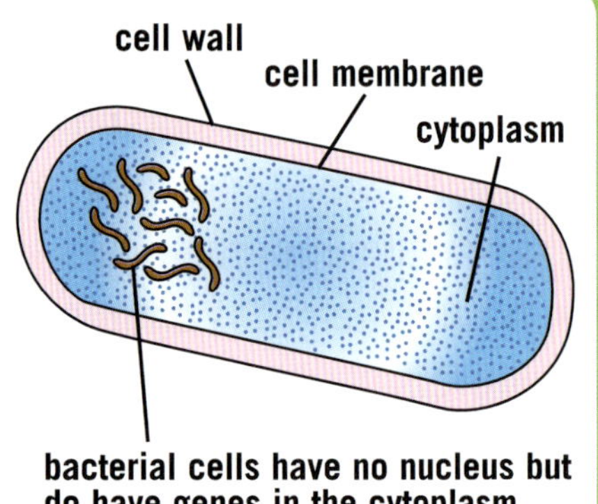

Fungi

- **Fungi** cause diseases such as athlete's foot and ringworm.
- Fungi reproduce by **making spores** that can be carried from person to person.
- Most fungi are useful as decomposers. Yeast is a fungus that is used when making bread, beer and wine.

Viruses

Viruses consist of a few genes surrounded by a **protein coat**.

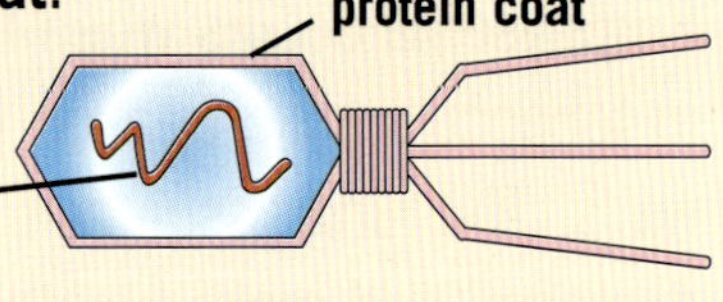

- Viruses are much smaller than bacteria.
- Viruses don't feed, move, respire or grow; they just reproduce.
- Viruses can only reproduce inside the cells of a living organism, releasing thousands of new viruses to infect new cells, and killing the cell in the process.
- Examples of diseases caused by viruses are HIV, flu, chicken pox and measles.

Defence against disease

- Infectious diseases are spread in various ways; through the air, via food and water, or contact with infected people.
- Microbes – bacteria, viruses and fungi – have to enter our body before they can do any harm.
- The body has many ways of preventing microbes from entering including skin, which provides a physical barrier, and various bodily fluids (such as tears) that kill some microbes.
- Stomach acid kills some microbes that are swallowed.
- If microbes do pass the barriers then your **immune system** springs into action.

Learn how the white blood cells fight infection.

The immune system response

If the microbes get into the body then your **white blood cells** travelling around in your blood spring into action.

- Some white blood cells **engulf** bacteria or viruses before they have a chance to do any harm.
- However, if the microbes are there in large numbers then another type of **white blood cell produces antibodies to fight them.**

Microbes have foreign antigens on their surface. Antibodies **attach to the microbes' antigens** and clump them together so they can then be engulfed and destroyed.

This type of white blood cell kills microbes by engulfing them

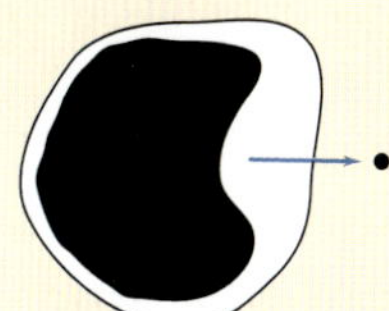

This type of white blood cell sends out antibodies which kill microbes

Natural immunity

- Making antibodies takes time, which is why you feel ill at first and then get better as the disease is destroyed by the white blood cells and antibodies.
- Once a particular antibody is made it stays in your body. If the same disease enters your body later, the antibodies are much quicker at destroying it and you feel no symptoms. **You are now immune to that disease**.

Artificial immunity

- Artificial immunity involves the use of vaccines.
- **A vaccine contains dead or harmless microbes**.
- These microbes still have antigens on them and your white blood cells respond to them as if they were alive by multiplying and producing antibodies.
- A vaccine is an advanced warning so that if the person is infected by the microbe the white blood cells can **respond immediately** and kill them.

Make sure you know the difference between natural immunity and artificial immunity.

KEY TERMS

Make sure you understand these terms before moving on!

- bacteria
- fungi
- viruses
- immune system
- antibodies
- vaccine

1. Name the three main types of microbes.
2. What chemicals do white blood cells produce?
3. What are vaccines?
4. Name two diseases caused by viruses.
5. Name two diseases caused by bacteria.

Photosynthesis

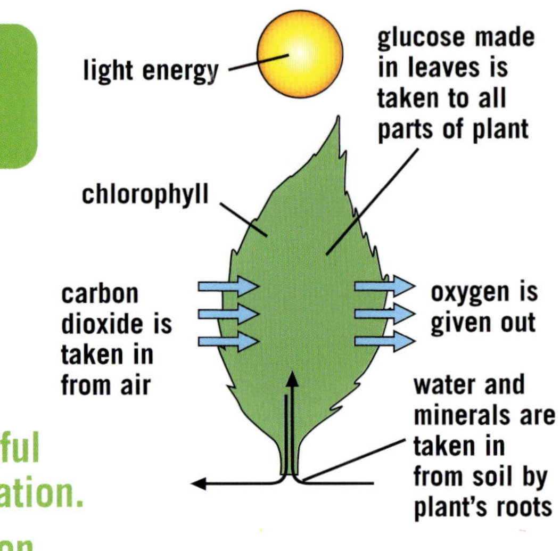

- **All living things need food: animals have to find their food and plants make their own.**
- **Photosynthesis is a chemical process that plants use to make their food (glucose) using energy from the Sun. It occurs in the leaves.**
- **Leaves then use this food to generate other useful substances and to obtain energy through respiration.**
- **Photosynthesis occurs in the light and respiration occurs all of the time.**

It is very important to learn the word equation for photosynthesis.

The word equation of photosynthesis:

$$\text{carbon dioxide} + \text{water} \xrightarrow[\text{chlorophyll}]{\text{light}} \text{glucose} + \text{oxygen}$$

The leaf – the organ of photosynthesis

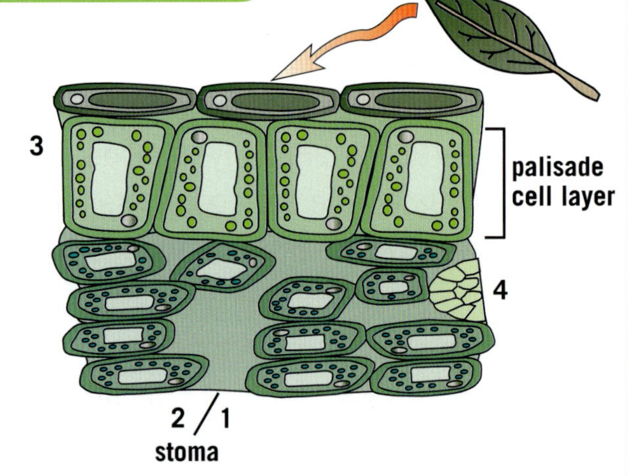

1 **Carbon dioxide** enters the leaf through tiny holes on the underside of the leaf. The holes are called **stomata**.
2 **Oxygen** that is produced by photosynthesis exits through the stomata by **diffusion**.
3 **Chloroplasts** are most abundant near the upper surface of the leaf in **palisade cells**. Chloroplasts contain **chlorophyll**.
   - **Chlorophyll** is a green pigment that **absorbs** energy from **sunlight**.
4 The root and stem of the plant lead to veins inside the leaf.
   - The veins contain **xylem** and **phloem**.
   - **Xylem** transports **water** from the root to the leaves.
   - **Phloem** transports the **glucose** up and down the plant to where it is needed, particularly the growing regions (the bud) and the storage areas (the roots).

Healthy growth

- The root is specially designed to absorb minerals dissolved in water from the soil.
- There are three **essential** minerals needed for healthy growth:

1 **Nitrates** are needed to make proteins.
2 **Phosphates** play an important role in photosynthesis and in helping the plant use some of its glucose for respiration.
3 **Potassium** is involved in making the enzymes used in respiration and photosynthesis work.

Factors affecting the rate of photosynthesis

There are **three** things that affect the rate of photosynthesis. They are:

Light

- If there is more light then the rate of photosynthesis will increase.

Carbon dioxide

- If the carbon dioxide concentration is increased then photosynthesis will increase.

Temperature

- The best temperature for photosynthesis is about 30°C.
- Photosynthesis slows down above 45°C.
- The rate of photosynthesis can be measured by how much oxygen is produced.
- These three factors can be controlled in a greenhouse. This means the plants have enough light and carbon dioxide, and just the right temperature to grow well.

Photosynthesis experiments

- A plant will store the glucose as starch once it has been made.
- We can test whether the leaf has photosynthesised or not by testing the leaf for starch.

1 Dip a leaf in boiling water for about a minute to soften it.
2 Put the leaf in a test tube of ethanol and stand in hot water for 10 minutes. (This removes the colour.)
3 Remove and wash the leaf.
4 Lay the leaf flat in a petri dish and add iodine solution.
5 If starch is present the leaf should go blue/black.

- You can repeat the experiment on a plant that has been kept in the dark for 24 hours or a leaf that has been kept in a flask without carbon dioxide.
- You should find that this time the iodine solution stays brown proving that light and carbon dioxide are needed for photosynthesis.

Make sure you understand these terms before moving on!

- photosynthesis
- stomata
- diffusion
- nitrates
- phosphates
- potassium

QUICK TEST

1. What four things does a plant need for photosynthesis?
2. What does a plant produce in photosynthesis?
3. Where does photosynthesis take place?
4. What do the plants do with the glucose they make?
5. What are the three main minerals a plant needs?

Plant reproduction

- **Plants have male and female sex cells just like animals.**
- **They reproduce to form seeds inside fruits.**
- **Reproduction consists of pollination, fertilisation, seed dispersal, and germination.**

The flower

- Many flowers contain male and female reproductive organs.
- **Carpels** are the female parts of the flower and consist of the **stigma**, which receives the pollen grains, **style** and **ovary**. The ovary contains the female sex cells called the **ovules**.
- Petals are nften brightly coloured to attract insects for pollination.
- **Stamen** are the male parts of the flower (**staMEN**) and consist of an **anther**, which produces the male sex cells called the **pollen grains**, and the **filament**.

Sepals protect the bud. They are green and are just below the flower petals.

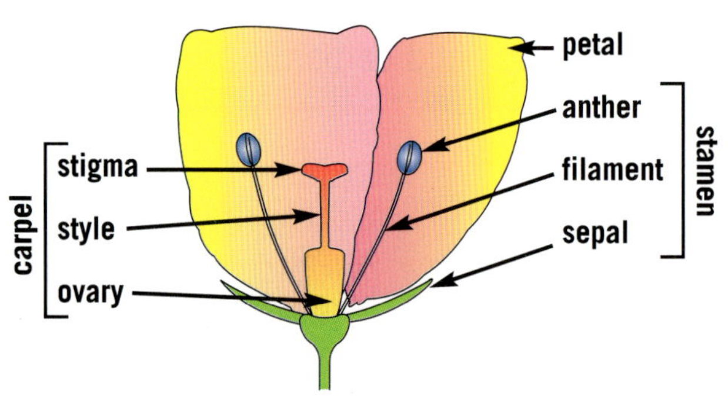

Pollination

- Pollination is the beginning of making a seed.
- The pollen grain from the anther must be transferred to the stigma; either of the same plant (**self-pollination**) or the stigma of another plant (**cross-pollination**).
- This transfer can be achieved by **wind**, by **insects** or sometimes by **water**.

Insect pollination

Insects such as bees carry pollen on their bodies from the anther to the sticky stigmas. Flowers that use insect pollination to reproduce usually:

- have brightly coloured petals
- have scented flowers
- contain sugary nectar.

Learn the differences between plants that use the wind to achieve pollination and the plants that use insects.

Wind pollination

Flowers that use wind pollination to reproduce usually have:

- less brightly coloured petals
- no scent
- no nectar
- filaments that hang the anthers outside the flower to catch the wind.

They produce more pollen than insect pollinated plants because there is much less chance of the pollen reaching the stigma.

Fertilisation

- **Fertilisation occurs when the male pollen grain joins with a female ovule.**
- **The pollen nucleus fuses with the ovule nucleus.** The ovule nucleus can then grow into a seed.

Steps

- The pollen grain lands on the stigma with help from insects or the wind.
- **A pollen tube** grows out of the pollen down the style towards the ovary.
- The pollen nucleus moves down the tube to join with the ovule nucleus. Fertilisation has occurred.
- The ovary turns into a fruit and inside it the ovule grows into a seed.

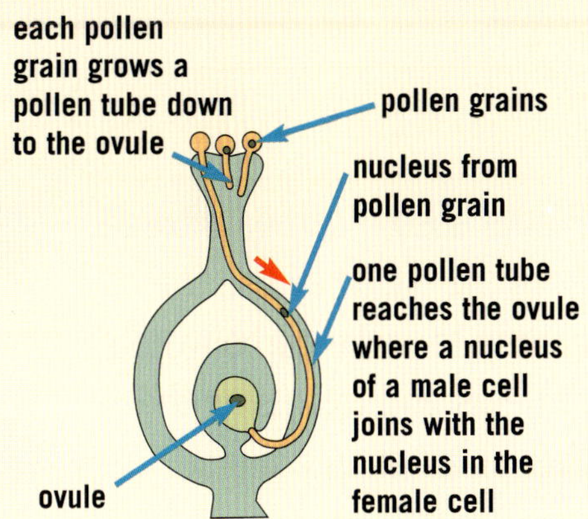

Seeds and seed dispersal

- Plants try to scatter their seed over as wide a range as possible so the seed has the opportunity to grow into plants with little competition for resources.
- **The scattering of seeds is called dispersal**. There are three different methods used by plants.

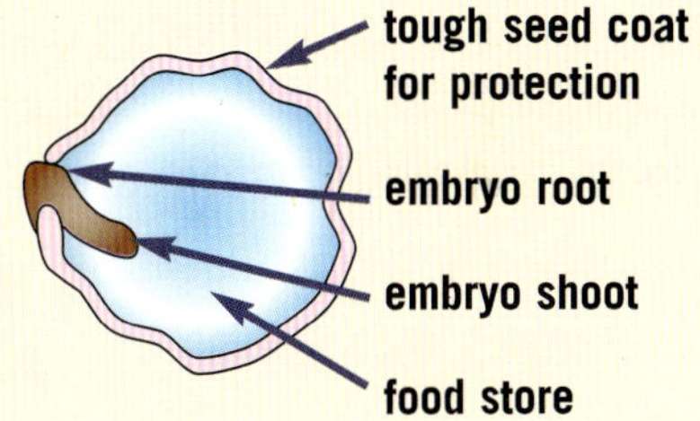

Wind dispersal

- The fruits of these plants are light and so are easily picked up by the wind.

Animal dispersal

- Animals eat the fruit (such as a tomato).
- The animals move to another place before producing droppings that contain the seeds.

Popping out

- Seed pods dry out and pop open to flick out the seeds.

Germination

- Once settled, the seeds will begin to grow into a new plant – but only if conditions are right.
- The conditions necessary for seeds to germinate are moisture, warmth and enough oxygen in the air.
- The root is sensitive to gravity and the shoot is sensitive to light so they will grow naturally in the right directions.

KEY TERMS

- carpels
- ovules
- stamen
- dispersal
- self-pollination
- cross-pollination
- stigma
- pollen grains
- germination

QUICK TEST

1. What is the female part of the flower called?
2. What is the male part of the flower called?
3. Name three ways that seeds are dispersed.
4. What is fertilisation in plants?

The carbon cycle

- **Carbon dioxide and nitrogen are atmospheric gases.**
- **The amount of each gas in the atmosphere should stay the same as they are constantly recycled in the environment.**

Photosynthesis

Plants absorb carbon dioxide from the air. They use the carbon to make carbohydrates, proteins and fats using the **Sun** as an energy source.

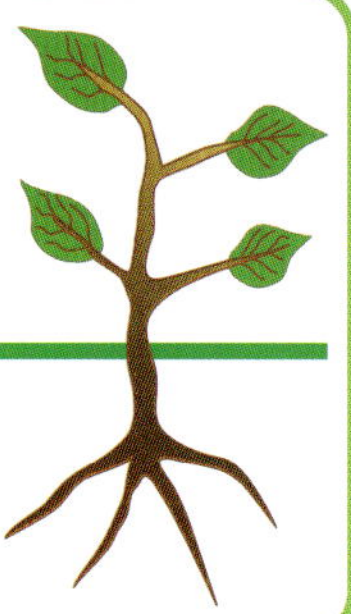

Feeding

Animals eat plants and so the carbon gets into their bodies.

Death and decay

Plants and animals die and produce waste. The carbon is released into the soil.

Death but no decay

Sometimes plants and animals die, but do not decay. Heat and pressure gradually, over millions of years, produce fossil fuels.

Remember, there is only one way carbon enters the cycle (photosynthesis) and two ways it is released back into the atmosphere (respiration and combustion).

Decomposers

Bacteria and fungi present in the soil break down dead matter, urine and faeces, which contain carbon. Bacteria and fungi release carbon dioxide when they respire.

The carbon cycle in the exam may look different, so make sure you learn the processes involved.

Burning and combustion

The burning of fossil fuels (coal, oil and gas) releases carbon dioxide into the atmosphere.

Respiration

- Plants, animals and decomposers carry out respiration and release carbon dioxide into the air.

Fossil fuels

Coal is formed from plants; oil and gas are formed from animals.

The nitrogen cycle

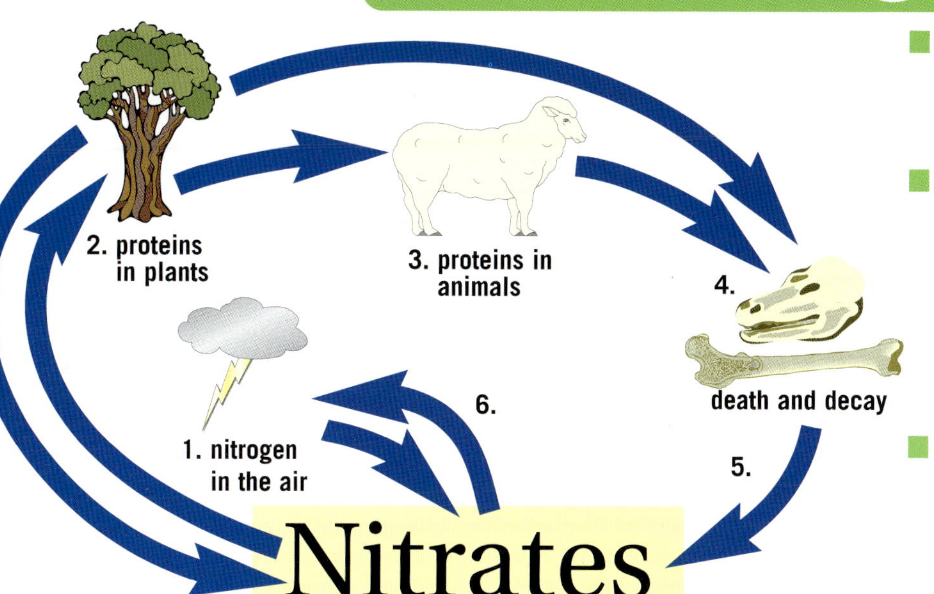

- **Nitrogen is an important element needed for making proteins.**
- **Plants and animals cannot use nitrogen in gas form, it has to be converted to nitrates before plants can use it to make protein.**
- **We eat plants to get the protein into our bodies.**

Nitrogen gas is changed into nitrates and back again in the nitrogen cycle

- **Nitrogen from the air is needed by plants and animals to make proteins in their bodies.**
- **Nitrogen** in the air has to be changed into **nitrates** first.
- Look at the diagram above and follow the points to see how the nitrogen cycle works.
  1. Lightning causes a chemical reaction in the air; the nitrogen oxides formed are washed into the soil by the rain to form nitrates.
  2. Plants take up the nitrates during photosynthesis and convert them into protein.
  3. Animals eat plants and make the protein part of their bodies.
  4. Animals and plants both produce waste and eventually die.
  5. Bacteria in the soil convert the waste and remains back into nitrates, ready for the plants to convert it back into protein.
  6. One type of bacteria works in waterlogged soils. These bacteria convert nitrates back into nitrogen gas that is released into the air.

KEY TERMS

Make sure you understand these terms before moving on!

- carbon
- fossil fuels
- nitrogen
- nitrates

QUICK TEST

1. Name the process that absorbs carbon dioxide from the air.
2. Name two ways that carbon is released back into the air.
3. What happens to the bodies of animals and plants that do not decay?
4. Why do plants need nitrogen?
5. What does nitrogen in the air have to be converted to first before it is used by living things?

Classification

- *Classification* is what scientists use to sort out all living organisms into groups.
- The organisms are put into groups according to the similarities between them.
- All living things are divided first into *kingdoms*.
- The two main kingdoms are the animal and plant kingdoms.

The animal kingdom

- Animals can be divided up into two groups, the **vertebrates** and the **invertebrates**.
- **Vertebrates** are animals **with a backbone**.
- **Invertebrates** are animals **without a backbone**.

Vertebrates

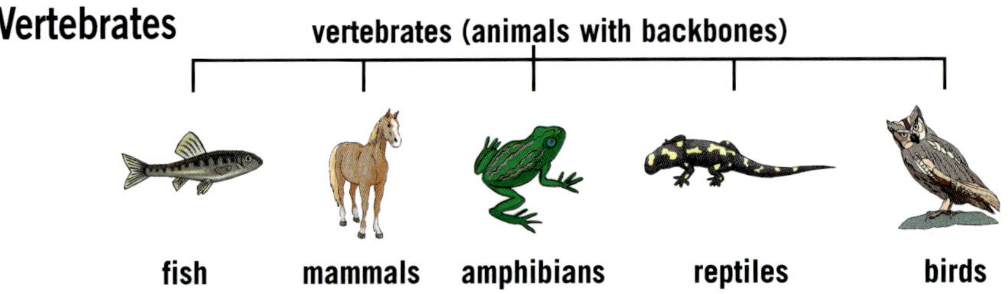

Vertebrates are divided into five groups and each of the groups has features that are specific only to them:

- **Fish** These live in water, have fins and scales, breathe through gills.
- **Mammals** These have hair on their bodies, are warm-blooded, give birth to live young and feed their young on milk from the mother.
- **Amphibians** These have smooth moist skin, live on water and land, but breed in water.
- **Reptiles** These have dry, scaly skin and most live on land.
- **Birds** These have feathers and wings, most can fly and they lay eggs.

Invertebrates

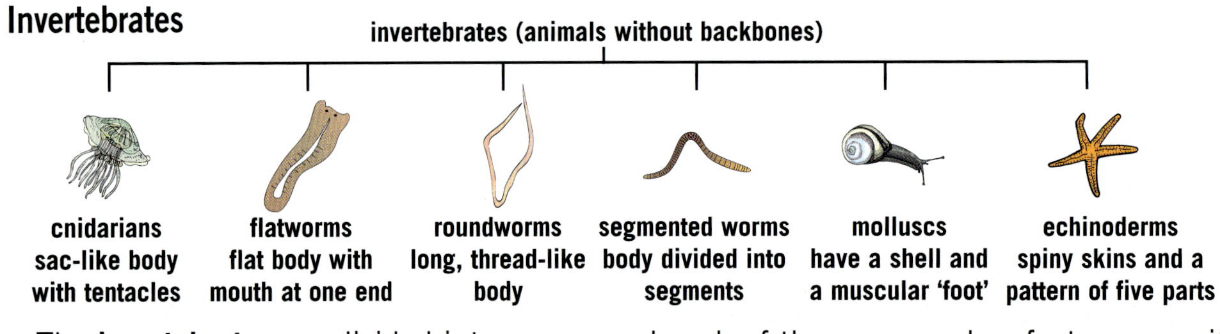

- The **invertebrates** are divided into groups and each of these groups has features specific only to them.

You may have found the organisms easy to identify just by looking at them, but they might not be so easy in the exam, so make sure you learn how to use both types of key.

The plant kingdom

Plants can be classified into the following groups:

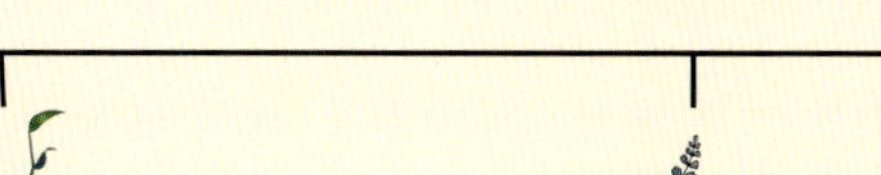

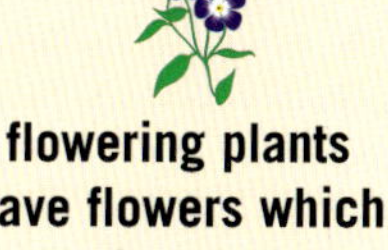

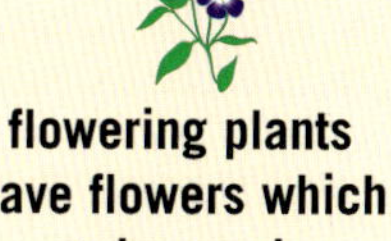

Using keys

- To help people **identify** living things we can use **keys**.
- Keys are a series of questions that have **two possible answers**.
- Eventually the questions divide the group until there is only one option.
- The option left will be the identification of the plant or animal.
- There are two main types of key.

Type 1

- Choose one organism, for example (**A**).
- Answer the first question: Has it got legs?
- The answer is no, so follow the 'no' arrow.
- Answer the next question: Has it got a shell?
- The answer is yes, so follow the 'yes' arrow.
  You can't go any further, so the answer is a snail.
- Go back to the start and choose another animal to identify.

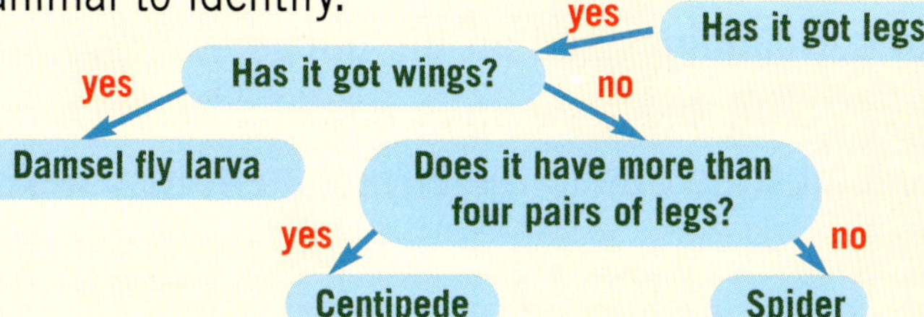

Type 2

- We can use a different type of key to identify the animals above.
- Again choose an organism, for example (**C**).
- Answer the first question for that organism and then follow the next instruction.

- classification
- kingdoms
- vertebrates
- invertebrates
- keys

QUICK TEST

1. What is classification?
2. What does invertebrate mean?
3. What does vertebrate mean?
4. Can you name the five vertebrate groups?

Variation

- **All living things vary in the way they look or behave.**
- **Living things that belong to the same species are all slightly different.**
- **Living things that belong to different species are totally different.**
- **Inheritance, the environment or a combination of both may cause these differences.**

Genetic variation

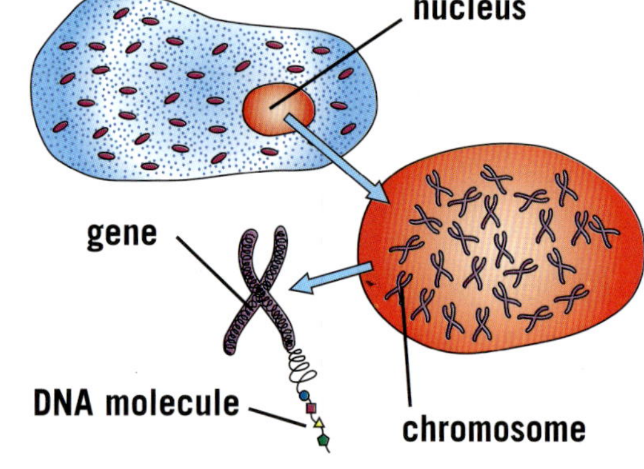

- Why do we look like we do? The answer is because we have inherited our characteristics from our parents.
- Brothers and sisters are not exactly the same as each other because they inherit different genes from their parents. It is completely random.
- Only identical twins have the same genes.
- **Genes** are made up of a chemical called **DNA** and are found on the **chromosomes** in cells.
- **Genes occur in pairs** and control all our inherited characteristics.
- **Chromosomes** are found in the nuclei of all our cells.
- Human body cells have **46 chromosomes** (23 pairs).
- Sperm and egg cells have **23 chromosomes**.
- When they fuse together during fertilisation the fertilised egg has 46 chromosomes with all the information to grow into a baby.

Environmental variation

- **The environment consists of your surroundings and all the things that may affect you**.
- Identical twins may be separated at birth and grow up in totally different environments. Any differences between the twins must be due to the environment they were brought up in as they have identical genes.
- Many of the differences between people are caused by a **combination** of genetic and environmental influences.

Variation in plants

- Plants inherit characteristics by their genes in the same way as animals do.
- However, plants are affected more than animals by small changes in the environment.
- Sunlight, temperature, moisture level and soil type are factors that will determine how well a plant grows.
- A plant grown in sunlight will grow much faster and may double in size compared to a plant grown in the shade, whereas an animal would not be affected.

Variation in animals

- We vary partly because of the random way our genes are **inherited**.
- The environment can affect most of our characteristics. It is usually a combination of genetics and environment that determines how we look and behave.
- There are some characteristics that are not affected by the environment at all:
  1 Eye colour 2 Natural hair colour 3 Blood group 4 Certain inherited diseases

Continuous and discontinuous variation

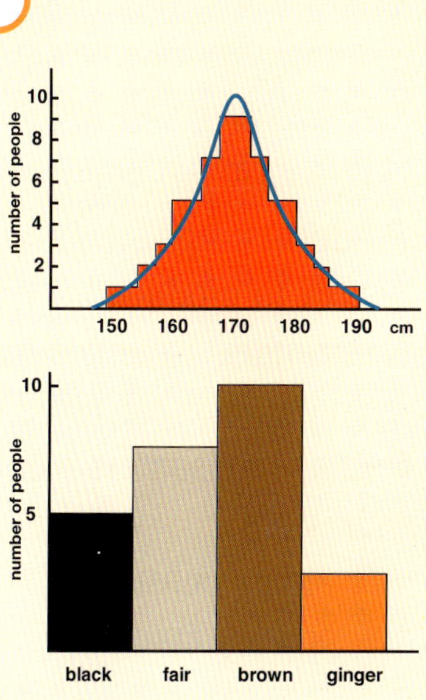

- Differences between animals and plants show two types of variation.
- If you measured the heights of people in your class you would find that they varied gradually from short to tall.
- **Height or weight follow continuous variation.**
- If you looked at the hair colour of people in your class, you would find there are only a few options, not a continuous range.
- Another example is whether a person can roll their tongue. You either can or you cannot; there is no in between.
- **Eye colour, hair colour, blood group and rolling tongues are examples of discontinuous variation.**

Learn examples of continuous and discontinuous variation.

Selective breeding

Selective breeding is where features that are wanted in a plant or animal are bred in and features that are not wanted are bred out. This is done by:

- Selecting the individuals with the **best characteristics** and breeding from them.
- Selecting and breeding the best offspring over generations until the **new varieties** have all the desired characteristics.

Humans carry out selective breeding to benefit themselves in some way. Examples include:

- Developing plants that are **resistant to disease or frost**, or fruit that tastes good.
- Breeding dogs for their **intelligence** or for **showing**.
- Breeding cows to produce **more milk** or **better tasting beef**.
- Breeding racehorses that can **run fast**.

- genes
- DNA
- chromosomes
- inherited
- continuous variation
- discontinuous variation

QUICK TEST

1. Is blood group inherited or caused by the environment?
2. Give two examples of continuous variation.
3. Give two examples of discontinuous variation.
4. What is selective breeding?

Food chains and webs

- **Food chains and webs begin with energy from the Sun.**
- **A food chain shows us what eats what in a community.**
- **A food web is made up of interconnected food chains.**

Food chains

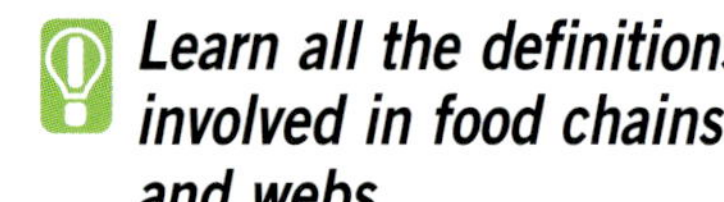
Learn all the definitions involved in food chains and webs.

- The **arrows** in a food chain show the transfer of food energy from organism to organism.
- **Food chains always begin with the Sun, then a green plant**; these can include seeds, fruits or even dead leaves.

Producers – green plants use the Sun's energy to produce food energy.
Consumers – animals that get their energy from eating other living things.
Primary consumers – animals that eat the producers.
Secondary consumers – animals that eat the primary consumers.
Tertiary consumers – animals that eat the secondary consumers.
Herbivores – animals that only eat plants.
Carnivores – animals that only eat animals.
Top carnivores – animals that are not eaten by anything else except decomposers after they die.

Loss of energy in food chains

- **Food chains** rarely have more than four or five links in them; this is because energy is lost along the way.
- The energy is used up for staying alive, moving, growing and keeping warm, and some of the energy is lost in urine and faeces.
- Not all of the animal material is eaten so not all of the energy is passed on.
- This loss of energy means that the mass of organisms gets less at each level up the food chain.

Pyramids of numbers

- If we look at the information a food chain tells us, it is simply what eats what.
- A **pyramid of numbers** tells us how many organisms are involved at each level in the food chain.
- Sometimes a pyramid of numbers doesn't look like a pyramid at all as it doesn't take into account the **size** of the organisms.
- A rosebush is one organism but it has many leaves to support many aphids.

fox
rabbit
grass

blackbird
ladybirds
aphids
rosebush

Pyramids of biomass

- A **biomass pyramid** takes into account the **mass of an organism** at each level of the food chain.
- A single rosebush weighs more than the aphids and lots of aphids weigh more than the few ladybirds that feed on them.

blackbird
ladybirds
aphids
rosebush

Food webs

- A **food web** gives us a more complete picture of what eats what.
- Most animals in a community eat more than one thing. If one kind of food runs out, they will be able to survive by eating something else.
- **Food webs are made up of many food chains linked together.**
- Food chains can be drawn for any environment.

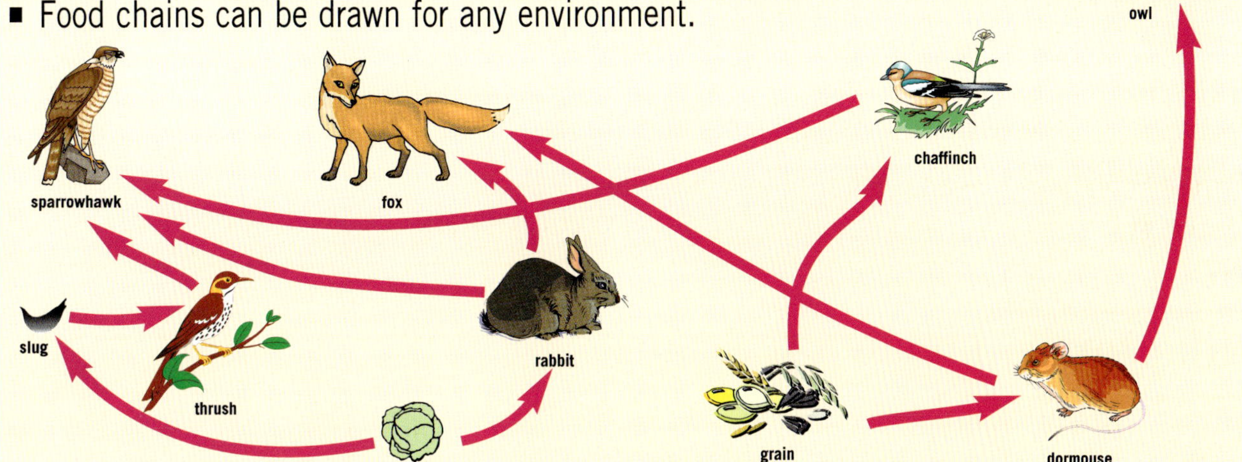

Typical exam questions

Exam questions often focus on what would happen to a food web if an animal was removed by disease or other factors.

- In the food web (above) what would happen if the rabbits were removed?
- What would increase in number due to not being eaten?
- Which species would go hungry due to its food source being removed?
- What effect would removing an organism have on the other animals and plants in the food web?

KEY TERMS

Make sure you understand these terms before moving on!

- producers
- consumers
- food chains
- pyramid of numbers
- biomass pyramid
- food web

QUICK TEST

1. What is a producer?
2. What is a consumer?
3. Where does the energy come from that begins a food chain?
4. What do pyramids of numbers show?
5. What do pyramids of biomass take into account?

Adaptation

- A *habitat* is where an organism lives; it has the conditions needed for it to survive.
- A *community* consists of living things in the habitat.
- Each community is made up of different populations of animals and plants.
- Each *population* is adapted to live in that particular habitat.

Sizes and populations

Population numbers cannot keep growing out of control; factors that keep the population from becoming too large are called **limiting factors**. The factors that affect the size of a population are:

- amount of food and water available
- predators or grazing – what may eat the animal or plant
- disease
- climate, temperature, floods, droughts and storms
- competition for space, mates, light, food and water
- human activity such as pollution or destruction of habitats.

Adaptation

A polar bear lives in cold, arctic regions of the world; it has many features that enable it to survive:

- It has a thick coat to keep in body heat, as well as a layer of blubber for insulation.
- Its coat is white so that it can blend into its surroundings.
- Its fur is greasy so that it doesn't hold water after swimming. This prevents cooling by evaporation.
- It has big feet to spread its weight on snow and ice; it also has big, sharp claws to catch fish.
- It is a good swimmer and runner to catch prey.
- It has a compact shape to keep the surface area to a minimum to reduce loss of body heat.

The adaptations of a cactus and a polar bear are popular examples for the exam but other plants and animals have adapted to live in other environments.

A cactus has adapted to live in the desert. It can cope with very hot and very cold temperatures as well as very little rainfall.

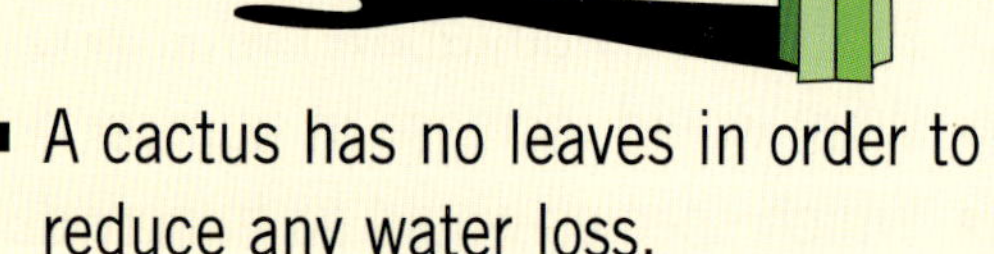

- A cactus has no leaves in order to reduce any water loss.
- The spines protect the cactus from being eaten.
- A cactus is able to store water in its thick stem for periods when there is no rainfall.
- A cactus root system is very well developed to search out water over a large area. The roots are also very strong to anchor the cactus in the sand.

Competition

- As the populations grow, there may be overcrowding and limited resources to support the growing numbers.
- Populations cannot keep growing out of control.
- Animals have to compete for space, food and water in their struggle to survive.
- Plants compete for space, light, water and nutrients.

Predator/prey graphs

- In a community, the number of animals stays fairly constant; this is partly due to the amount of food limiting the size of the populations.
- A **predator** is an animal which hunts and kills another animal.
- The **prey** is the hunted animal.
- Populations of predator and prey go in cycles.

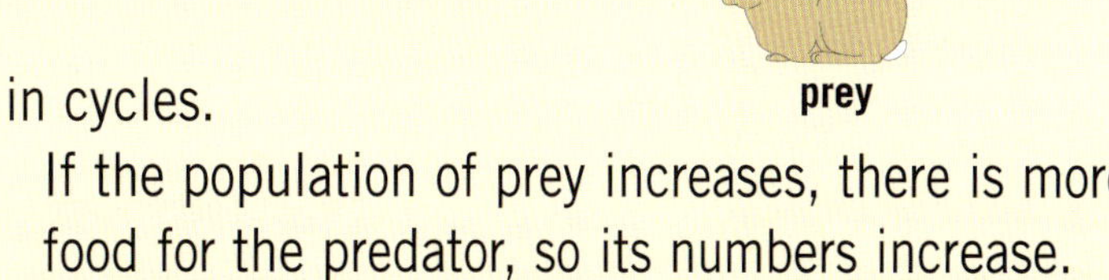

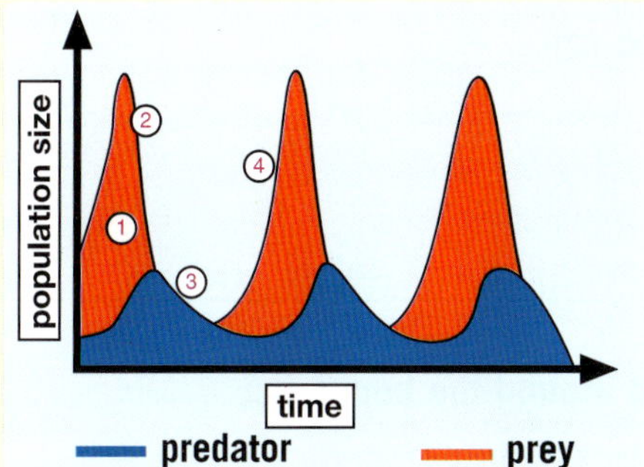

1 If the population of prey increases, there is more food for the predator, so its numbers increase.
2 This causes the number of prey to decrease as they are eaten.
3 This causes the number of predators to decrease, as there is not enough food.
4 If the predator numbers fall, the prey numbers can increase again, as they are not being eaten, and so on.

- Predators have adapted to survive by being strong, agile and fast. They may have good vision and a camouflaged body. They also tend to hunt in packs, have a variety of prey, and often hunt the young, sick and old.
- Prey have also adapted; the best adapted escape and breed.
- Adaptations of prey include being able to hide, run, swim and fly fast. They also tend to stay in large groups. They may have a horrible taste, warning colours and camouflage.

KEY TERMS

Make sure you understand these terms before moving on!

- habitat
- community
- population
- competition
- predator
- prey

QUICK TEST

1. What is a habitat?
2. What things do animals compete for?
3. What things do plants compete for?
4. Why do the numbers of prey and predators in a community stay fairly constant?
5. What factor determines whether animals or plants survive in their environments?

Practice questions

Use the questions to test your progress. Check your answers on page 124.

1. Identify the labels a), b) and c) of this animal cell

   a ....

   b ....

   c ....

2. Which part of the plant cell absorbs the Sun's energy for photosynthesis?

   ....

3. What type of cell is this and what does it do?

   ....

   ....

4. Match each cell with its function:

1. white blood cell	a absorbs water from the soil
2. nerve cell	b fights disease
3. root hair cell	c carries signals

5. Name the five parts that make up a plant. ....

6. Which human organ system is responsible for transporting blood around the body? ....

7. Where are (i) the male sex cells and (ii) the female sex cells in a flower? ....

8. Finish this word equation for photosynthesis

   carbon dioxide + a) ______ $\xrightarrow[\text{b) \_\_\_\_\_\_}]{\text{light}}$ glucose + c) ______

9. Which group of vertebrates have dry, scaly skin and mostly live on land? ....

10. What happens to food in the stomach? ....

11. Where is the information stored that controls your characteristics? ....

12. What happens to undigested food?

    ....

13. Where in the body is digestion completed?

    ....

14. Put this food chain in the correct order:
    snail blackbird oak-tree leaves

    ....

15. Name three diseases associated with smoking ....

16. Complete the equation for respiration:

Glucose + a) .... ⟶ Carbon dioxide + b) .... + c) ....

17. What four parts make up the human blood? ....

18. What are the differences between an artery and a vein? ....

....

19. Explain two ways in which white blood cells fight disease-causing microbes ....

....

20. List as many ways as you can in which the baby is protected in the womb ....

....

21. What are the three main functions of the skeleton? ....

....

22. Replace the letters a–f on the diagram of the breathing system below.

a .... b .... c .... d .... e .... f ....

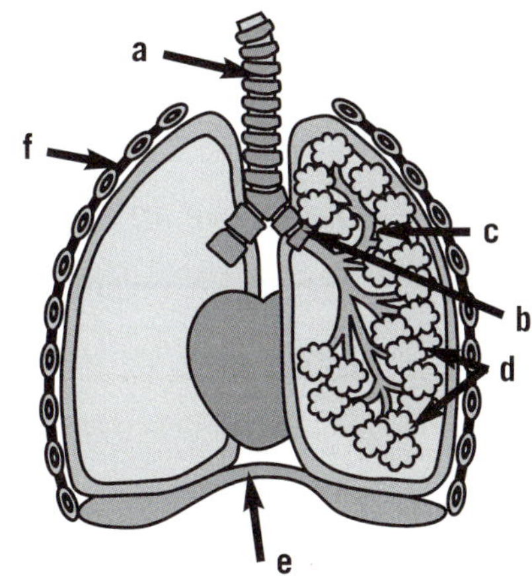

23. What is natural immunity? ....

24. Which three minerals are needed for healthy growth in a plant? ....

25. What is a carpel and what does it consist of? ....

....

26. What is the name of the process which farmers use to improve their crops or livestock? ....

27. List the ways in which the air we breathe in is different to the air we breathe out.

....

28. How many chromosomes does a human body cell have? ....

29. What is pollination? ....

30. Name the seven food groups that make up a balanced diet ....

....

How well did you do? ✗ 1–6 Try again 7–17 Getting there 18–24 Good work 25–30 Excellent! ✓

Rocks

Rocks can be classified into 3 groups: igneous, sedimentary and metamorphic.

Igneous rocks

granite has large crystals

- **All igneous rocks are formed from molten rock which has cooled and solidified.** Molten rock below the surface of the Earth is called magma. Above the Earth's surface it is called lava.
- **Igneous rocks** are very hard and have **crystals**.
- **Extrusive igneous rocks** have **small crystals** because they have formed very quickly above ground. Basalt is an example of an extrusive igneous rock.
- **Intrusive igneous rocks** have **large crystals** because they solidified slowly below the ground. Granite is an example of an intrusive igneous rock.

 ***Name the three types of rock and be able to give an example of each.***

Metamorphic rocks

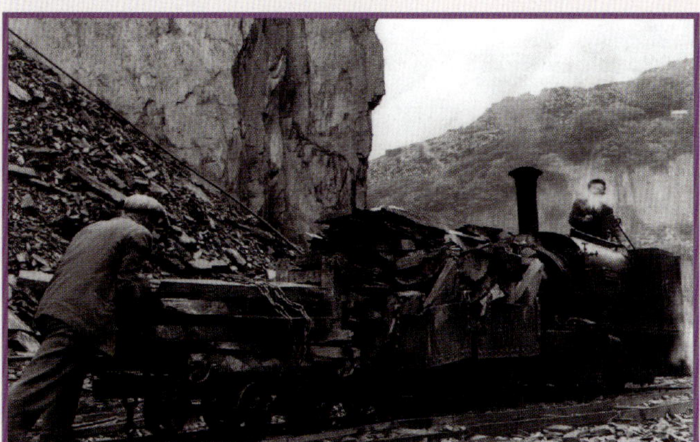
schist (schist and gneiss are examples of metamorphic rocks)

Metamorphic rocks are usually hard and may contain banded crystals.
Metamorphic rocks are formed by high temperature and pressure on existing rocks over a long period of time.
Metamorphic rocks are created when:

- rock is **stressed** as mountains are formed
- **hot magma** comes into contact with rock causing alteration of the existing rocks.

Slate is a metamorphic rock formed from mud. It can be split into layers and used to make roof tiles. Marble is a metamorphic rock formed from limestone.

Sedimentary rocks

- **Sedimentary rocks tend to be crumbly and sometimes contain fossils.** Sandstone and limestone are examples of sedimentary rocks.
- **Sedimentary rocks** form from **layers of sediment** found in seas or lakes. Over millions of years these layers are buried by further sediment. **The weight of these layers squeezes out the water and the particles become cemented together.**
- At least 50% of a rock must be calcium carbonate for it to be called limestone. This mineral is mainly formed from the **calcium-rich skeletons of sea creatures**.
- The exact **composition** of the limestone allows scientists to work out the conditions in which limestone was **formed**. **Some limestones contain almost pure calcium carbonate**. This shows that the water in which they formed must have been **very clear and clean**.

sandstone

limestone

- **Fossilised remains** may give evidence about the environment in which the limestone formed. Some limestones contain **mud and silt**. This shows that they must have been formed in **muddy water**, perhaps **near river deltas**.
- Sometimes there is such a lot of mud and silt that the rock changes from being a limestone and is instead classified as a **shale** or even a **mudstone**.
- Sedimentary rocks like sandstone can be porous. This means that there are gaps between the grains of sand in the sandstone and water is able to soak into these gaps.
- Some sedimentary rocks are called evaporates. These, like **rock salt**, formed when **water in lakes or landlocked seas evaporated**, leaving behind salts which had previously been dissolved.

QUICK TEST

1. Which type of rock is formed when molten rock cools and solidifies?
2. Which type of rock is the hardest?
3. Which sort of igneous rock has small crystals and was formed quickly?
4. Which sort of igneous rock has large crystals and was formed slowly?
5. What two factors can cause existing rock to be changed into metamorphic rock?
6. Which type of rock may contain fossils?
7. Over what time period do sedimentary rocks form?
8. Give two examples of sedimentary rocks.
9. Give two examples of igneous rocks.
10. Give two examples of metamorphic rocks.

KEY TERMS

- igneous
- crystals
- metamorphic
- temperature
- pressure
- sedimentary
- fossils

The rock cycle

Rocks are continually being broken down and then built up again. During the rock cycle, one type of rock is changed into another.

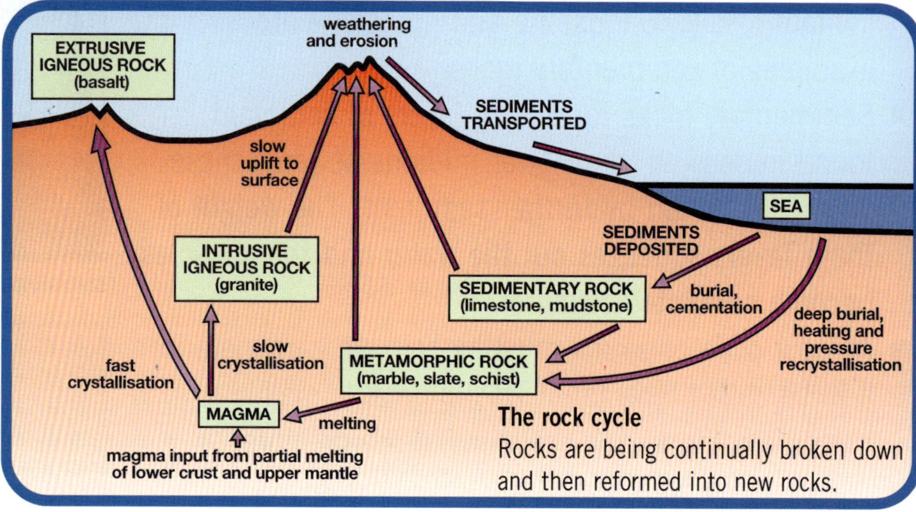

The rock cycle
Rocks are being continually broken down and then reformed into new rocks.

Stages of the rock cycle

- **During weathering large rocks are broken down into smaller pieces.**
- **Erosion** is the wearing down of rock by, for example, wind, waves and rain.
- **Transportation** is the movement of the eroded pieces of rock, usually by rivers and streams, but also by wind and glaciers.
- **Deposition** occurs when sediment is laid down as water can no longer carry it along.
- Rivers cannot carry large grains as far as they can carry smaller grains.
- As the grains are transported they rub against each other and the river bed and become increasingly **more rounded, smoother and smaller**.
- Our ideas about the rock cycle have changed over time. Scientists look at the evidence that is available and use the evidence to make a model to explain what is happening. As new evidence is discovered the models are adapted and changed.

angular, jagged larger grains
river
rounded, smoother smaller grains
sea

The rock cycle involves the same particles being reused over and over again. These processes happen over very long periods of time.

Weathering 1

Weathering is the breaking down of larger rocks into smaller pieces. There are two important ways in which rocks at the Earth's surface are weathered. These are: physical weathering and chemical weathering.

Physical weathering
This happens when rocks are subjected to changes in temperature.

Weathering 2

Freeze thaw

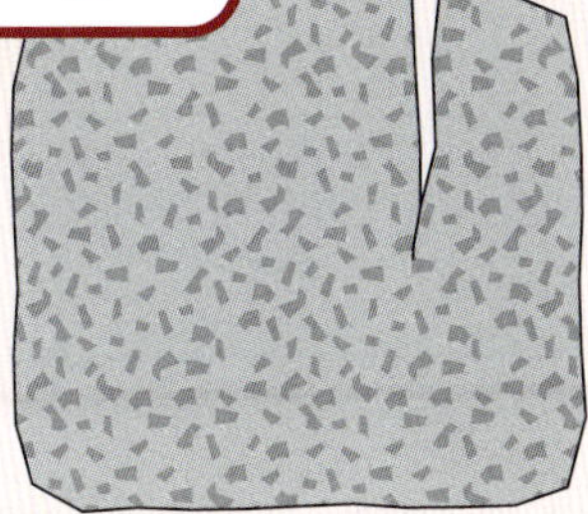
a rock with a small crack

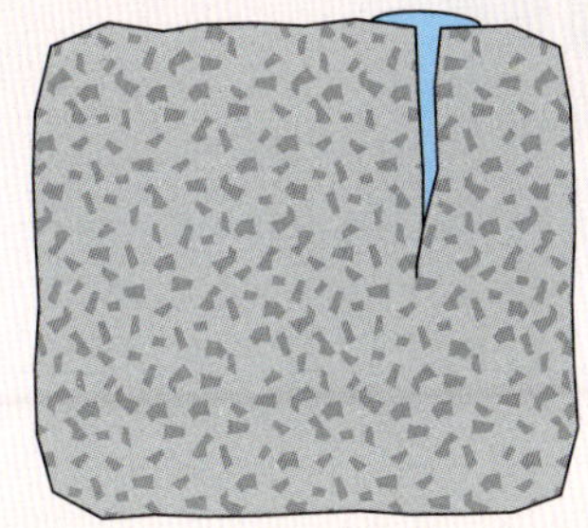
the crack fills with water

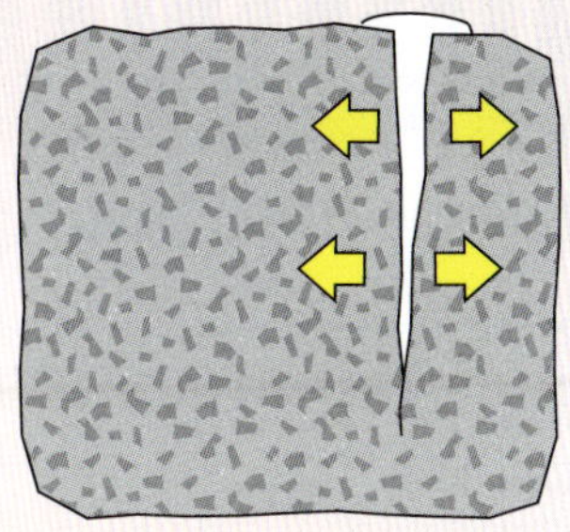
the water freezes and expands, widening the crack

- This type of weathering involves water.
- **Water expands when it freezes**.
- Water enters into a crack in the rock. When this water freezes it expands and gradually forces the crack in the rock wider apart.

Effect of the Sun

- **This type of weathering again involves changes in temperature. Rocks are very poor conductors of thermal energy**. During the day the rock is gradually warmed up by the heat of the Sun, and the outer layer of the rock expands slightly. At night the temperature drops and the outside of the rock tries to contract, but cannot. Eventually the rock will be broken down.

Chemical weathering

- This type of weathering involves a chemical reaction.
- **Chemical weathering damages statues, buildings and gravestones**. It is worst in areas of high pollution.
- As rain falls from the sky **carbon dioxide** in the air dissolves in the rain to form a weak acid which attacks rocks containing calcium carbonate; these rocks include **limestone, chalk and marble**.
- In polluted areas other gases – including **sulphur dioxide** – also dissolve in the rain water, making it even more acidic.

KEY TERMS

Make sure you understand these terms before moving on!

- weathering
- erosion
- transportation
- deposition
- carbon dioxide
- sulphur dioxide

QUICK TEST

1. What is weathering?
2. What is involved in all types of physical weathering?
3. Which substance is involved in freeze-thaw weathering?
4. What happens during freeze-thaw weathering?
5. Why is chemical weathering worst in polluted areas?
6. What is transportation?
7. What normally carries the eroded rock pieces during transportation?
8. In which process are the pieces of rock laid down as sediment?

Pollution

The atmosphere is being polluted in many ways.

Acid rain

- Fossil fuels may contain some **sulphur**.
- When these fuels are burnt sulphur dioxide is produced and released into the atmosphere.
- This gas dissolves in rain water to produce acid rain.
- This acid rain can harm statues and buildings which are made of rock that contains calcium carbonate, like **limestone**, **chalk** and **marble**.
- Acid rain can also attack exposed metals.
- Acid rain can damage – and even kill – trees. It can also harm animals and plants.

Formation of limestone caves

At least 50% of any limestone is the mineral **calcium carbonate**. **Limestone reacts with acids**. Many geologists carry small bottles of hydrochloric acid to test if a particular rock contains limestone. Limestone reacts with the acid to produce carbon dioxide, water and a salt. **If the rock fizzes** when a little acid is dropped on it, **the rock contains calcium carbonate**. Most other sedimentary rocks show no reaction.

When carbon dioxide dissolves in rain water it forms a weak acid which reacts with limestone. The limestone dissolves away and may form fissures and caves.

Reducing the amount of fossil fuels that are burnt will decrease the amount of sulphur dioxide and carbon dioxide put into the environment.

Catalytic converters

The **exhaust** fumes produced by cars contain many **pollutants**. Catalysts are chemicals that speed up chemical reactions, but are not, themselves, used up. Catalytic converters are devices fitted to the exhaust systems of cars. These catalytic converters are made of precious metals like platinum or rhodium. The catalysts convert harmful pollutants such as carbon monoxide, oxides of nitrogen and unburned hydrocarbons into harmless carbon dioxide, water vapour and nitrogen.

Monitoring pollution

The levels of **pollutants** in water and the air are carefully monitored. If they rise above acceptable limits people in nearby areas are warned and steps taken to reduce the pollution, if possible. **Some living organisms can act as good indicators**. Lichen only grows well when there are low levels of air pollutants. **If the lichen starts to die, this is a warning that the air has become polluted.**

Carbon dioxide and the greenhouse

- The **greenhouse effect** is slowly heating up the Earth as a result of human activity.
- When fossil fuels are burnt **carbon dioxide** is produced.
- Although some of this carbon dioxide is removed from the atmosphere when the gas dissolves in the oceans, the overall amount of carbon dioxide in the atmosphere has gradually increased over the last 200 years.
- Carbon dioxide traps heat that has reached the Earth from the Sun.
- Global warming means that ice in the polar regions will melt and cause extensive flooding.

The greenhouse effect is caused by carbon dioxide.

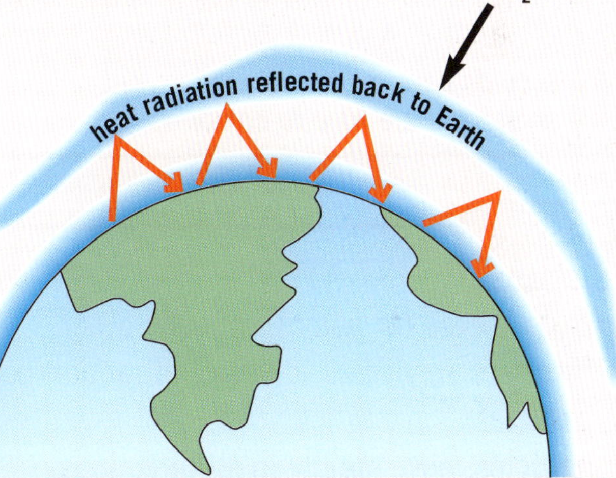

KEY TERMS

Make sure you understand these terms before moving on!

- sulphur
- limestone
- chalk
- marble
- caves
- exhaust
- pollutants
- greenhouse effect
- carbon dioxide

QUICK TEST

1. What is formed when sulphur in fossil fuels is burnt?
2. What does the gas from 1 form when it dissolves in rain water?
3. What environmental problems does this cause?
4. Which rocks are attacked by acid rain?
5. Which gas is responsible for global warming?
6. Why are the amounts of carbon dioxide in the environment increasing?
7. How is carbon dioxide removed from the atmosphere?
8. What is the effect of global warming on the environment?
9. Why is this a problem?

States of matter

There are three *states of matter*: *solid*, *liquid* and *gas*.

Solids

- **particles** are very close together
- particles are held together by strong forces of attraction
- particles vibrate but have fixed positions

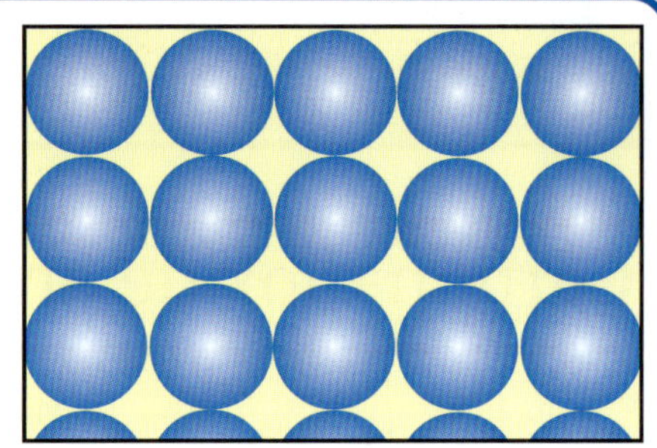

 ***Solids have a definite shape and volume and are hard to compress.***

Liquids

- particles are close together
- particles are held together by forces of attraction
- **particles move relative to each other**

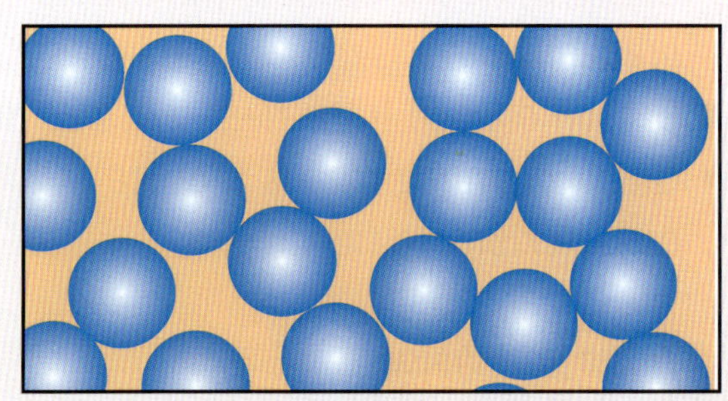

 ***Liquids have a definite volume, but not a definite shape and are hard to compress.***

Gases

- particles are far apart from each other
- there are very small forces of attraction between particles
- **particles move rapidly in all directions**

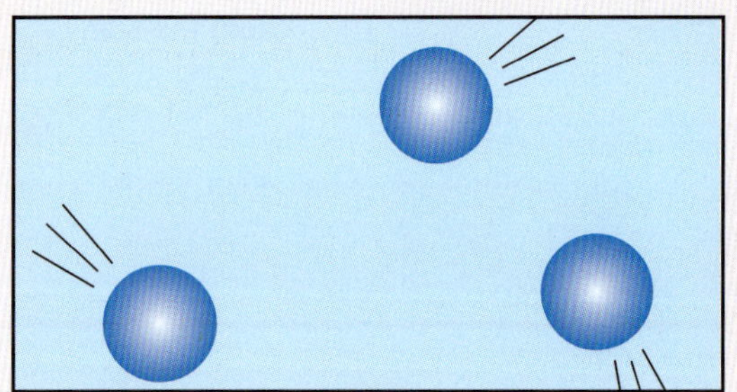

 ***Gases do not have a definite shape or volume and are easy to compress.***

Expansion and contraction

When a solid is heated it expands because the particles begin to move around more and take up more space. Railway tracks are built with small gaps to allow for the metal to expand during hot weather – otherwise they would buckle.

When a solid material is cooled it gets smaller or 'contracts'. Structures like the Eiffel Tower are **slightly shorter on cold days**. Liquids also expand on heating. **We use mercury in thermometers because it is the only metal which is liquid at room temperature** and it expands significantly on heating. It is a silver liquid so it is easier to read the exact temperature.

Changes of state

When changing from one state to another there is no change in mass.

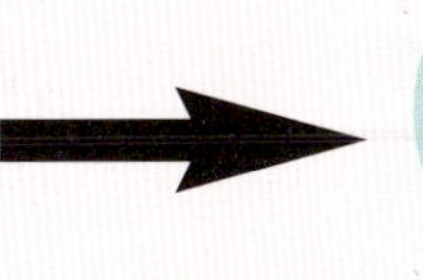

solid (ice) liquid (water)

temperature increases

a) The particles of the solid are heated and vibrate more.

b) The vibration of the particles overcomes the forces of attraction between the particles, enabling them to move more freely.

c) The particles of the liquid are heated and move more quickly.

d) The movement of the liquid particles overcomes the forces of attraction between the particles.

e) The particles in the gas move faster.

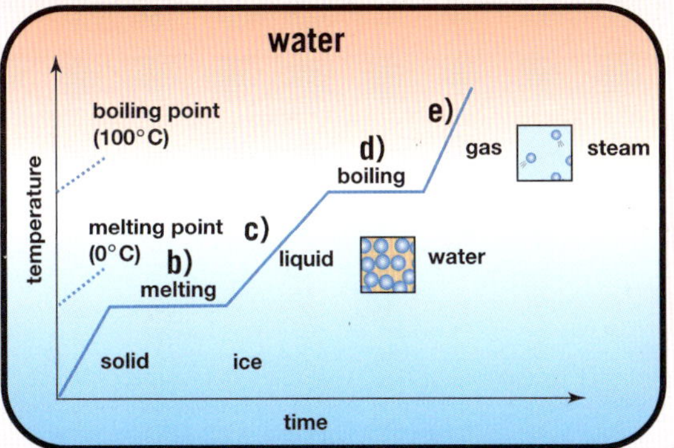

Melting and boiling points

- Above its **boiling** point a substance is a gas.
- Between its **melting** point and its boiling point a substance is a liquid.
- Below its melting point a substance is a solid.

Substance	Melting point °C	Boiling point °C
Iron	1535	2750
Mercury	–39	357
Oxygen	–218	–183

- At 25°C (room temperature) oxygen is a gas.
  25°C is above the boiling point of oxygen.
- At 25°C mercury is a liquid.
  25°C is above the melting point but below the boiling point of mercury.
- At 25°C iron is a solid.
  25°C is below the melting point of iron.

The particles themselves do not get bigger on heating, they just move around more.

KEY TERMS

Make sure you understand these terms before moving on!

- particles
- liquid
- melting
- states of matter
- solid
- gas
- boiling

QUICK TEST

1. Name the three states of matter.
2. Do solids have a definite volume?
3. In which state are particles held together by forces of attraction, but the particles move relative to each other?
4. Can liquids be compressed?
5. Can gases be compressed easily?
6. In which process do liquids turn into gases?
7. In which process do solids turn into liquids?
8. Draw a temperature–time graph to show solid ice melting to form liquid water.

Dissolving

- **If a solid dissolves in a liquid it forms a solution.**
- **However, the overall mass stays the same.**

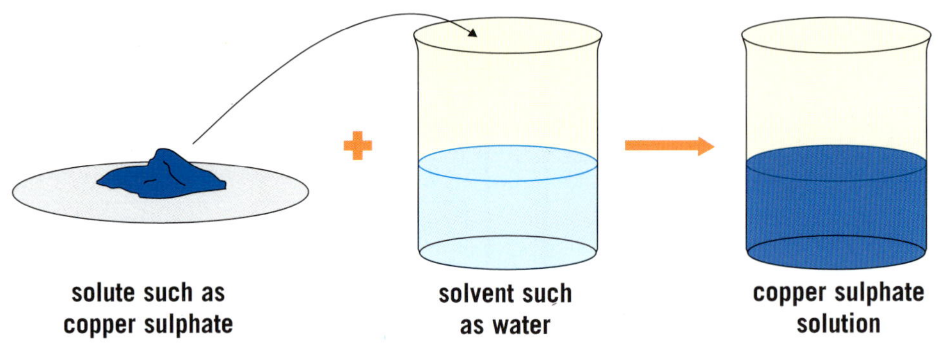

Dissolving solids

What happens when a solid dissolves in a solvent?
Salt is soluble, it dissolves in water to form a solution. The salt particles intermingle with the water particles. In total there is the same number of particles before and after the salt dissolves, so the total mass is the same.

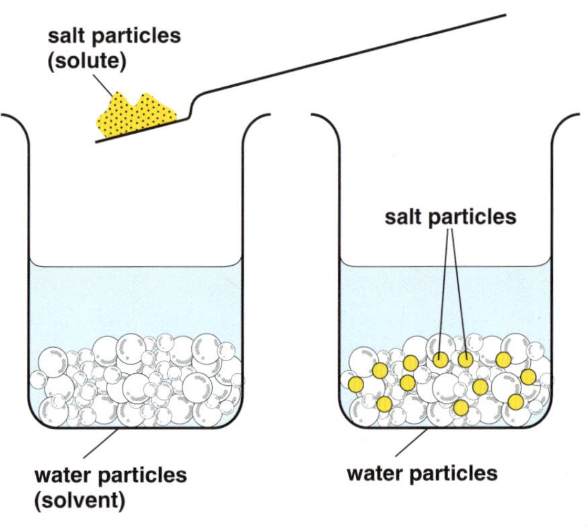

Solvents and solutions

- Once a substance, usually a solid, has dissolved, the liquid (often water) is called the **solvent**.
- The dissolved substance is then called the **solute**.

solute + solvent ⇨ solution

- If a substance dissolves in the solvent it is **soluble**.
- If a substance does not dissolve in the solvent it is **insoluble**.
- The insoluble substance may dissolve in a different solvent.

Nail varnish is insoluble in water, but soluble in nail varnish remover.

How soluble?

- If a substance dissolves well in a solvent it has a high solubility. To measure how soluble a particular substance is we can find how many grams of it will dissolve in a particular solvent.
- The graph shows how the solubility of two solutes, sodium nitrate and potassium nitrate, changes as the **temperature** increases.
- Both of them become more soluble as the temperature rises.
- If no more solute can dissolve in a solvent it is known as a **saturated** solution (at that temperature).
- Temperature affects solubility.
- Normally, the higher the temperature the more soluble the substance becomes.
- Temperature can also affect how quickly something dissolves.
- At a higher temperature the particles are moving faster, so the substance will dissolve faster.
- Sugar will dissolve faster in hot water than cold water.

solubility in grams of solute per 100g of water: 0, 200, 400, 600, 800, 1000, 1 200
temperature in °C: 0, 20, 40, 60, 80, 100
sodium nitrate
potassium nitrate

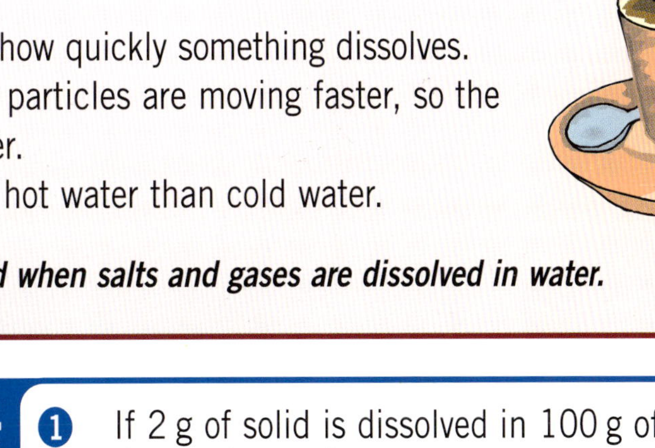

Seawater is a solution formed when salts and gases are dissolved in water.

KEY TERMS

Make sure you understand these terms before moving on!

- solvent
- solute
- solution
- soluble
- insoluble
- temperature
- saturated

QUICK TEST

1. If 2 g of solid is dissolved in 100 g of water, what is the total mass?
2. What is the solid called?
3. What is the liquid called?
4. If a substance dissolves in a solvent, what is formed?
5. What is a solid which can dissolve called?
6. How does increasing temperature affect how much dissolves?
7. What is a saturated solution?
8. Referring to the graph above, what is the solubility of potassium nitrate at 20° C ?
9. What is the solubility of sodium nitrate at 20° C ?
10. What happens to the solubility of potassium nitrate if it is heated?

Particle theory

Particle theory can be used to explain many everyday situations.

Expansion

- When particles are heated they move around more.
- The substance grows bigger (or expands) if it can.
- **The particles themselves do not get larger, they just take up more space because they are moving more.**
- Solids, liquids and gases all **expand** on heating.
- Solids expand the least because the particles are tightly held. Liquids usually expand more than solids.
  Gases expand the most of all the states.
- **On cooling, substances become smaller (or** contract).
- Expansion can exert a lot of force. Concrete roads are constructed with gaps in to allow for expansion in hot weather.

Diffusion

The mingling of particles is called **diffusion**. Gases diffuse or mix together quickly, because the **particles are moving very quickly in all directions**.

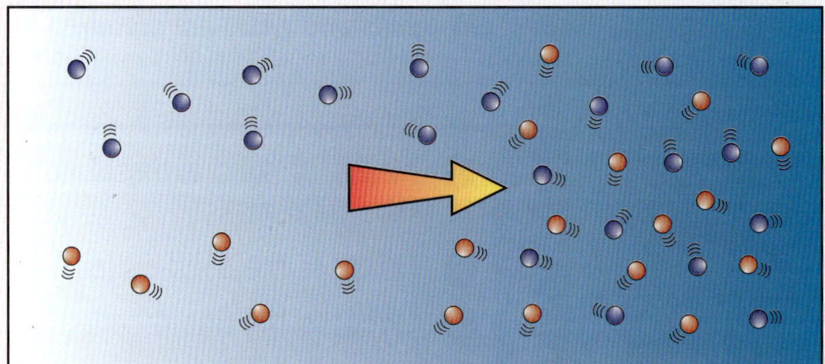

You can smell a perfume because the **scent particles diffuse through the air** to your nose. Many perfumes and aftershaves contain alcohol. The boiling point of alcohol is about 78°C. Body temperature is 38°C. This means that alcohol can evaporate from the skin quite easily. Liquids can mix without being stirred because liquid particles, like gas particles, can diffuse. **Liquids diffuse more slowly than gases** because the particles are moving more slowly.

Gas pressure

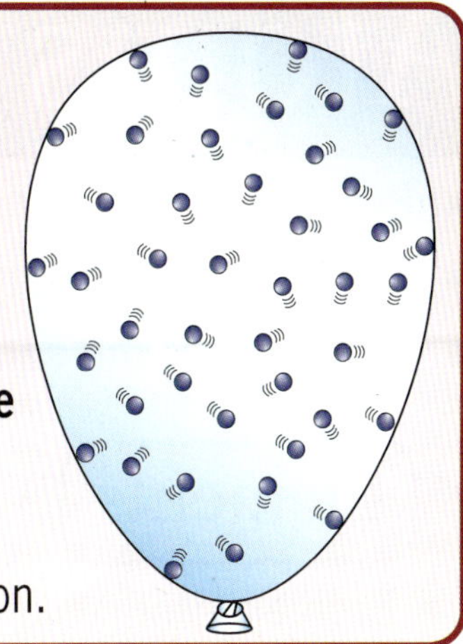

- Gas particles are moving very quickly in all directions.
- If a gas is put into a container the gas particles crash into the walls of the container.
- The force of these collisions creates **gas pressure**.
- If the **temperature is increased the gas particles collide with more force** and more often with the walls of the container, **so the pressure increases**.
- You can feel the effect of gas pressure when you blow up a balloon.

Atmospheric pressure

As you read this page the gas particles in the air continually collide with you. The particles exert a pressure called **atmospheric pressure**. We are so used to this pressure that we don't often think about it, but it is very strong.

The effects of atmospheric pressure can be shown by the collapsing can experiment.

An 'empty' can is not really empty at all – it is full of air!

Normally the pressure on the inside and the outside of the can is equal. If some air particles from inside the can are removed, then the pressure inside the can suddenly becomes less than the pressure on the outside. This causes it to collapse dramatically, due simply to atmospheric pressure.

KEY TERMS

Make sure you understand these terms before moving on!

- expand
- contract
- diffusion
- gas pressure
- atmospheric pressure

QUICK TEST

1. Why can you smell a flower across a room?
2. Why do gases diffuse quickly?
3. Can liquids diffuse?
4. What causes pressure?
5. Why does increasing temperature increase the pressure?
6. What happens to the particles as they are heated?
7. Which expands more – a solid or a liquid?
8. Do the particles themselves expand?
9. Why are concrete roads built with gaps in them?

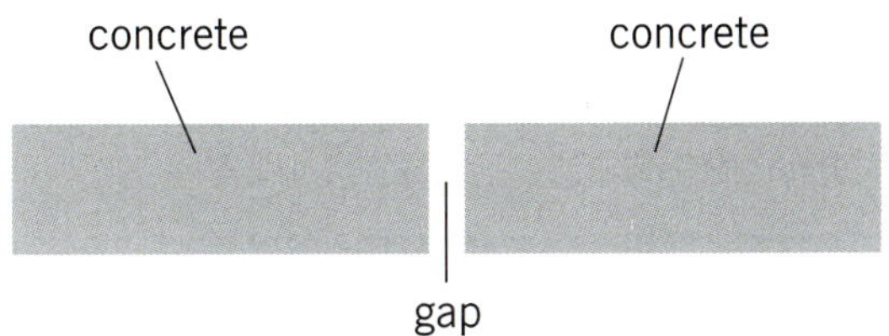

Atoms and elements

- **Everything is made up of atoms.**
- **Atoms are extremely small.**
- **All atoms of the same element have identical numbers of protons.**

Elements

- **Each element contains only one type of atom**. There are about 100 different **elements**.
- The **periodic table** is a helpful way of showing all the elements.
- **Each element has a symbol** which can be used to identify it.
- For example, carbon can be identified by the symbol C.

Group	1	2											3	4	5	6	7	0
Period																		
1	H 1																	He 2
2	Li 3	Be 4											B 5	C 6	N 7	O 8	F 9	Ne 10
3	Na 11	Mg 12											Al 13	Si 14	P 15	S 16	Cl 17	Ar 18
4	K 19	Ca 20	Sc 21	Ti 22	V 23	Cr 24	Mn 25	Fe 26	Co 27	Ni 28	Cu 29	Zn 30	Ga 31	Ge 32	As 33	Se 34	Br 35	Kr 36
5	Rb 37	Sr 38	Y 39	Zr 40	Nb 41	Mo 42	Tc 43	Ru 44	Rh 45	Pd 46	Ag 47	Cd 48	In 49	Sn 50	Sb 51	Te 52	I 53	Xe 54
6	Cs 55	Ba 56	57 – 71*	Hf 72	Ta 73	W 74	Re 75	Os 76	Ir 77	Pt 78	Au 79	Hg 80	Tl 81	Pb 82	Bi 83	Po 84	At 85	Rn 86
7	Fr 87	Ra 88	89 – 103**	Rf 104	Db 105	Sg 106	Bh 107	Hs 108	Mt 109	Uun 110	Uuu 111	Uub 112	Uut 113	Uuq 114	Uup 115	Uuh 116	Uus 117	Uuo 118

***Lanthanides**	La 57	Ce 58	Pr 59	Nd 60	Pm 61	Sm 62	Eu 63	Gd 64	Tb 65	Dy 66	Ho 67	Er 68	Tm 69	Yb 70	Lu 71
****Actinides**	Ac 89	Th 90	Pa 91	U 92	Np 93	Pu 94	Am 95	Cm 96	Bk 97	Cf 98	Es 99	Fm 100	Md 101	No 102	Lr 103

Note that elements 113, 115 and 117 are not yet known, but are included in the table to show their respective positions. Elements 114, 116 and 118 have only been reported recently.

Key: Non-metal, Metalloid, Metal, Transitional, Rare-earth element (Lanthanide) and radioactive rare-earth element (Actinide), Transactinide, 'Missing' element

- In the modern periodic table the elements are arranged in order of **increasing atomic number**.
- Most of the elements in the periodic table are metals. All the **metallic** elements are solids at room temperature with the exception of mercury, which is a liquid. Bromine is the only non-metal element which is a liquid at room temperature.

The nucleus

- Atoms have a **nucleus** in the centre, which is surrounded by electrons.
- **The nucleus contains neutrons and protons.**
- Neutrons have no electric charge and protons have a positive charge.
  This means that overall the nucleus has a positive charge.
- The electrons are very, very small, and carry a negative charge as they spin rapidly around the nucleus.

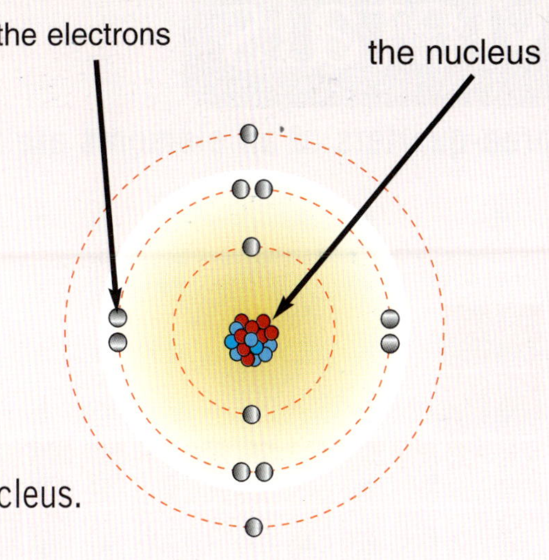

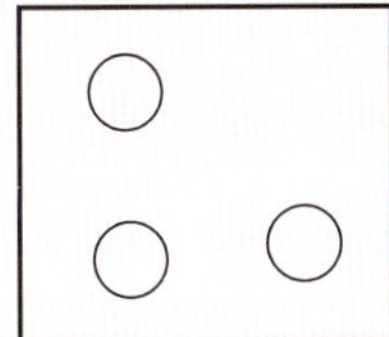

Atoms of the element neon

An element is made up of only one type of atom.

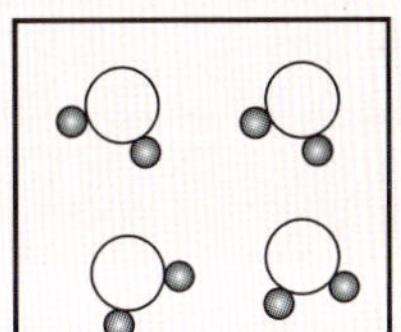

Carbon and oxygen atoms are joined together to form the compound carbon dioxide

A compound is made up of at least two different types of atom that have been joined together.

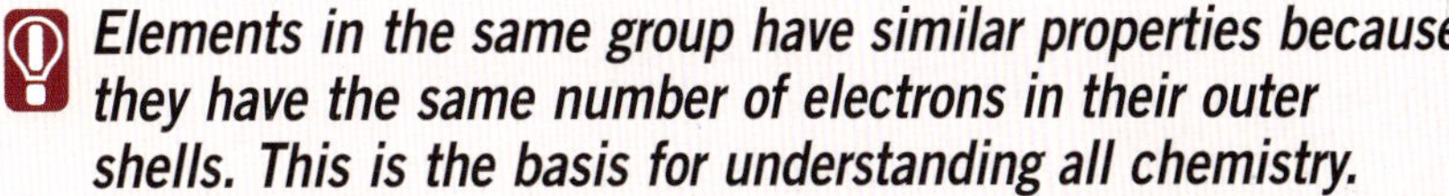

Elements in the same group have similar properties because they have the same number of electrons in their outer shells. This is the basis for understanding all chemistry.

KEY TERMS

Make sure you understand these terms before moving on!

- atom
- elements
- periodic table
- symbol
- increasing atomic number
- metallic
- nucleus

QUICK TEST

1. What is special about an element?
2. How many elements have been discovered?
3. How are the elements often displayed?
4. How are elements arranged in the periodic table?
5. What is the centre part of an atom called?
6. Which particles are found in the nucleus of an atom?
7. Which particles are found in shells around the nucleus?
8. What charge do electrons have?

Metals

Three-quarters of all elements are metals.

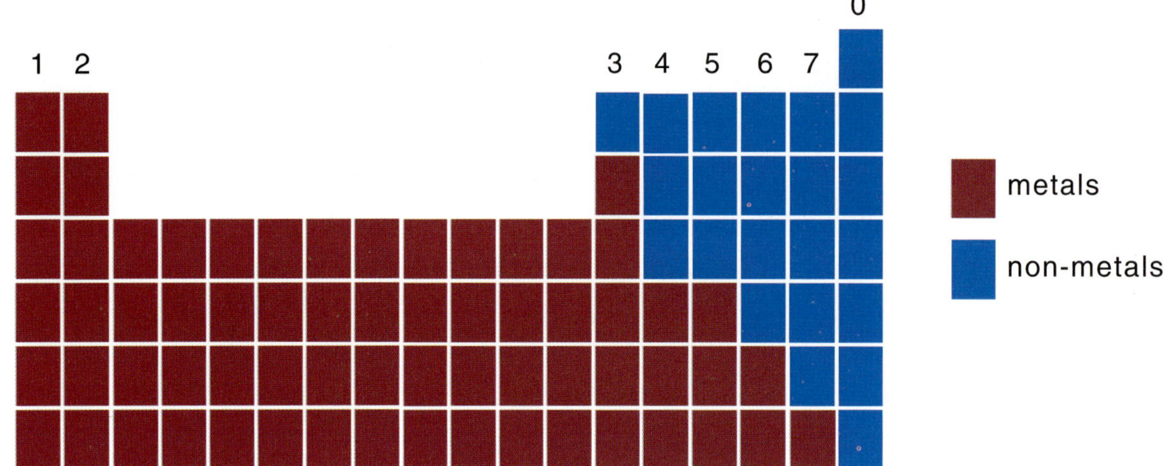

Properties of metals

Metals are good conductors of **heat**.

Metals have high melting and boiling points. All the metals are solids except mercury which is **liquid** at room temperature.

Metals are shiny (when freshly cut).

Metals are sonorous (ping when hit).

Metals may be mixed together to form useful **alloys**.

Metals are good conductors of **electricity**.

Metals are strong and dense, but they are also malleable (can be hammered into shape) and ductile (can be drawn into wires).

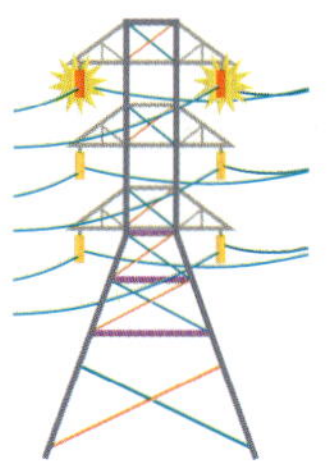

Some metals are **magnetic** (like iron and steel).

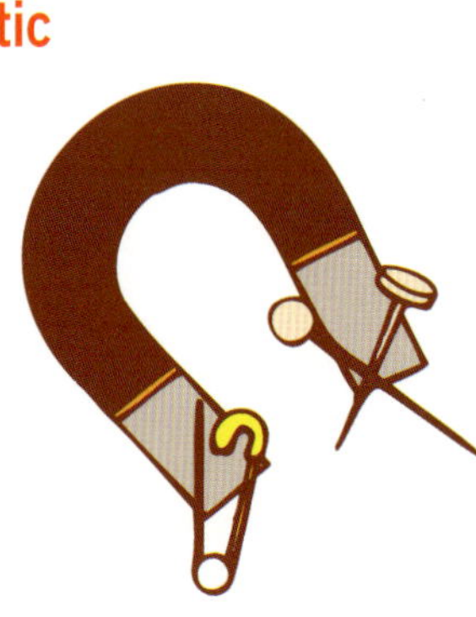

Learn the characteristics of metals then cover these pages and write them down. Do the same for non-metals.

Aeroplanes are made of alloys which are light and strong.

Non-metals

- About one-quarter of the elements are non-metals.

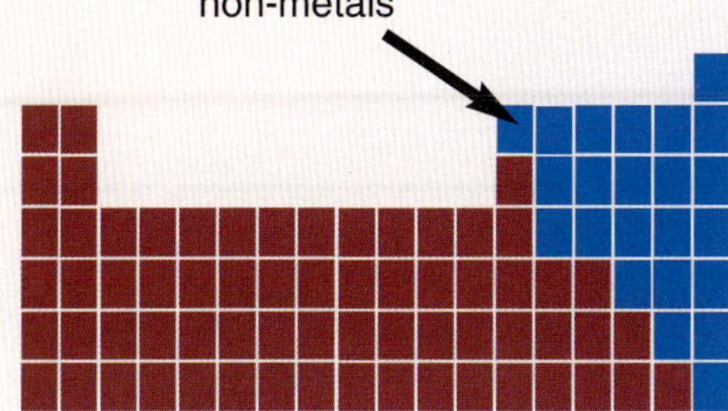

- Non-metals usually have low melting points and boiling points; 11 of them are gases at room temperature.
- Bromine is the only liquid non-metal at room temperature.
- **Non-metals are not shiny, malleable, strong, ductile or sonorous.**
- If hit they are **brittle** and tend to break.
- They appear **dull**.

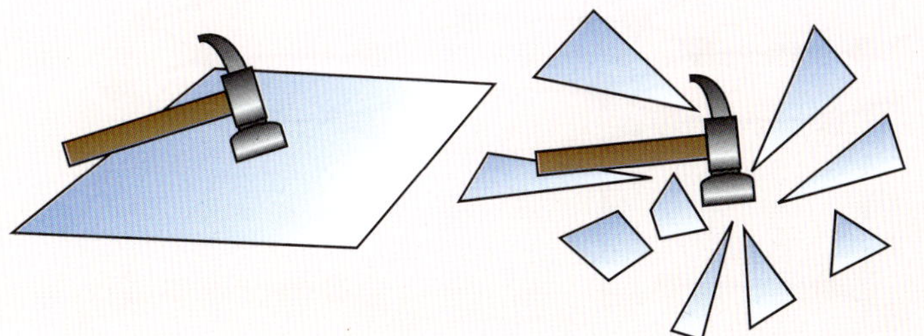

- **Non-metals have low densities.**
- Non-metals are poor conductors of heat.
- Non-metals usually do not conduct electricity.
- An exception is carbon which, when in the form of graphite, does conduct.

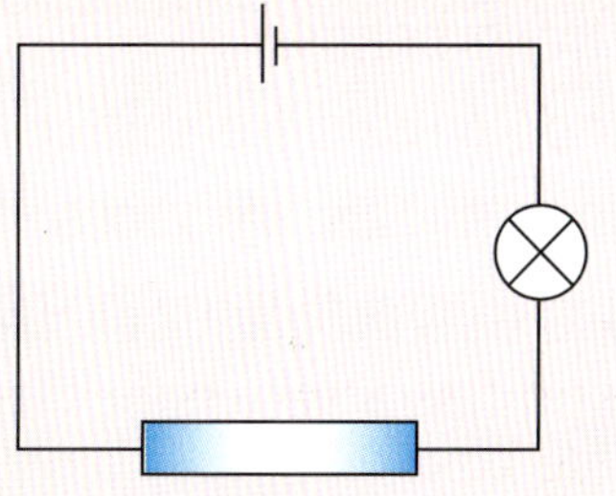

electricity cannot flow and the lamp does not light

Metal oxides dissolve in water to form alkaline solutions. Non-metal oxides dissolve in water to form acidic solutions.

KEY TERMS

Make sure you understand these terms before moving on!

- heat
- melting
- boiling
- liquid
- alloys
- electricity
- magnetic
- brittle
- dull
- low densities

QUICK TEST

1. Sketch the periodic table and shade the metal elements.
2. Roughly what fraction of the elements are metals?
3. Name the only metal which is not a solid at room temperature.
4. What does sonorous mean?
5. Name the properties that are common to all metals.
6. Roughly what fraction of elements are non-metals?
7. Which non-metal is a liquid at room temperature?
8. Comment on the density of non-metals.
9. Do non-metals generally conduct electricity?
10. Which non-metal conducts electricity?

Unusual elements

Metals and non-metals have characteristic properties; however, there are certain elements which have unexpected properties.

Non-metals

Carbon can exist as diamond or graphite.

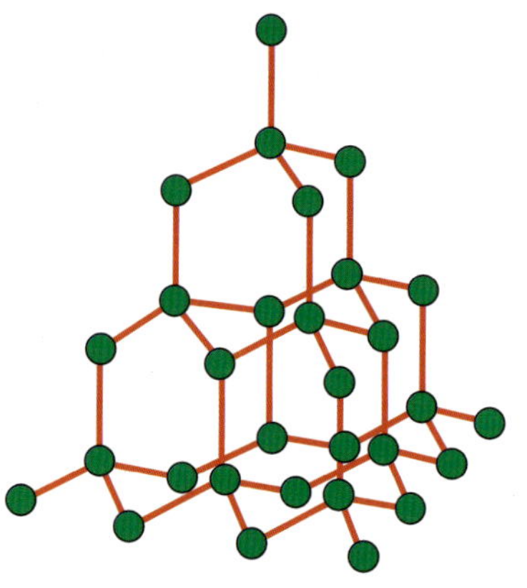

diamond

Diamond

- Diamond is a form of the element carbon.
- In diamond all the carbon atoms are held together with very strong bonds.
- Most non-metals are soft or brittle: diamond is very hard.
- Most non-metals are gases, one is a liquid and a few are solids with low melting points.
- Diamond has a very high melting point – over 3500°C.

Graphite

- Graphite is also a form of the element carbon.
- It is made of the same carbon atoms as diamond, but **graphite has a layered structure**.
- Most non-metals do not conduct electricity. Graphite is unusual because it can conduct electricity.
- 'Pencil lead' is actually graphite.

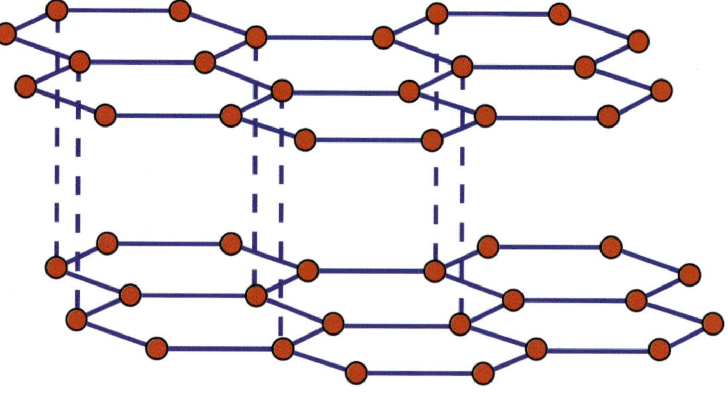

graphite

Bromine

- Bromine is the only non-metal element which is a liquid at room temperature.

Carbon has two forms: diamond and graphite.

Unusual metals

Mercury

Mercury is the only metal which is a liquid at room temperature. All the other metals are solid. Liquids expand more than solids when they are heated, one reason mercury is useful in thermometers.

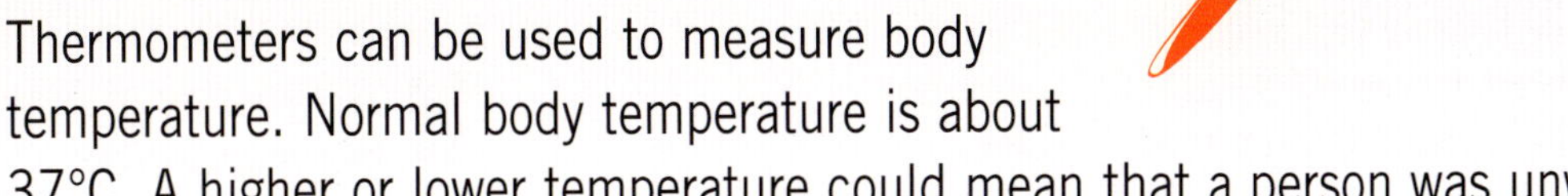

Thermometers can be used to measure body temperature. Normal body temperature is about 37°C. A higher or lower temperature could mean that a person was unwell.

Sodium

Sodium is an unusual metal.

- Most metals have a high density: sodium has a much lower density and will even float on water.
- Most metals are hard and strong: sodium is soft and can be cut with a knife.
- Most metals react slowly or not at all with water: **sodium reacts very vigorously with water giving off a gas (hydrogen) and forming an alkaline solution (sodium hydroxide)**.

Potassium and lithium behave in a similar way to sodium.

KEY TERMS

Make sure you understand these terms before moving on!

- carbon
- diamond
- graphite
- bromine
- liquid
- mercury
- sodium
- vigorously

QUICK TEST

1. What state are most metals at room temperature?
2. Which is the only metal element which is a liquid at room temperature?
3. What happens to solids and liquids on heating?
4. What is mercury used in?
5. Why does sodium float on water?
6. What happens in the reaction between sodium and water?
7. Name two forms of carbon.
8. Why is diamond unusual for a non-metal?
9. Why is graphite unusual for a non-metal?
10. Which is the only non-metal which is liquid at room temperature?

Chemical reactions

The rusting of iron and steel is an important everyday chemical reaction.

It is not a useful reaction, and we try to slow down or stop the reaction.

Burning (or combustion) is another everyday reaction. When substances are burned in a controlled way it can be a very useful reaction.

Corroding of iron

Iron corrodes (or **rusts**) faster than most metals.
Three test tubes are set up in an experiment and left for a few days.

The rusting of iron has a very slow rate of reaction.

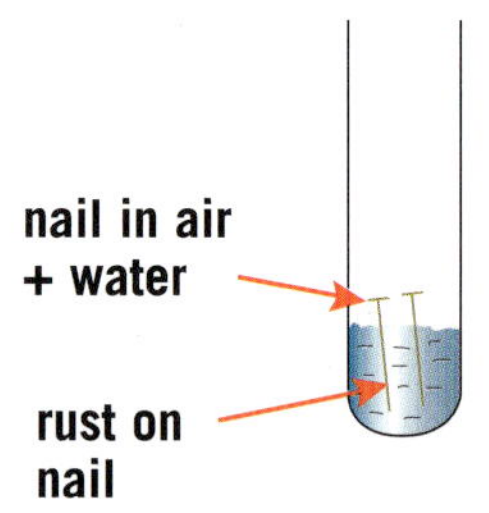

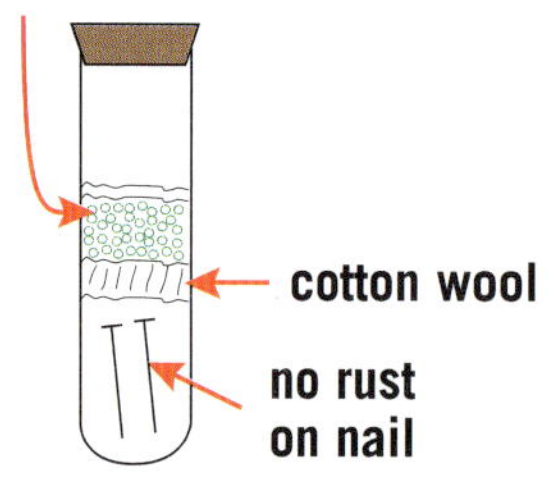

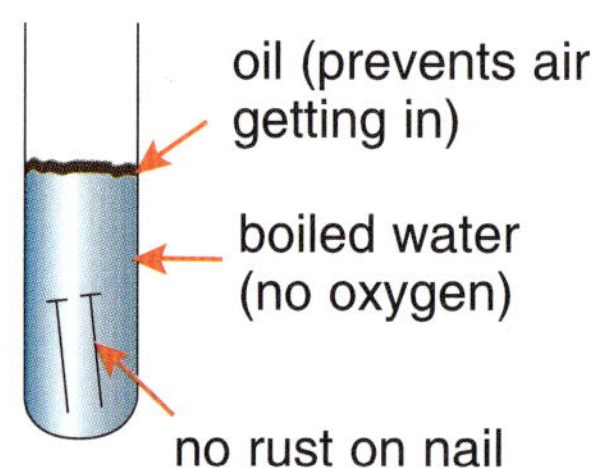

Test tube 1
Air (which contains oxygen) and water are both present.

Test tube 2
Air is present but there is no water. **Anhydrous calcium chloride removes any water from the air.**

Test tube 3
The nails are resting in water. Although there is air in the test tube, any air dissolved in the water has been removed by boiling it. **A layer of oil on top of the water stops any air from reaching the water.**
Water is present

After a few days **rusting has only occurred in test tube 1**. Therefore both **oxygen and water must be present** for rusting to happen.
If either the oxygen or the water is completely removed then the iron will not rust.

Water and oxygen must both be present for rusting to occur.

Burning

When a substance is **burned** it reacts with the oxygen in the air to form a new substance called an oxide.
When magnesium is burned in air it reacts with oxygen to form the compound magnesium oxide.

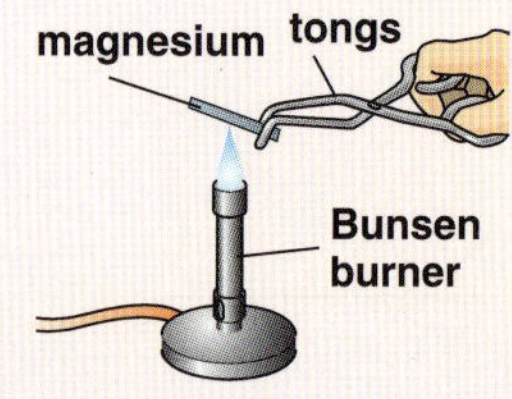

This chemical reaction can be represented by the word equation:

magnesium + oxygen → magnesium oxide

Burning fuels

Fuels are substances that release energy (normally in the form of heat) **when they are burned.**

The fuel methane is burned in a Bunsen burner. Methane has the formula CH_4.

This shows that it contains the elements carbon and hydrogen.

When methane is burned carbon reacts with oxygen to form carbon dioxide, while hydrogen reacts to form water vapour.

Preventing rusting

Coating iron or steel

- **Painting** or coating iron in plastic or oil can stop oxygen and water from reaching the iron. If the coating is damaged, the iron will rust.

iron is protected by paint

if the layer is scratched water and air reach the iron

no rusting occurs

rusting occurs

Tin plating

- If iron is plated with tin or chromium it will not rust. Tin and chromium are both less reactive than iron. However, if the protective layer is damaged then it will begin to rust.

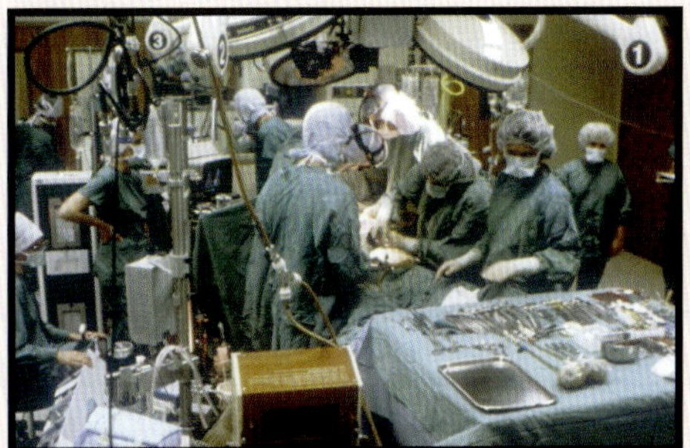

surgical instruments can be made from stainless steel

Alloying the metal

- If iron is mixed with other metals such as chromium it will form the alloy stainless steel.
- This does not rust.

Sacrificial protection

- If a metal which is more reactive than iron, such as zinc or magnesium, is connected to iron then corrosion will be prevented. Because zinc is more reactive, zinc reacts instead of iron.
- Iron is protected at the expense of the more reactive metal. For this reason it is called sacrificial protection.

KEY TERMS

Make sure you understand these terms before moving on!

- rusts
- fuels
- burned
- painting
- tin plating
- alloying
- release energy
- sacrificial protection

QUICK TEST

1. What does anhydrous calcium chloride do?
2. Why is the water boiled in test tube 3 of the experiment described on page 62?
3. Why is a layer of oil placed on top of the water in test tube 3?
4. What is needed for iron to rust?
5. How is stainless steel made and what are its advantages?
6. What is sacrificial protection?

Reactivity series

Some metals are more reactive than others. The metals can be placed in order of reactivity.

Reactivity series

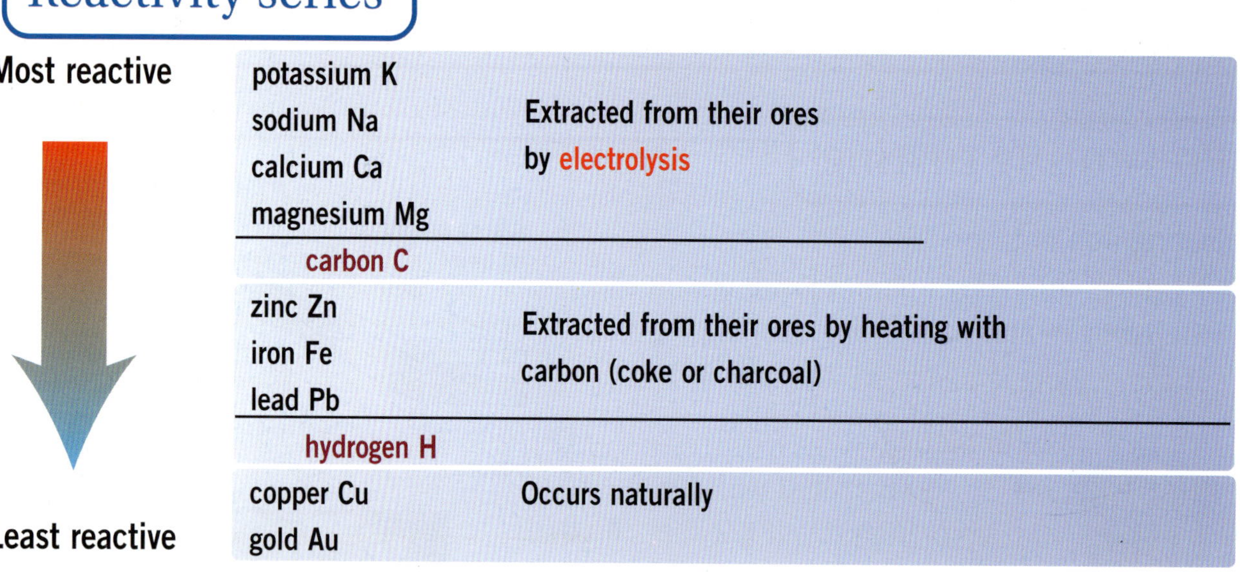

Most reactive		
	potassium K sodium Na calcium Ca magnesium Mg	Extracted from their ores by electrolysis
	carbon C	
	zinc Zn iron Fe lead Pb	Extracted from their ores by heating with carbon (coke or charcoal)
	hydrogen H	
Least reactive	copper Cu gold Au	Occurs naturally

The order of reactivity has been worked out by observing how vigorous the **reactions** are between the metals and: ▪ air; ▪ water; and ▪ dilute acid.

Reacting the metals with air

When metals are heated with air they may react with the oxygen present.

metal + oxygen ➪ **metal oxide**

magnesium + oxygen ➪ magnesium oxide

$2Mg(s) + O_2(g) \Rightarrow 2MgO(s)$

Most reactive		
	potassium K sodium Na calcium Ca magnesium Mg	These metals react vigorously. They burn fiercely.
	carbon C zinc Zn iron Fe lead Pb hydrogen H copper Cu	These metals react slowly with air.
Least reactive	gold Au	No reaction

Reacting the metals with water

Some metals react with water to produce a **metal hydroxide** and hydrogen.

metal + water ➪ metal hydroxide + hydrogen

sodium + water ➪ sodium hydroxide + hydrogen

potassium copper

When potassium, sodium and calcium are reacted with water, bubbles can be seen. **These bubbles show us that a gas is being made**. The gas made in this reaction is hydrogen.

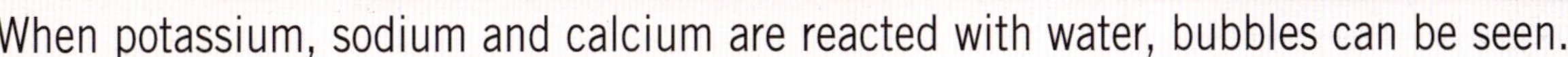

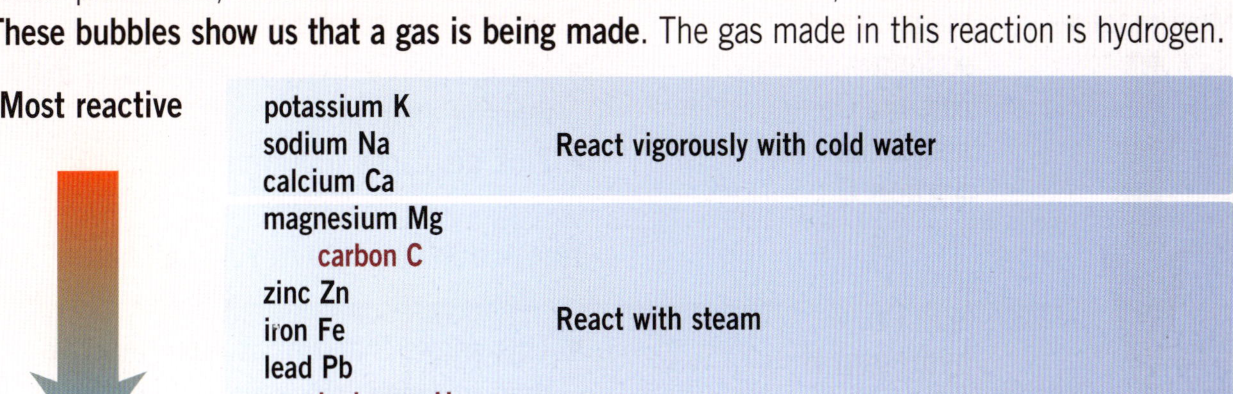

Most reactive ↓ Least reactive	Metal	Reaction with water
	potassium K sodium Na calcium Ca	React vigorously with cold water
	magnesium Mg carbon C zinc Zn iron Fe lead Pb hydrogen H	React with steam
	copper Cu gold Au	No reaction

Reacting the metals with dilute acids

Some metals (those more reactive than hydrogen) react with dilute acids to produce **salts** and hydrogen.

metal + acid ➪ salt + hydrogen

calcium + hydrochloric acid ➪ calcium chloride + hydrogen

When magnesium reacts with acid the temperature of the acid increases. A change in temperature is evidence that a chemical reaction is taking place. The bubbles formed when magnesium reacts with dilute acid show us that a gas is being made. The gas is hydrogen.

Most reactive ↓ Least reactive	Metal	Reaction with dilute acid
	potassium K sodium Na	React violently with dilute acid
	calcium Ca magnesium Mg	React fast with dilute acid
	carbon C zinc Zn iron Fe lead Pb hydrogen H	React more slowly with dilute acid
	copper Cu gold Au	No reaction

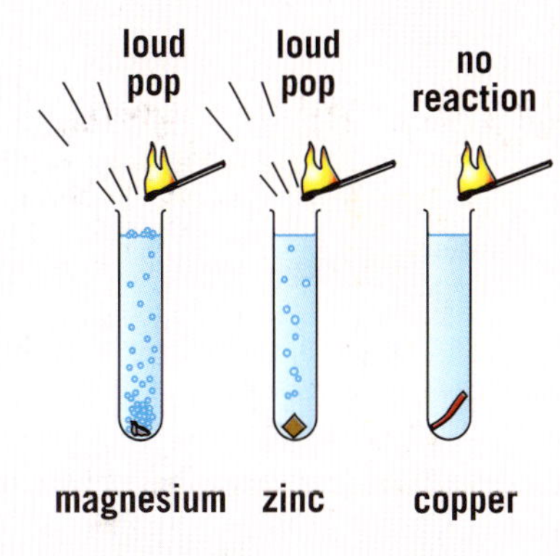

KEY TERMS

- electrolysis
- reaction
- metal oxide
- metal hydroxide
- salts

QUICK TEST

1. How should metals more reactive than carbon be extracted from their ores?
2. How should metals less reactive than carbon be extracted from their ores?
3. How was the reactivity series compiled?

Displacement

A more reactive metal will displace a less reactive metal from a compound.

Reactivity series

Most reactive	potassium K
	sodium Na
	calcium Ca
	magnesium Mg
	carbon C
	zinc Zn
	iron Fe
	lead Pb
	hydrogen H
	copper Cu
Least reactive	gold Au

Iron and copper sulphate

Iron is **more reactive** than copper.

- When an iron nail is placed in a solution of copper sulphate, the nail changes colour from silver to orange-pink.
- The nail has been **coated with copper**.
- The solution changes colour from blue to a very pale green.
- The solution now contains iron sulphate.

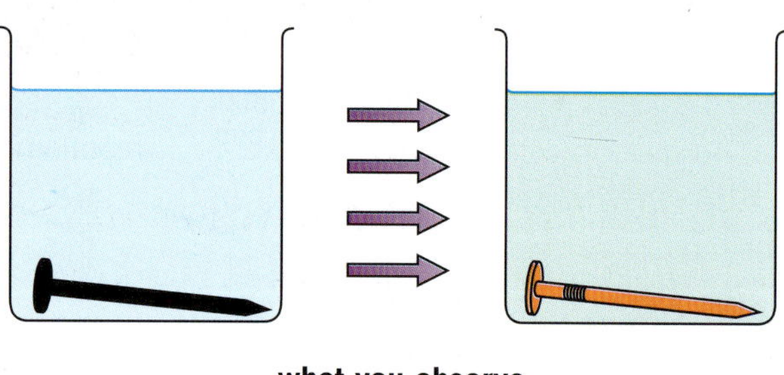

what you observe

Zinc and iron sulphate

- Using the reactivity series, zinc is **more reactive** than iron.
- Zinc **displaces** iron from the solution.

zinc + iron sulphate ⇨ zinc sulphate + iron

- This shows that zinc is **more reactive** than iron and iron is **more reactive** than copper.

The order of reactivity is:

most reactive	zinc
	iron
least reactive	copper

An understanding of the reactivity series and displacement reactions helps you to predict and explain many chemical reactions.

iron + copper sulphate ⇨ copper + iron sulphate
iron is more reactive copper is less reactive

This is an example of a **displacement reaction**. The **more reactive** metal, iron, **displaces** the **less reactive** metal, copper, from its compound, copper sulphate.
Iron displaces the copper from the solution.

Copper and magnesium sulphate

magnesium sulphate
copper

If the metal which is added is **less reactive** than the metal in the compound then no reaction will occur.

copper + magnesium sulphate ⇨ no reaction

We can use displacement reactions to investigate the reactivity of metals. The table below shows some results from displacement reactions. A cross shows that no reaction takes place. A tick shows a reaction does take place.

Metal/metal solution	Magnesium sulphate	Iron sulphate	Copper sulphate
Magnesium		✓	✓
Iron	✗		✓
Copper	✗	✗	

Magnesium is the most reactive metal because it displaces iron from iron sulphate and copper from copper sulphate.

The thermite reaction

This is a very useful displacement reaction.

It is used to produce **molten** iron to mend railway tracks.

- Aluminium is heated with iron oxide.
- Aluminium is more reactive than iron, so the aluminium displaces the iron.
- Aluminium oxide and iron are produced.

The reaction gives out a lot of heat, it is very **exothermic**; the iron produced is molten and can therefore be poured into gaps in the rails.

aluminium + iron oxide ⇨ aluminium oxide + iron

Exothermic reactions give out heat energy.

KEY TERMS

Make sure you understand these terms before moving on!

- reactive
- displace
- displacement reaction
- molten
- exothermic

1. What is the rule for displacement reactions?
2. Which metal is more reactive: iron or copper?
3. Write a word equation for the reaction between iron and copper sulphate.
4. Which metal is the more reactive: iron or zinc?
5. Write a word equation for the reaction between zinc and iron sulphate.
6. Which metal is more reactive: copper or magnesium?
7. Write a word equation for the reaction between magnesium and copper sulphate.
8. What happens when copper is placed in a solution of zinc sulphate?

Acids and alkalis

Indicators are used to show whether a solution is acidic, alkaline or neutral by changing colour.

Indicators

There are many different **indicators**.

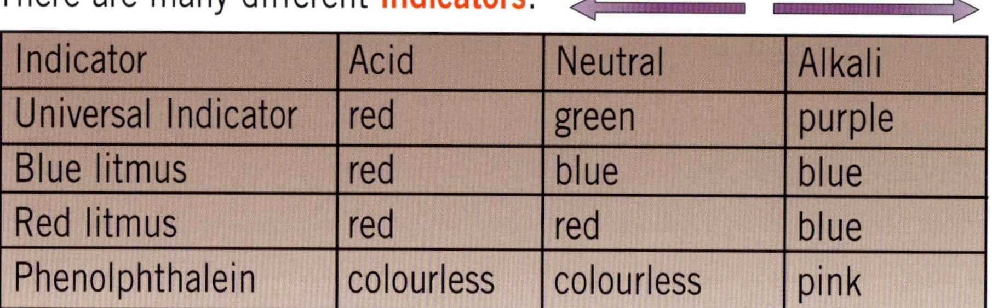

Indicator	Acid	Neutral	Alkali
Universal Indicator	red	green	purple
Blue litmus	red	blue	blue
Red litmus	red	red	blue
Phenolphthalein	colourless	colourless	pink

Wasp stings are alkaline.

Acids

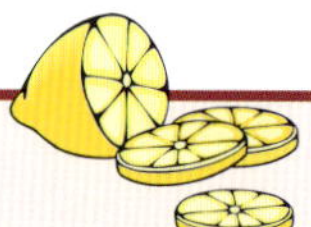

Acidic solutions have a pH less than 7.
The strongest acids have a pH of 1.
The weakest acids have a pH of 6.
Many foods such as **lemons and vinegar contain acids**. These foods **taste sour**.

Common laboratory acids are:

- hydrochloric acid
- sulphuric acid
- nitric acid

The soluble oxides of non-metals form acidic solutions.

Many soft drinks like cola and lemonade are quite acidic.

Alkalis

Alkalis are also called **bases**.
Alkalis are soluble bases.
Alkalis have a pH of more than 7.
The strongest alkalis have a pH of 14.
The weakest alkalis have a pH of 8.
Alkalis often make good cleaning materials.

Common alkalis are:

- sodium hydroxide
- potassium hydroxide
- calcium hydroxide

Many people do not realise that alkalis are often more corrosive than acids. Always wear goggles when handling acids and alkalis.

Treating soils

- Many plants only grow really well at a certain **pH.**
- Food crops in particular do not thrive if the soil is too acidic.
- Farmers add **lime** to the soil to neutralise the acid so the pH of the soil is right for the plant that is being grown.

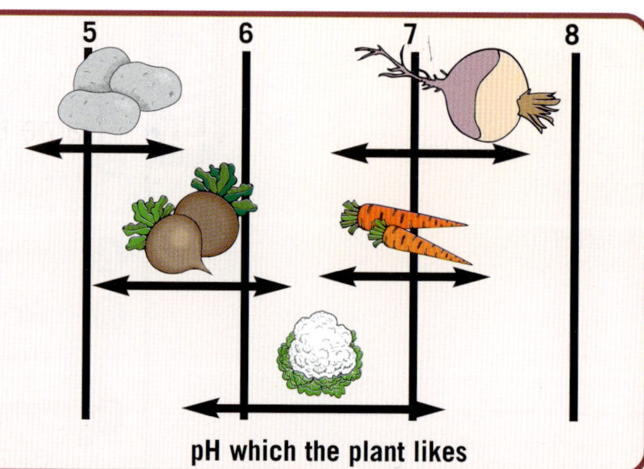

Treating indigestion

- **Your stomach contains hydrochloric acid.**
- It helps you to digest your food.
- If more acid than usual is produced you get indigestion.
- To stop the indigestion this extra acid needs to be neutralised with an alkali.
- Some indigestion tablets contain calcium carbonate.

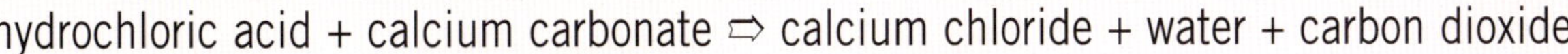

hydrochloric acid + calcium carbonate ⇨ calcium chloride + water + carbon dioxide

extra acid in the stomach	**base in the indigestion tablet**	**salt**		

Hydrogen, H^+ ions make solutions acidic.

Neutralisation

The reaction between an acid and a base is called **neutralisation**.

acid + alkali ⇨ a neutral salt + water

Learn what colour indicators will be in different types of solution.

The type of salt produced depends on the metal in the alkali used and on the acid used.

KEY TERMS

Make sure you understand these terms before moving on!

- indicators
- acidic
- alkalis
- bases
- pH
- lime
- neutralisation

QUICK TEST

1. What colour is Universal Indicator in neutral solution?
2. What colour is blue litmus in neutral solution?
3. What colour is blue litmus in an acid?
4. What is the pH of a neutral solution?
5. What is the pH of a strong alkali?
6. What is the pH of a weak acid?
7. What colour is Universal Indicator in water?
8. What colour is red litmus in water?
9. How are alkalis and bases related?
10. Name three common acids.

Making salts

Metal hydroxides

We have seen that metal hydroxides can be neutralised with acids to make salt and water:

metal hydroxide + acid ➪ salt + water

Some uses of salts

Potassium nitrate
This **salt** is widely used in fertiliser.

Copper sulphate
This salt is used in electroplating, in the dyeing of textiles and as a wood preservative.

Silver nitrate
Silver nitrate is used in photography.

Metal carbonates

Metal carbonates can be **neutralised** by acids.
Most carbonates are insoluble.
When carbonates neutralise an acid carbon dioxide is given off:

metal carbonate + **acid** ➪ **salt** + **water** + **carbon dioxide**

copper carbonate + hydrochloric acid ➪ copper chloride + water + carbon dioxide

zinc carbonate + sulphuric acid ➪ zinc sulphate + water + carbon dioxide

Sulphuric acid makes sulphate salts. Hydrochloric acid makes chloride salts. Nitric acid makes nitrate salts.

Making copper chloride

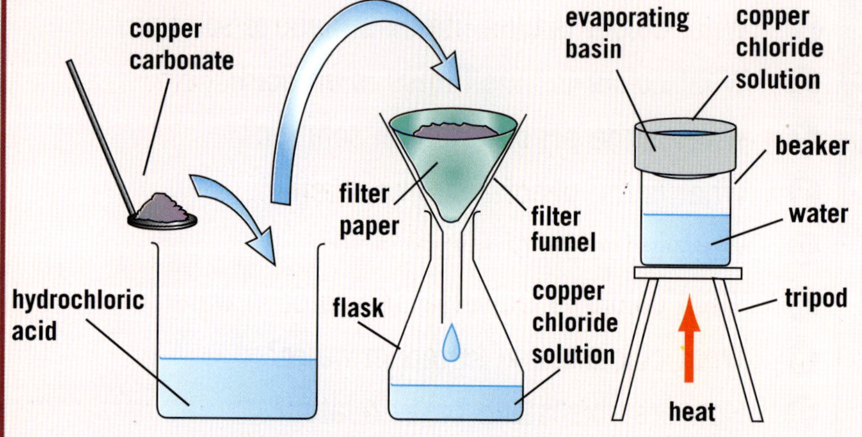

When bubbles are observed during a chemical reaction it shows that a gas is being made.

- Copper carbonate is added to the acid until it stops fizzing.
- The unreacted copper carbonate is then removed by filtering.
- The solution is poured into an evaporating dish.
- It is heated until the first crystals appear.
- The solution is then left for a few days for the copper chloride to crystallise.

When acids react with metals, a salt and the gas hydrogen is produced. When acids react with metal carbonates, a salt, water and the gas carbon dioxide are produced.

Metals

Some metals can react with acids to form a salt and hydrogen:

■ **metal**	+	**acid**	➪	**salt**	+	**hydrogen**
zinc	+	hydrochloric acid	➪	zinc chloride	+	hydrogen
magnesium	+	sulphuric acid	➪	magnesium sulphate	+	hydrogen

Metal oxides

Metal oxides are bases. They react with acids to make salts and water:

■ **metal oxide**	+	**acid**	➪	**salt**	+	**water**
copper oxide	+	hydrochloric acid	➪	copper chloride	+	water
zinc oxide	+	sulphuric acid	➪	zinc sulphate	+	water

Metal hydroxides

Metal hydroxides are bases. They react with acids to make salts and water:

■ **metal hydroxide**	+	**acid**	➪	**salt**	+	**water**
sodium hydroxide	+	hydrochloric acid	➪	sodium chloride	+	water
potassium hydroxide	+	sulphuric acid	➪	potassium sulphate	+	water

QUICK TEST

1. What is formed when hydrochloric acid reacts with potassium hydroxide?
2. What is formed when sulphuric acid reacts with sodium hydroxide?
3. Which gas is given off when carbonates react with acid?
4. What is formed when hydrochloric acid reacts with zinc carbonate?
5. What is formed when sulphuric acid reacts with magnesium carbonate?
6. How could you get a sample of a soluble salt?
7. What is formed when hydrochloric acid reacts with magnesium?
8. What is formed when sulphuric acid reacts with zinc?
9. What is formed when hydrochloric acid reacts with zinc oxide?
10. What is formed when sulphuric acid reacts with copper oxide?

KEY TERMS

Make sure you understand these terms before moving on!

- metal hydroxide
- salt
- metal carbonates
- neutralised

Chemical tests

Common tests

Carbon dioxide

The gas is bubbled through **limewater**. Carbon dioxide turns limewater **milky**.

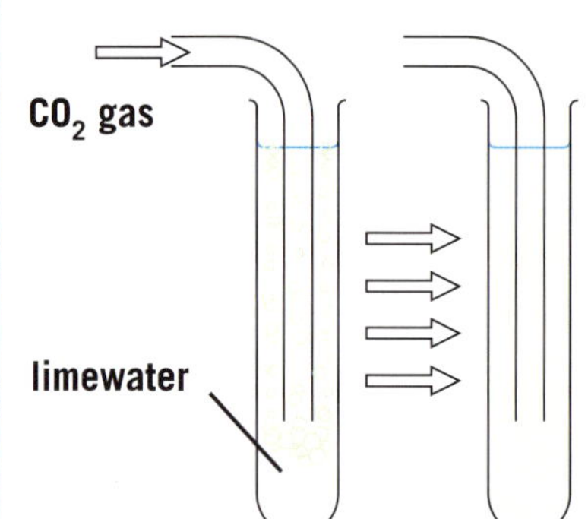

Hydrogen

If a lighted splint is nearby hydrogen will burn with a 'squeaky pop'.

Oxygen

Oxygen **relights** a glowing **splint**.

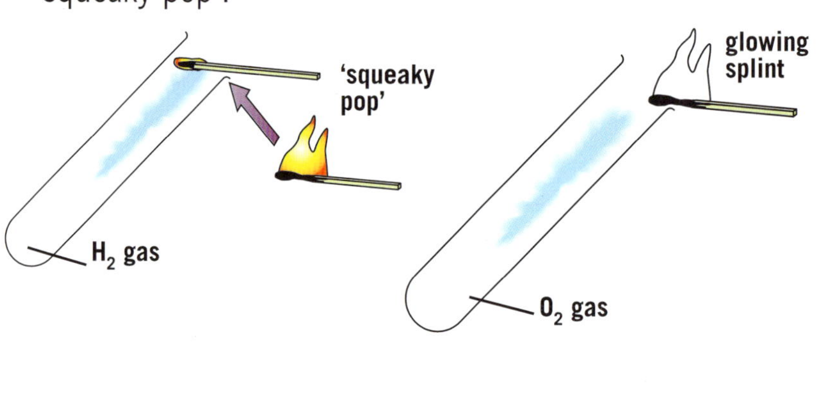

Apparatus

Below is some of the apparatus found in the science laboratory.

conical flask

measuring cylinder

triangle

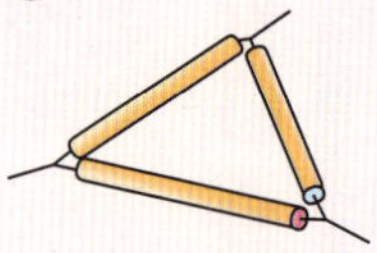

beaker

evaporating basin

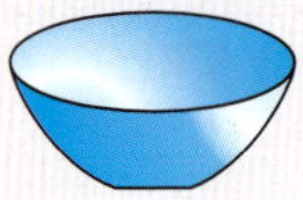

spatula

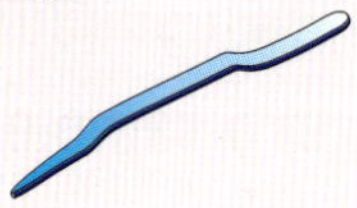

tripod

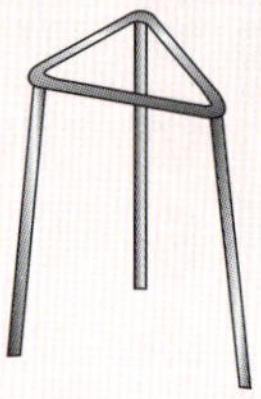

Bunsen burner

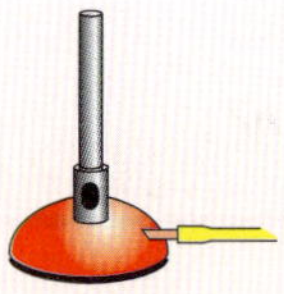

filter funnel

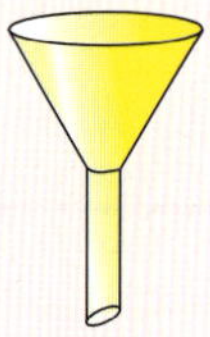

test tube

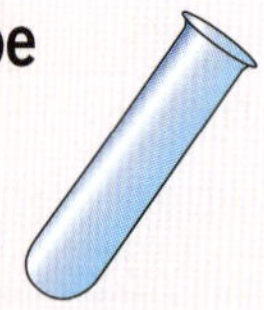

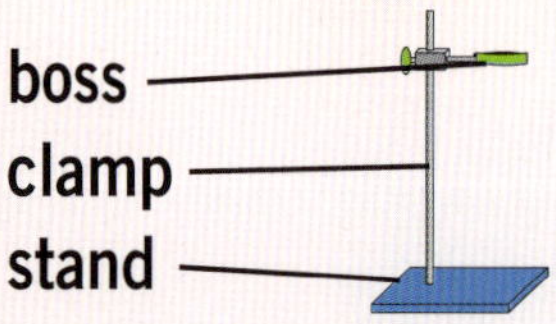

boss

clamp

stand

gauze

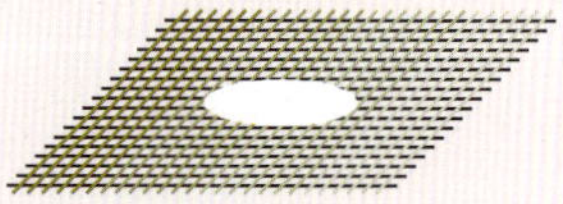

thermometer

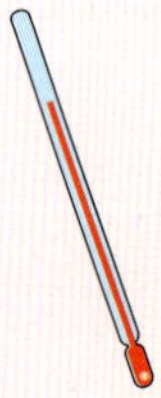

Choose apparatus which is suitable for the experiment.

Safety hazard signs

Oxidising
- Provides oxygen which allows other materials to burn more fiercely.

Toxic
- Can cause death if swallowed, breathed in or absorbed through the skin.

Corrosive
- Attacks and destroys living tissues, including eyes and skin.

Highly flammable
- Catches fire easily.

Harmful
- Similar to toxic but less dangerous.

Irritant
- Not corrosive but can cause reddening or blistering of the skin.

Some chemicals carry more than one hazard.

Common gases

Carbon dioxide

Carbon dioxide is a compound with the formula CO_2. It is **produced when fuels containing carbon are burned in oxygen**. The fuel methane contains the elements carbon and hydrogen.

The combustion of methane.
methane + oxygen → carbon dioxide + water

Carbon dioxide is also produced when metal carbonates react with acids.

The bubbles of carbon dioxide show that a chemical reaction is taking place. As the carbon dioxide escapes from the flask, the mass of the flask decreases.

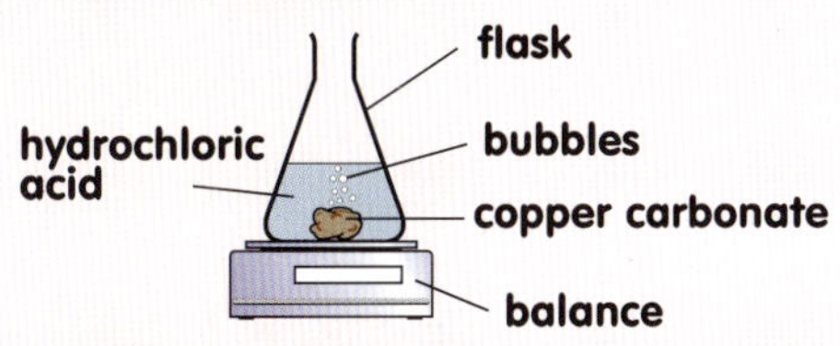

Hydrogen

Hydrogen is produced when metals react with acids.

The bubbles of hydrogen show that a chemical reaction is taking place. The mass of the test tube decreases as the hydrogen is lost. The temperature of the acid also increases, another sign that a chemical reaction is taking place.

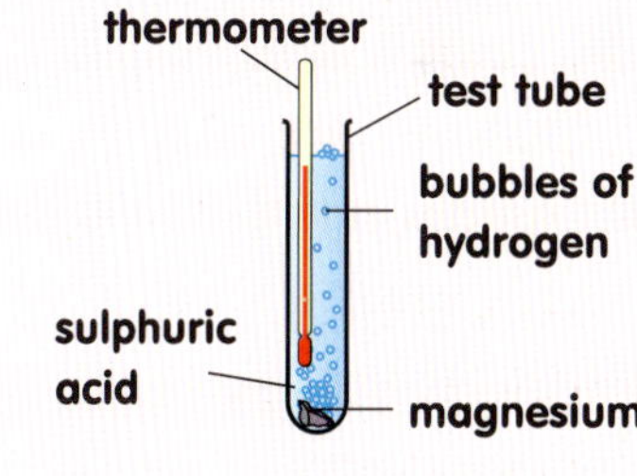

Oxygen

Oxygen is the second most abundant gas in the air. **Oxygen is required for burning and rusting**. When a metal is burned it forms a metal oxide.

None of this is hard, it is just a case of learning all the points.

KEY TERMS
- oxidising
- toxic
- corrosive
- highly flammable
- harmful
- irritant

QUICK TEST

1. Sketch the hazard symbol for harmful.
2. What is the test for carbon dioxide?
3. What is the test for hydrogen?
4. What would you use to measure the volume of a liquid?
5. What would you use to separate a solid from a liquid?

Mixtures

If there are two or more different atoms, but they are not combined, they are a mixture of different elements.

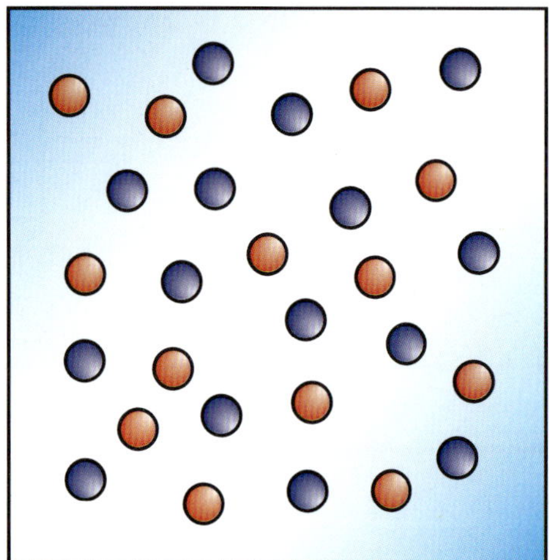

If there are two or more different compounds, they are a mixture of compounds.

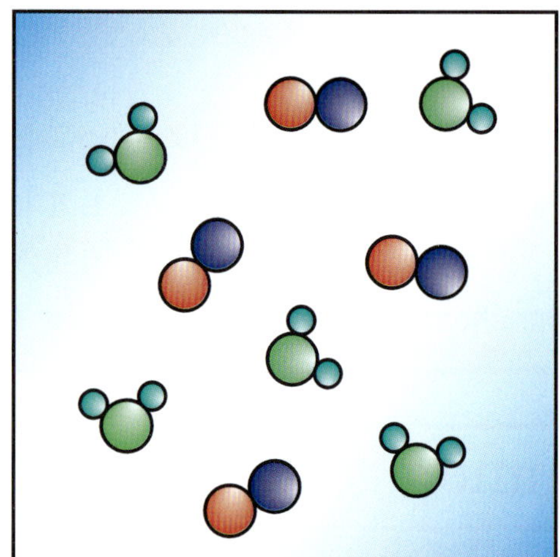

Mixtures and compounds

- **Mixtures are easy to separate.**
- **Compounds** are much harder to separate.
- Mixtures **do not have a fixed composition.**
- Compounds have a fixed composition.

Sea water

Sea water is a mixture. It contains particles of water, salts and gases. These particles are mixed together, but they are not combined.

Rocks

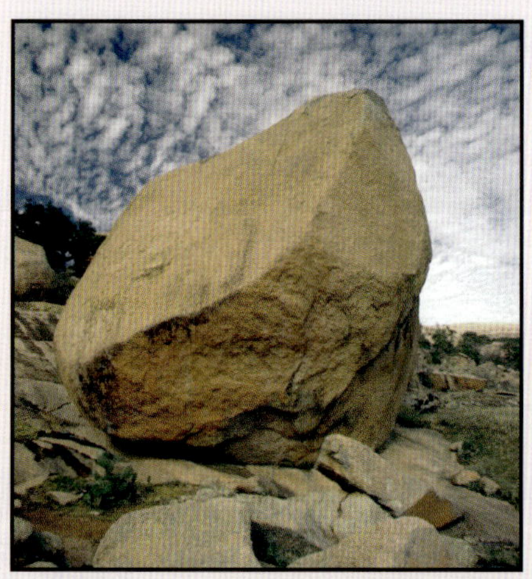

- Most rocks contain a mixture of different minerals.
- **Minerals** are compounds because they have a fixed composition.
- Granite is an igneous rock.
- It contains a mixture of minerals.
- It consists mainly of the minerals feldspar, quartz and mica.
- The exact proportion of these minerals is not fixed, and will vary from rock to rock.

Air

- Air is a mixture of gas particles. Air is composed of about 80% nitrogen molecules and about 20% oxygen molecules.
- There are also very small amounts of carbon dioxide, water vapour and noble gases, including argon and neon.
- These gas particles are mixed together, but they are not combined.
- Air can be separated by the fractional distillation of liquid air.

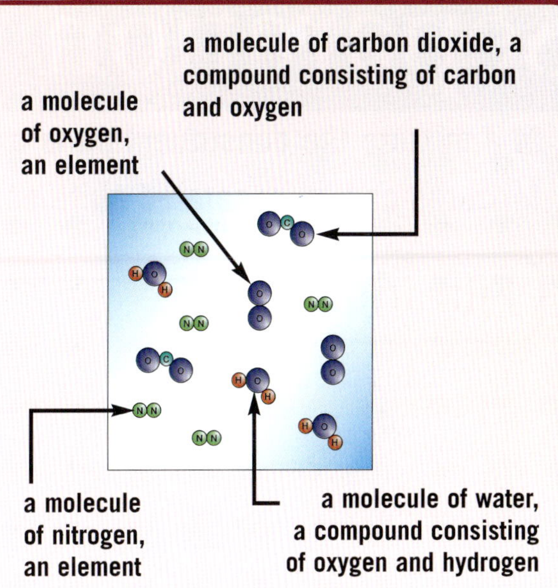

Melting points

Pure substances melt and boil at certain temperatures. Ice melts to form water at 0°C and water boils to form steam at 100°C. The melting point of ice is 0°C. The boiling point of water is 100°C.Mixtures do not melt at one fixed temperature. Instead, **each component in the mixture melts at its own particular melting point**.

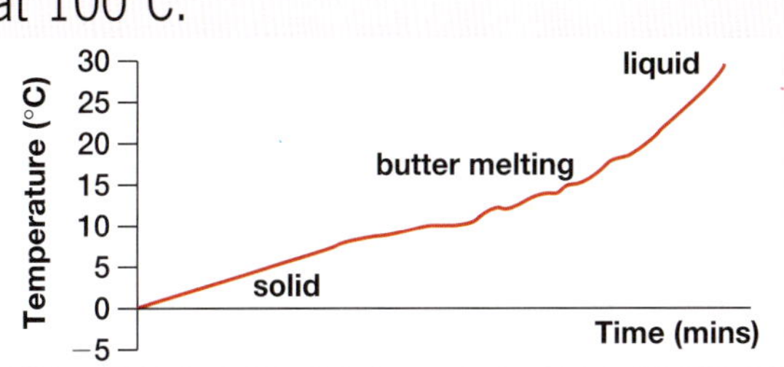

Butter is a good example of a mixture. On a warm day butter will begin to melt. If you look carefully, some of it will have already melted while other parts are still solid.

Mixtures melt over a range of temperatures.

KEY TERMS

Make sure you understand these terms before moving on!

- mixtures
- compounds
- fixed composition
- minerals

QUICK TEST

1. Can mixtures be separated easily?
2. Why is a mixture different from a compound?
3. Can you have a mixture of compounds?
4. Do compounds have a fixed composition?
5. Do mixtures have a fixed composition?
6. Is sea water a mixture?
7. What does sea water contain?
8. What does air contain?
9. What percentage of air is nitrogen?
10. What are most rocks a mixture of?

Separation techniques

- **In a mixture the constituent parts are not joined together.**
- **Mixtures can be separated quite easily.**

Filtration

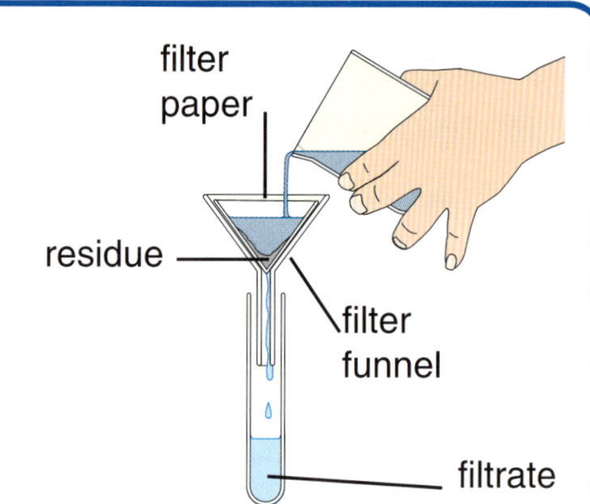

- Filtration is used to **separate** a mixture of a solid and a liquid.
- The mixture is poured through a filter paper. Only the liquid passes through and is called the **filtrate**. The solid is collected on the filter paper and is called the **residue**.

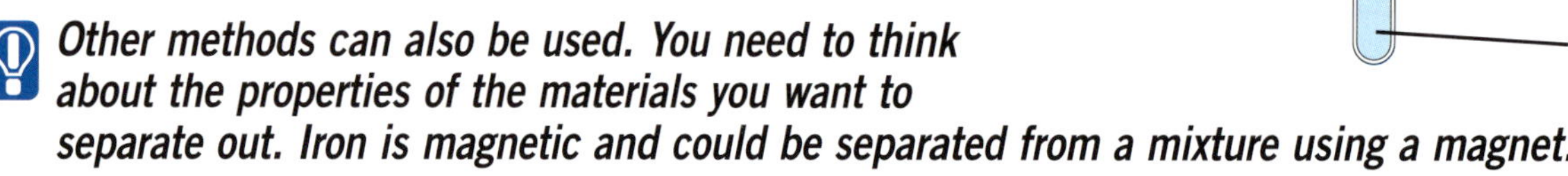

Other methods can also be used. You need to think about the properties of the materials you want to separate out. Iron is magnetic and could be separated from a mixture using a magnet.

Filtration and evaporation

- A mixture of salt and sand can be separated using these two techniques.
When water is added and the mixture is stirred, the salt will dissolve.
The **insoluble sand** does not dissolve.
The mixture can then be filtered: the dissolved salt passes through the filter, while the sand can be collected from the filter paper.

- Solutions of solvents and solutes can be separated by evaporation. The solvent, in this case water, can be **evaporated**, leaving the solute (salt) behind.
The salt forms crystals; this process is called crystallisation.

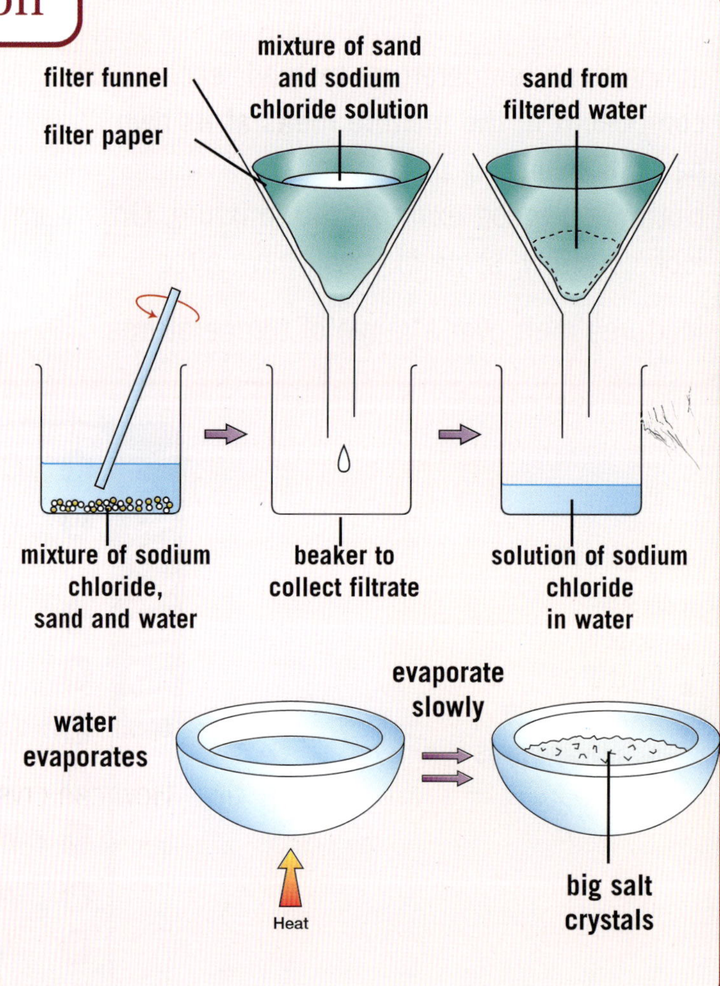

Chromatography

- **Chromatography** can be used to separate mixtures of different coloured dyes.
  The different dyes have different solubilities.
- This method can be used to find which dyes make up black ink:
  - A spot of ink is placed on a piece of filter paper and this is placed in a beaker containing some solvent.
  - The solvent travels across the filter paper carrying the dyes with it.
  - Each dye has a slightly different solubility, so travels a slightly different distance across the paper.
  - This black dye contains red, blue and yellow dyes.

Distillation

Distillation

- **Distillation** can be used to **separate a solvent from a solution.**
- It can be used to separate water from a solution of salt and water.
- The solution is heated.
- The water boils and water vapour is formed.
- The water vapour cools and condenses to form liquid water which is collected in a beaker.
- This water is called 'distilled water' and is very pure.

Fractional distillation

- Fractional distillation can be used to separate a mixture of two or more liquids.
- It can be used to separate alcohol and water.
- The liquids still boil at their own boiling temperatures, even though they are now in a mixture. The alcohol boils at 78°C. Some water will also evaporate, but it will condense in the fractionating column and fall back into the flask.
- Only the alcohol passes into the condenser, where it forms pure liquid alcohol which is collected in the beaker.

KEY TERMS

Make sure you understand these terms before moving on!

- separate
- filtrate
- residue
- evaporation
- crystals
- chromatography
- distillation

QUICK TEST

1. In a mixture are the constituent parts joined?
2. In a compound are the constituent parts joined?
3. How should a mixture of solid and liquid be separated?
4. How can crystals of a salt be obtained from a mixture of salt and water?
5. Which technique should be used to separate a mixture of different coloured dyes?
6. Why do different dyes travel different distances?
7. How can water be separated from a mixture of salt and water?

Compounds

Atoms may form *molecules*. A molecule consists of two or more atoms joined together.

- **If the atoms are of the same element, they form molecules of the element.**
- **If atoms of two or more elements are joined together, they form molecules of a compound.**

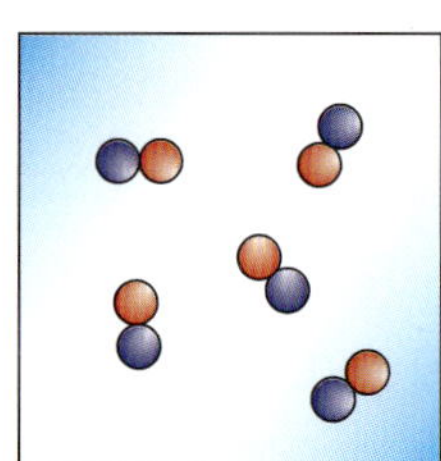

Forming compounds

- During a chemical reaction a new substance is made.
- These new chemicals are the **products** of the reaction. The starting chemicals are called the **reactants**.
- The **products can have very different properties from the reactants.**
  Heating iron with sulphur gives iron sulphide.

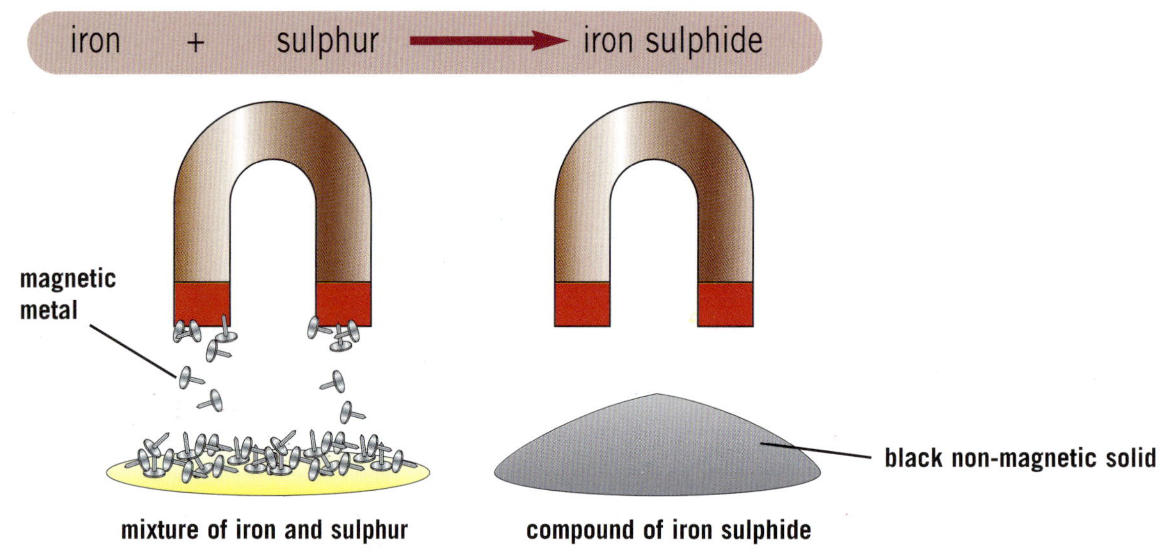

mixture of iron and sulphur

compound of iron sulphide

- A compound has a fixed composition.
  Iron sulphide FeS contains one atom of iron and one atom of sulphur joined together.

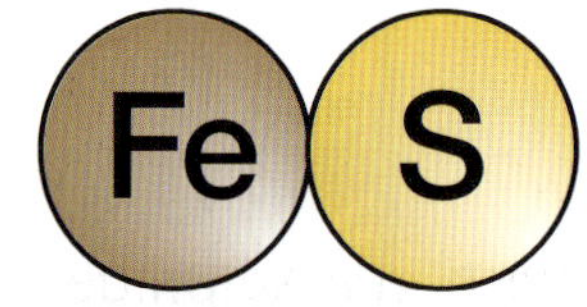

Things to look out for to show a chemical reaction is happening:
- *bubbles – these show a gas is being made*
- *a change in colour*
- *a change in temperature – usually an increase as most reactions are exothermic*

Can compounds react?

We have seen that chemical reactions can take place between elements. Chemical reactions can also take place between compounds. If a chemical reaction takes place new substances are made.

There are three things to look out for that show that a chemical reaction is occurring.

Temperature change

Most chemical reactions **give out heat energy**, so we can **measure an increase in temperature**.

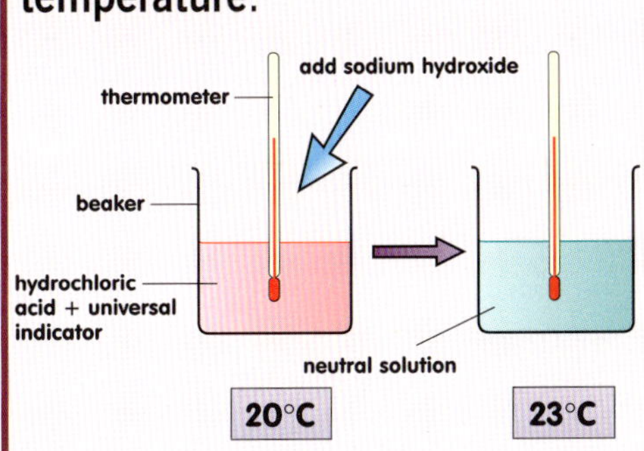

Gas is produced

Bubbles show that gas is being produced. If the reaction is carried out in a beaker placed on a mass balance then the **mass of the beaker will go down** as the **gas produced (which has mass) escapes into the air**.

beaker

dilute sulphuric acid

magnesium carbonate

mass balance

130.00 g

129.80 g

Change in colour

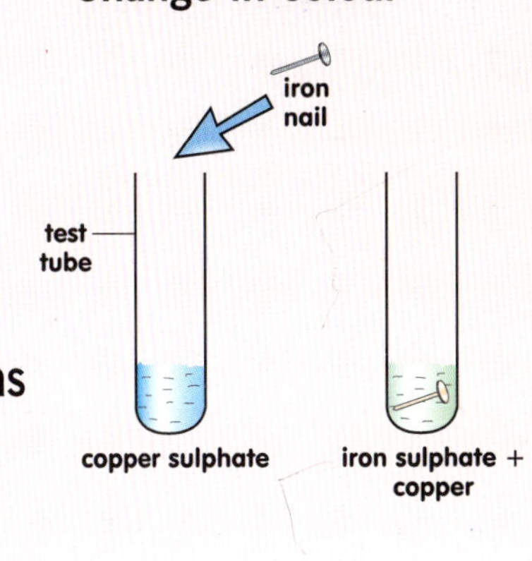

If bubbles are produced during a reaction only name the gas if you are sure what it is. If you are not sure, just say that a gas has been produced.

QUICK TEST

1. What does this represent? 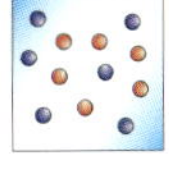
2. What does this represent? 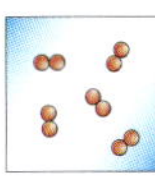
3. What does this represent? 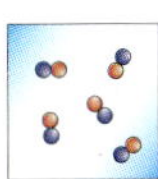
4. If you saw bubbles during a chemical reaction, what is being made?
5. What piece of apparatus would you use to find if the temperature had increased?
6. What are the chemicals at the start of a chemical reaction called?
7. What are the chemicals made by a chemical reaction called?
8. How can you tell if a chemical reaction has occurred when iron and sulphur are heated to form iron sulphide?
9. Do compounds have a fixed composition?
10. Can the elements in a compound be separated easily?

- molecules
- reactants
- products
- properties

Naming compounds

When atoms of two or more elements join together they form a compound.

Changing names

If atoms of two elements join together in a **chemical reaction**, it can be represented in a **word equation**:

This can also be represented using symbols:

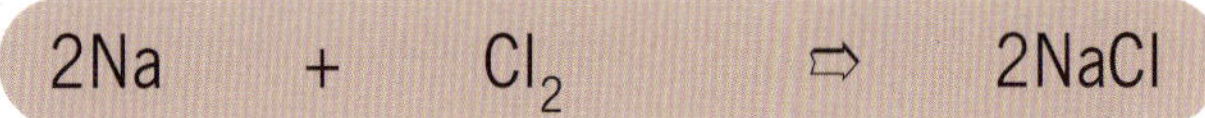

The name of the compound is given by the two elements that have joined, sodium **chloride**.

- The chlorine has changed to chloride.

The names of non-metals change when they react with one other element.

chlorine	⇨	chloride
oxygen	⇨	oxide
fluorine	⇨	fluoride
bromine	⇨	bromide
iodine	⇨	iodide
sulphur	⇨	sulphide

Therefore,

or

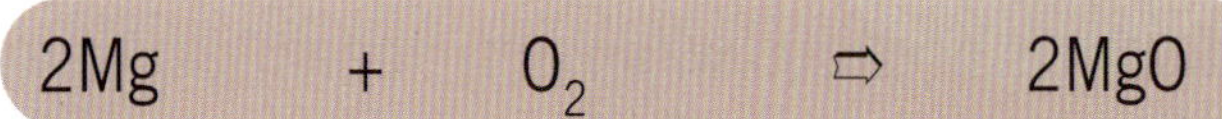

In all chemical reactions the overall mass does not change.
Overall mass before the reaction = overall mass after the reaction.

Carbon dioxide (CO_2)

Carbon dioxide is formed from one carbon and two oxygen atoms.

- carbon + oxygen ⇨ **carbon dioxide**

The **di-** shows that there are **two** oxygen atoms.

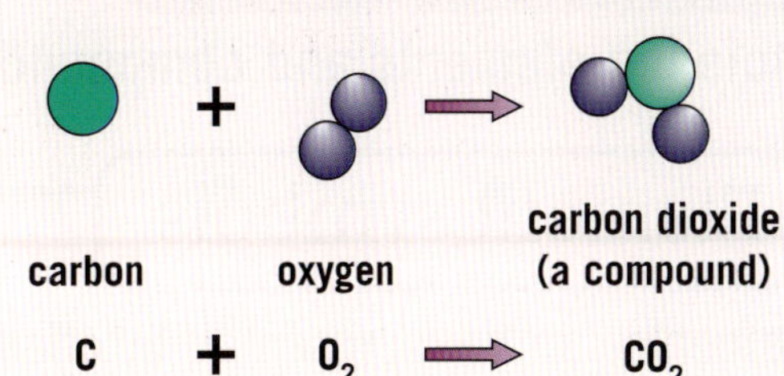

Water (H_2O)

Water is formed from **two hydrogen** atoms and **one oxygen** atom.

- hydrogen + oxygen ⇨ water

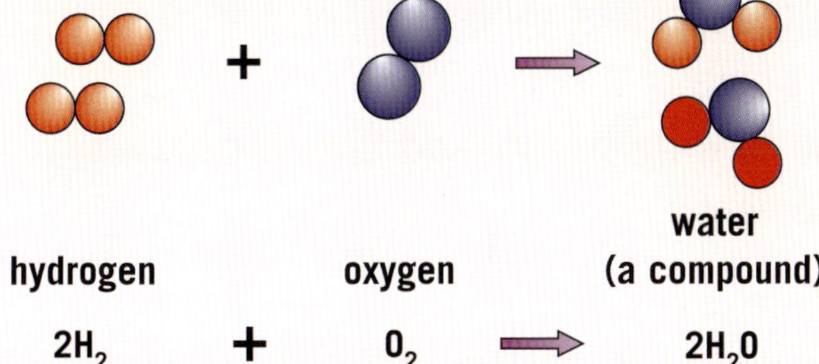

Other useful names

- OH is called hydroxide, so NaOH is sodium hydroxide.
- SO_4 is called sulphate, so $CuSO_4$ is copper sulphate.
- CO_3 is called carbonate, so $MgCO_3$ is magnesium carbonate.

If a name ends with 'ate' it shows that oxygen is present, for example calcium carbonate has the formula $CaCO_3$.

KEY TERMS

Make sure you understand these terms before moving on!

- chemical reaction
- word equation
- chloride
- carbon dioxide

QUICK TEST

1. What is a compound?
2. What is the name of the compound formed when magnesium reacts with oxygen?
3. What is the name of the compound formed when magnesium reacts with bromine?
4. In the compound magnesium chloride, $MgCl_2$ how many atoms of magnesium and chlorine are present?
5. In the compound carbon monoxide CO, how many atoms of carbon and oxygen are present?
6. Write a word equation for the reaction between sodium and chlorine.
7. Write a word equation for the reaction between hydrogen and oxygen.
8. Write a word equation for the reaction between magnesium and oxygen.

Symbols

In science elements and compounds can be represented by simple symbols.

Element symbols

Elements can be represented by **chemical symbols**. Each symbol is **unique** to one particular element, so there are over 100 different symbols. The same symbol is used to represent each element everywhere in the world. **The symbols are easier to write and to read than the names of elements.**

In some cases the symbol for an element is simply the **first letter** of that element's name. This letter must be a capital.

The element sulphur is represented by the symbol **S**.

The element carbon is represented by the symbol **C**.

The element iodine is represented by the symbol **I**.

However, sometimes the names of two or more elements begin with the same letter. When this occurs the first letter of the name is used together with another letter from the name. The first letter must be a capital letter and the second letter must be lower case.

The element magnesium is represented by the symbol **Mg**.

The element manganese is represented by the symbol **Mn**.

Occasionally an element may take its symbol from its old Latin name. When this happens the first letter must be a capital letter and the second letter must be lower case.

The element mercury can be represented by the symbol **Hg**. This comes from the Latin name for mercury which was ***h**ydrar**g**yrum*.

The element sodium can be represented by the symbol **Na**. This comes from the Latin name for sodium which was ***na**trium*.

Only use the symbol instead of the name of an element or compound if you are sure you know what it is.

If you are asked to write or complete a word equation – use the name NOT the symbol.

Chemical formulae of compounds

- Chemical **formulae** show the relative number of atoms present.
- The chemical formula for water is H_2O.
- This means that every water **molecule** consists of two hydrogen atoms and one oxygen atom.

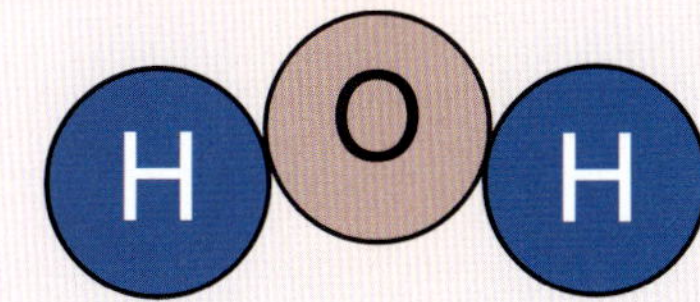

- The chemical formula for carbon monoxide is CO.
- This means that every water molecule consists of one carbon atom and one oxygen atom.
- The chemical formula for copper sulphate is $CuSO_4$.
- This means that copper sulphate consists of copper atoms, sulphur atoms and oxygen atoms in the ratio 1:1:4.

QUICK TEST

1. Give the chemical symbol for the element sulphur.
2. Name the element which has the chemical symbol Na.
3. What is wrong with this chemical symbol for carbon – c?
4. What is wrong with this chemical symbol for magnesium – MG?

Consider $CaCO_3$

5. How many calcium atoms are present?
6. How many carbon atoms are present?
7. How many oxygen atoms are present?

Consider H_2SO_4

8. How many hydrogen atoms are present?
9. How many sulphur atoms are present?
10. How many oxygen atoms are present?

KEY TERMS

Make sure you understand these terms before moving on!

- symbols
- unique
- formulae
- molecule

Practice questions

Use the questions to test your progress. Check your answers on page 125.

1. The table shows the pH of four solutions.
   Which of the solutions is
   a) an acid
   b) a neutral solution
   c) an alkali?

Solution	pH of solution
A	10
B	6
C	2
D	7

2. Melting and condensing are the names of two changes of state. Explain the changes these terms represent.
   a) melting ....
   b) condensing ....

3. The diagram shows a cross section of rock. Which rock is probably the oldest?
   E is an igneous intrusion cutting across the existing rocks.

a cross section of rock

4. A magnet was used to find out which objects were magnetic.
   Complete the results:

   Object tested — Attracted to magnet
   plastic knife ....
   steel pin..
   iron nail ....
   wooden ruler..
   aluminium foil ....

5. a) Fill in the missing word:
   When a solid is dissolved in a solvent it forms a ....
   b) A beaker containing water is placed on a balance. It has a mass of 100.0 g.
   5.5 g of salt is dissolved in the water. It can no longer be seen.
   What is the mass of the beaker now?...

6. Why is copper used in electrical wiring? Choose one answer.
   a) copper is shiny b) copper does not react with water
   c) copper is a good conductor of electricity.

7. Three inks, yellow, blue and green, were compared using chromatography (see diagram).
   a) Which ink is made of two substances?..
   b) Name the two colours this ink is made from...

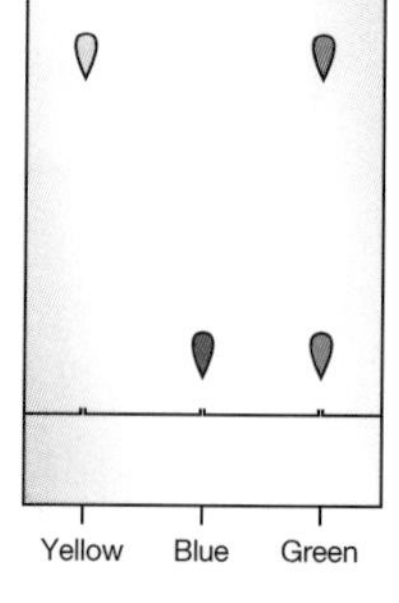

8. The table below shows the melting and boiling temperatures of four halogens.

Element	Melting temperature °C	Boiling temperature °C
fluorine	–220	–188
chlorine	–101	–34
bromine	–7	59
iodine	114	184

Using the table name one substance which at room temperature (25°C) is:
a) a solid...
b) a liquid..
c) a gas..

9. A student heated some magnesium in a crucible.
She did not lose any of the magnesium oxide that was formed.
The mass of the crucible was measured before and after heating.

30.00 g — empty crucible
30.24 g — crucible and magnesium
30.40 g — crucible and magnesium oxide

a) Why has the mass of the contents increased during this reaction?

....

b) Write a word equation for the reaction ....

10. Iron oxide reacts with carbon monoxide to form iron and carbon dioxide.

a) Name three compounds in this reaction ....

b) Name a substance that is an element in the reaction..

11. Limestone is mainly calcium carbonate. It decomposes on heating to form calcium oxide and the gas carbon dioxide.

Write a word equation for this reaction ....

12. Four metals were placed in solutions of different metal sulphate solutions. The results are shown in the table below. (If a reaction occurred a tick is shown, if no reaction took place a cross is shown.)

Metal	Magnesium sulphate	Copper sulphate solution	Iron sulphate solution	Zinc sulphate solution
magnesium	–	✓	✓	✓
copper	✗	–	✗	✗
iron	✗	✓	–	✗
zinc	✗	✓	✓	–

a) Using the table write down the order of reactivity of these four metals. Write the most reactive metal first.

....

b) Give a word equation for the reaction between magnesium and zinc sulphate.

....

13. Methane (natural gas) is burnt in Bunsen burners.
Complete a word equation for methane burning in plenty of oxygen.

....

14. The diagram shows a cross section of a rock. T is a small igneous intrusion.

a) Why are the crystals at T smaller than those at S? ....

b) Which compound to limestone and sandstone have in common?

....

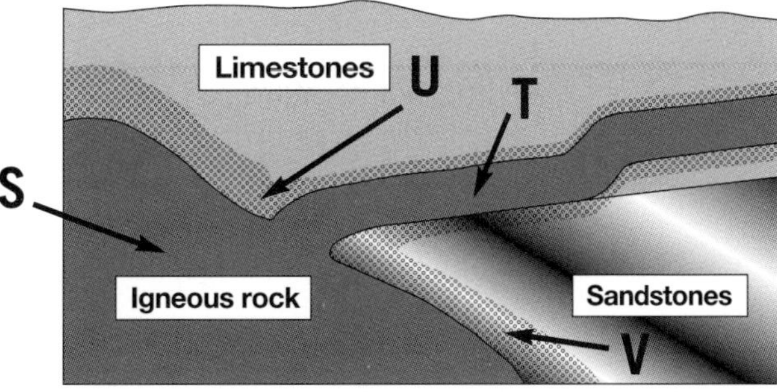

Speed

The speed of an object is a measure of how fast it is moving.

Calculating speeds

To find the **speed** of an object we need to know how far it has travelled and how long it took to travel this distance. Then we use the equation.

$$\text{speed} = \frac{\text{distance}}{\text{time}} \text{ or } s = \frac{d}{t}$$

Example

Calculate the speed of a sprinter who runs 100 m in 10 s.

$$s = \frac{d}{t} = \frac{100\,\text{m}}{10\,\text{s}} = 10\,\text{m/s}$$

This answer tells us that the sprinter, on average, ran 10 m every second.

Whenever you do a calculation be sure to write down the units of your answer. An answer of 10 to the question may not gain you full marks. An answer of 10 m/s will get you all the marks available.

Example

Calculate the speed of a car which travels 300 km in 5 hours.

$$s = \frac{d}{t} = \frac{300\,\text{km}}{5\,\text{h}} = 60\,\text{km/h}$$

The car, on average, travels 60 km each hour.

Acceleration

If an object is speeding up it is **accelerating**. If an object is slowing down it is **decelerating**.

Calculating distances and times

Some questions may give you the speed of an object and ask you to calculate either:

a) the distance it travels in a certain time

or

b) the time it takes to travel a certain distance.

Both of these are very easy to do once you know how to use the formula triangle.
We draw the triangle with the letters in the same place as they are in the formula.

So $s = \frac{d}{t}$ is drawn in the **formula triangle** as:

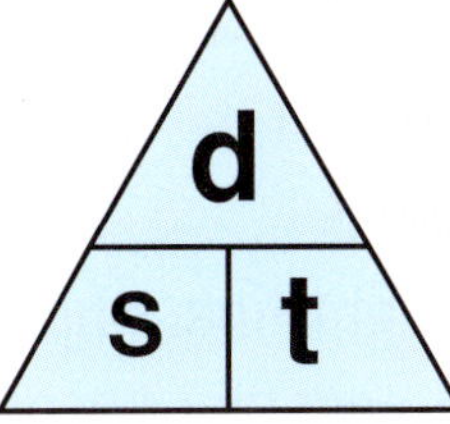

To find the formula to calculate the distance we simply cover the d in the triangle:

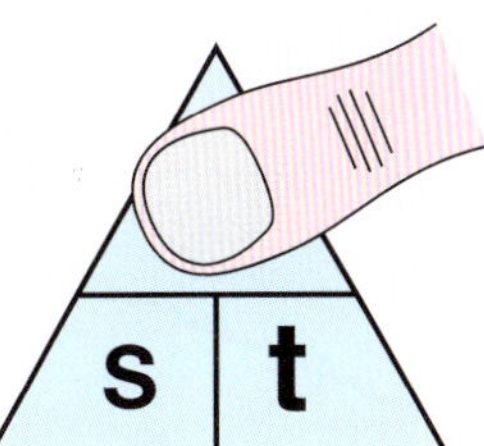

Now we can see that $d = s \times t$

Example

A cannonball after being fired travels at 75 m/s for 4 s. How far has the ball travelled?

$d = s \times t = 75\ \text{m/s} \times 4\ \text{s} = 300\ \text{m}$

To find the formula to calculate time we simply cover the *t* in the triangle

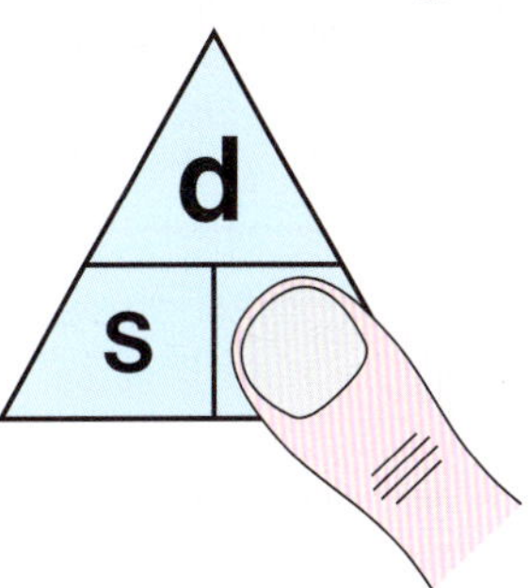

Now we can see that $t = \frac{d}{s}$

Example

A cyclist travels 80 km at an average speed of 20 km/h. How long does the journey take?

$t = \frac{d}{s} = \frac{80}{20} = 4$ hours

Practise using your formula triangle. It is very useful for lots of formulae you will need in your exams.

KEY TERMS

Make sure you understand these terms before moving on!

- speed
- accelerating
- decelerating

QUICK TEST

1. What two measurements do you need to calculate the speed of an object?
2. Name two units you could use to measure the speed of an object.
3. Calculate the speed of a woman who runs 400 m in 80 s.
4. How long will it take a boy cycling at 20 m/s to travel 400 m?
5. How far will a bus travel in 5 hours if its speed is 60 km/h?

Graphs of motion

It is often useful to show the journey of an object in the form of a graph. There are two types of graph: the *distance–time graph* and the speed or *velocity–time graph*.

Distance–time graphs

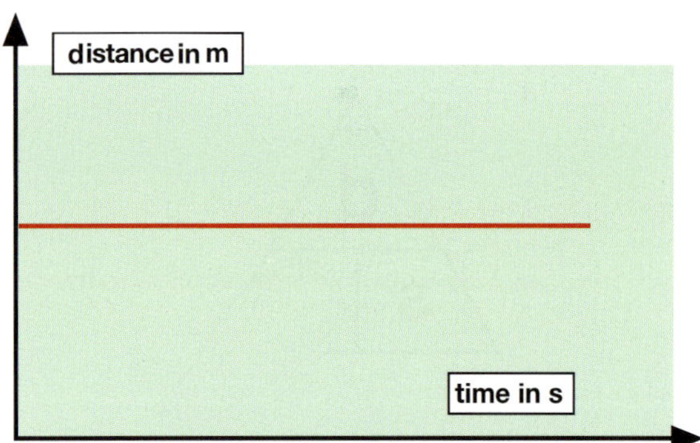

Horizontal line: object is not moving.

Make sure you understand what is happening to an object when its distance–time graph is a) horizontal, b) a gently sloping straight line and c) a steeply sloping straight line.

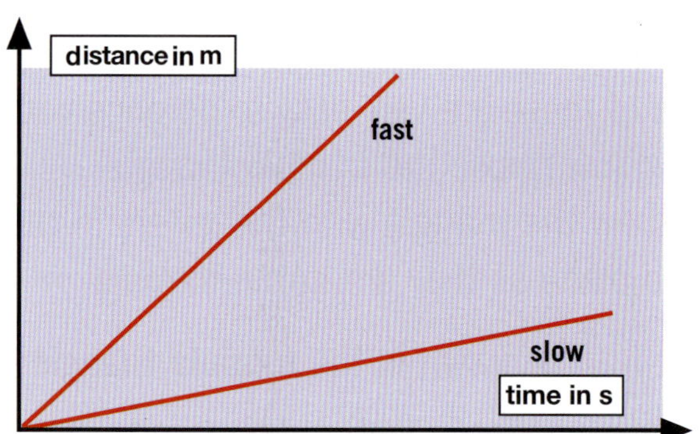

Sloping straight line: object moving at **constant speed**.

Steeper straight line: object moving at a greater constant speed.

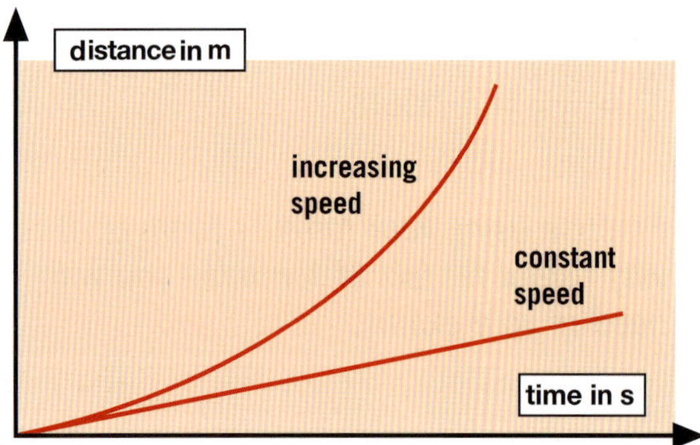

If the gradient of the line is not straight then speed of object is not constant.

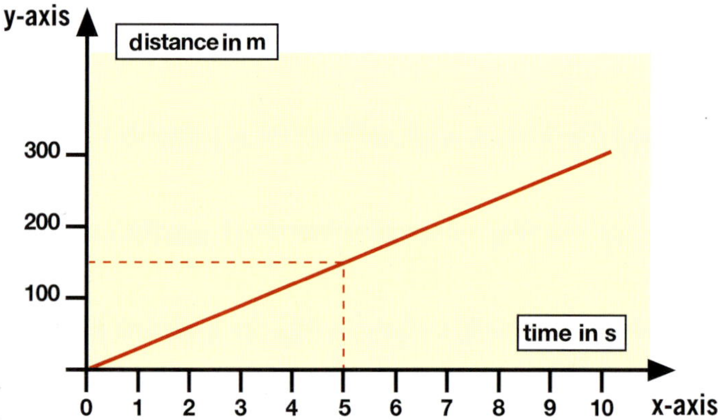

Speed of an object is equal to the gradient of the line.

Speed of object $= \frac{y}{x} = \frac{150}{5} = 30\,\text{m/s}$

Example

A motorcyclist moving at a constant speed travels 400 m in 10 s. He then stops for the next 10 s before travelling 600 m at a constant speed in the next 10 s.

a) Draw a distance–time graph to show the journey.

b) What is the motorcyclist's average speed?

c) $\frac{1000}{30} = 33\frac{1}{3}$ m/s

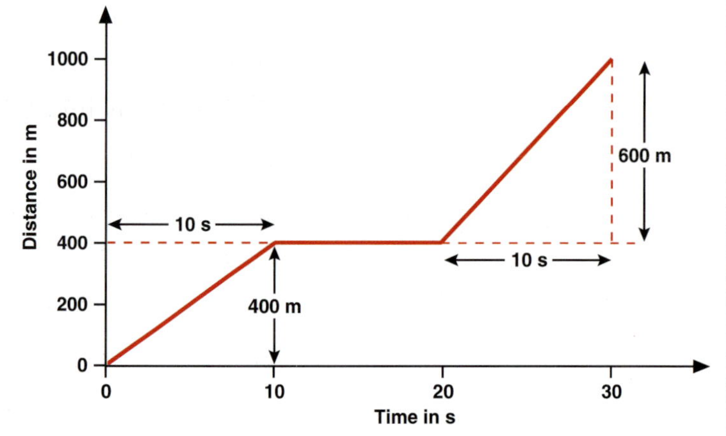

Speed– or velocity–time graphs

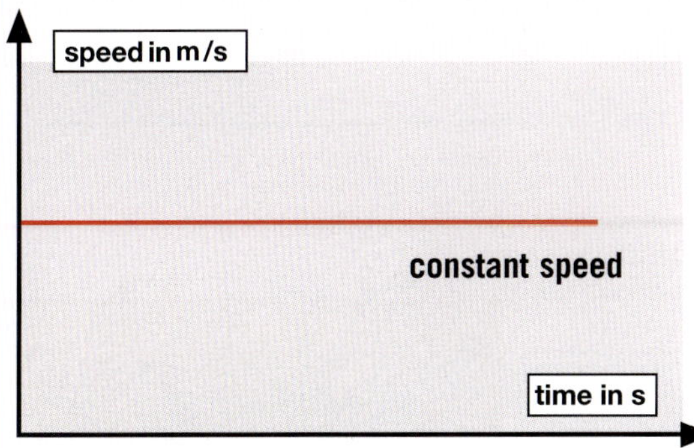

Horizontal line: object moving at constant speed.

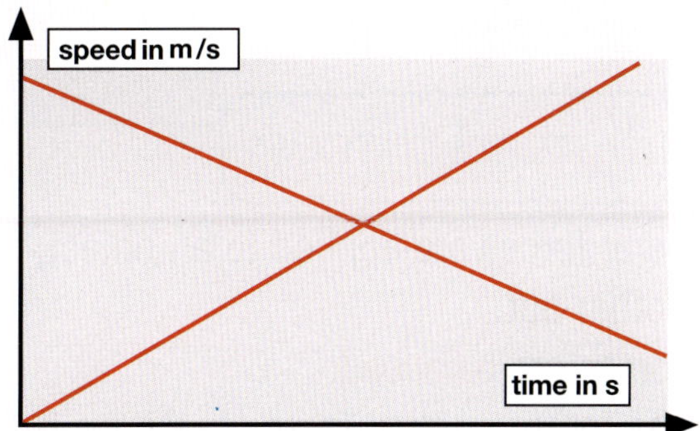

Line sloping upwards: object increasing speed, i.e. **accelerating**.
Line sloping downwards: object decreasing speed, i.e. **decelerating**.

Example
A bus starting from rest accelerates to a speed of 40 m/s in 4 s. It travels at this speed for 10 s before decelerating to a halt in 8 s.

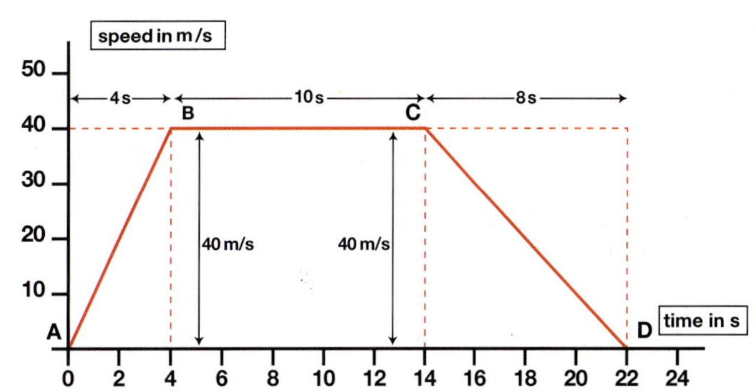

QUICK TEST

1. On a distance–time graph what do the following show?

   a) a horizontal line b) a steeply sloping straight line

   c) a straight line sloping just a little.
2. Draw a distance–time graph to show the following journey:

   A bus moving at a constant speed travels 2000 m in 100 s. It stops for 50 s to pick up passengers. It then continues its journey moving at a constant speed, travelling 1000 m in the next 100 s.
3. On a speed–time graph what do the following show?

   a) a horizontal line b) a straight line sloping steeply upwards

   c) a straight line sloping gently downwards.
4. Draw a speed–time graph to describe the following journey:

   A sprinter starting from rest accelerates to a speed of 10 m/s in 2 s.

   He travels at this speed for the next 8 s then decelerates to 2 m/s in 4 s.

   He continues to jog at this speed for the next 6 s.

KEY TERMS

Make sure you understand these terms before moving on!

- distance–time graph
- velocity–time graph
- constant speed
- gradient

Forces

Balanced forces

balanced forces: no motion

If several forces are applied to an object, they may cancel each other out.
The forces are **balanced**.

- If the forces applied to an object are balanced they will have no effect on its motion.
- If the object is **stationary** it will remain stationary.

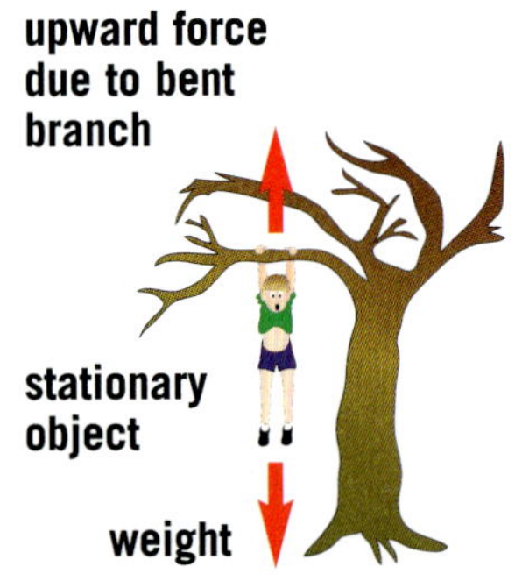

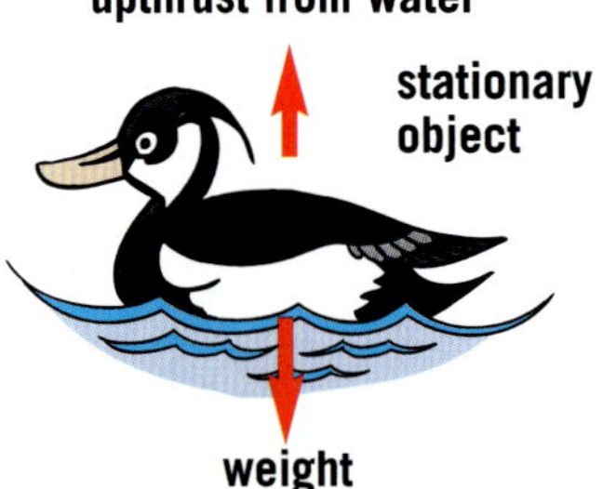

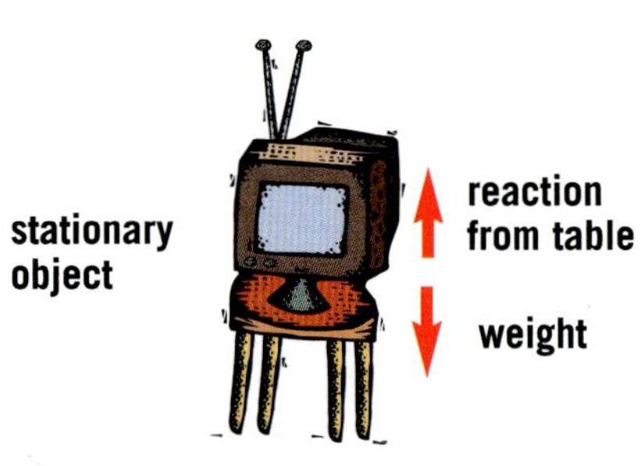

- If the object is moving it will continue to move in the same direction and at the same speed.

If the driving force of this aircraft equals the drag, it will travel at a constant speed. If the lift force equals the weight, the aircraft will stay at a constant height.

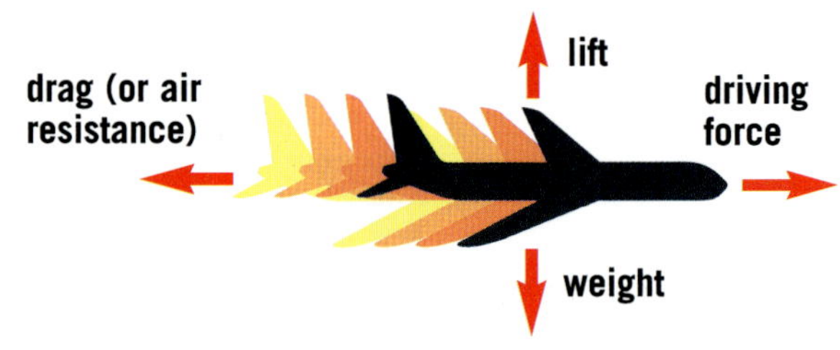

Measuring forces

- We measure forces in **Newtons** (N). An average-sized apple has a weight of about 1 N.
- We can measure the size of a force using a **Newton meter**.
- This consists of a spring and a scale; the scale measures how much the spring stretches when a force is applied to it.
- **The larger the force the more the spring extends.**

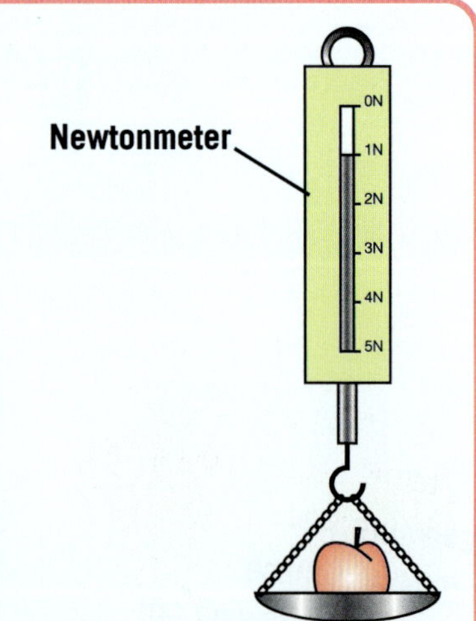

Effects of forces on objects

When forces like these are applied to an object they may cause an object to:

- start moving if it is stationary

- stop moving if it is already moving

- speed it up

- slow it down

- change its direction

- change its shape.

Sometimes a force can be applied to an object without any physical contact.

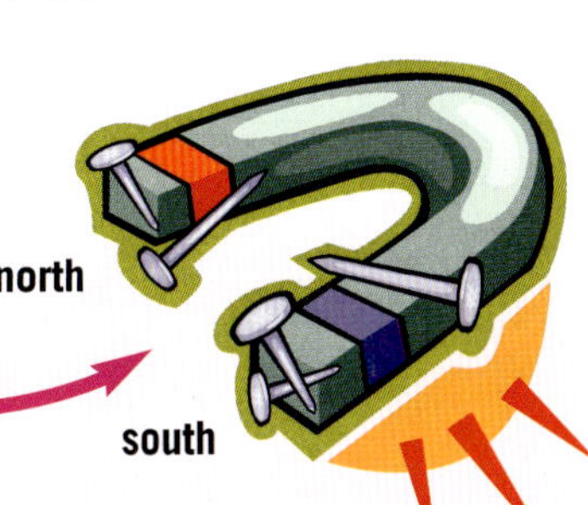

This diver is being pulled downwards by a force we call gravity. The size of this gravitational attraction we call **weight**.

These objects have been attracted by the magnet.

Unbalanced forces

- If the forces applied to an object do not cancel each other out, i.e. they are **unbalanced**, they will affect its motion.

Stationary object made to move. Unbalanced forces.

KEY TERMS

Make sure you understand these terms before moving on!

- weight
- Newton meter
- Newton
- balanced
- unbalanced
- stationary

1. Name three possible effects of applying a force to an object.
2. Name two forces that can be applied to an object without any physical contact.
3. What do we measure with a Newton meter?
4. What effect do balanced forces have on the motion of an object?
5. What effect do unbalanced forces have on the motion of an object?
6. Explain what is meant by the phrase 'the weight of the object is 12 N'?

Friction and terminal velocity

Friction

Whenever an object moves or tries to move, **friction** is present.

All moving objects cause friction to occur.

Friction between surfaces can make them hot and wear them away.

worn brake block
rim of tyre
high temperature

Friction between the tyres of a car and the surface of a road is very important. If there is insufficient grip it is impossible to stop or steer the car safely.

Reducing friction by streamlining and lubricating

- As a bobsleigh travels down a run it gains speed.
- There are large **frictional forces** at work between the sleigh and the air, and between the runners and the ice.
- To keep these forces to a minimum the bobsleigh is:
  a) **streamlined** – it is shaped so it **cuts through the air with less resistance**.
  b) the runners are coated with a **lubricant**, such as wax.

Moving through air

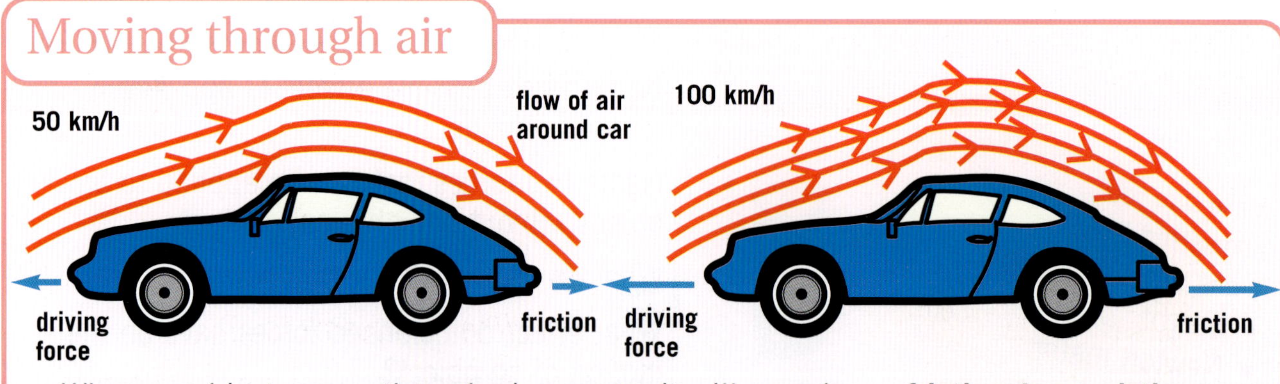

- When an object moves through air or water it will experience **frictional or resistive forces (drag)** which will try to prevent its motion.
- The **faster** the object moves the **larger these resistive forces** become.

Terminal velocity: cars

Action	Result
The driver begins the journey by pressing the accelerator.	The driving force from the engine makes the car accelerate.
The accelerator is kept in the same position.	As the speed of the car increases the air resistance increases. The car will have a smaller acceleration.
The accelerator is kept in the same position.	The air resistance and the driving force are equal and balanced. The car travels at a constant speed, known as its **terminal velocity**.

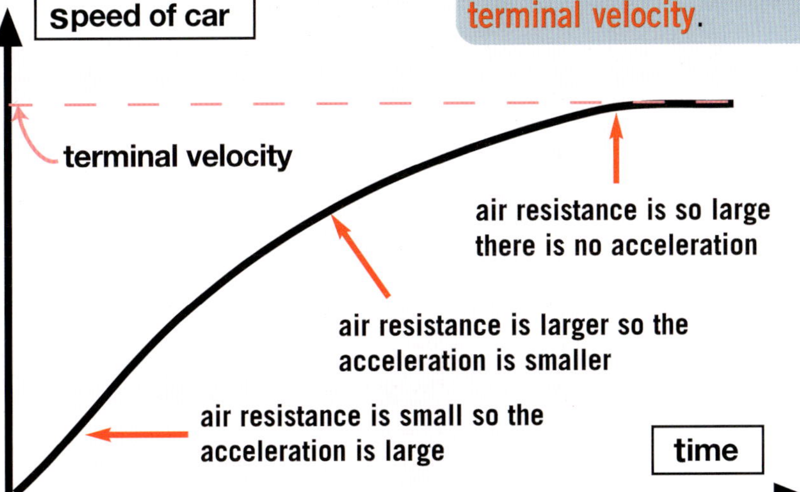

Remember – streamlining and lubricating reduce friction. Rough surfaces and high speeds increase friction.

Make sure you can give examples of situations where the presence of friction is an advantage or disadvantage.

KEY TERMS

Make sure you understand these terms before moving on!

- friction
- frictional forces
- streamlined
- lubricant
- terminal velocity

QUICK TEST

1. What is friction?
2. In which direction does friction act?
3. What is streamlining?
4. What happens to a moving object if the driving force and the resistive forces are balanced?
5. Name two possible effects of friction between two surfaces.

Moments

- Forces sometimes make objects turn or rotate.
- The turning effect of a force is called a moment.
- You created a moment with your fingers when you opened this book.

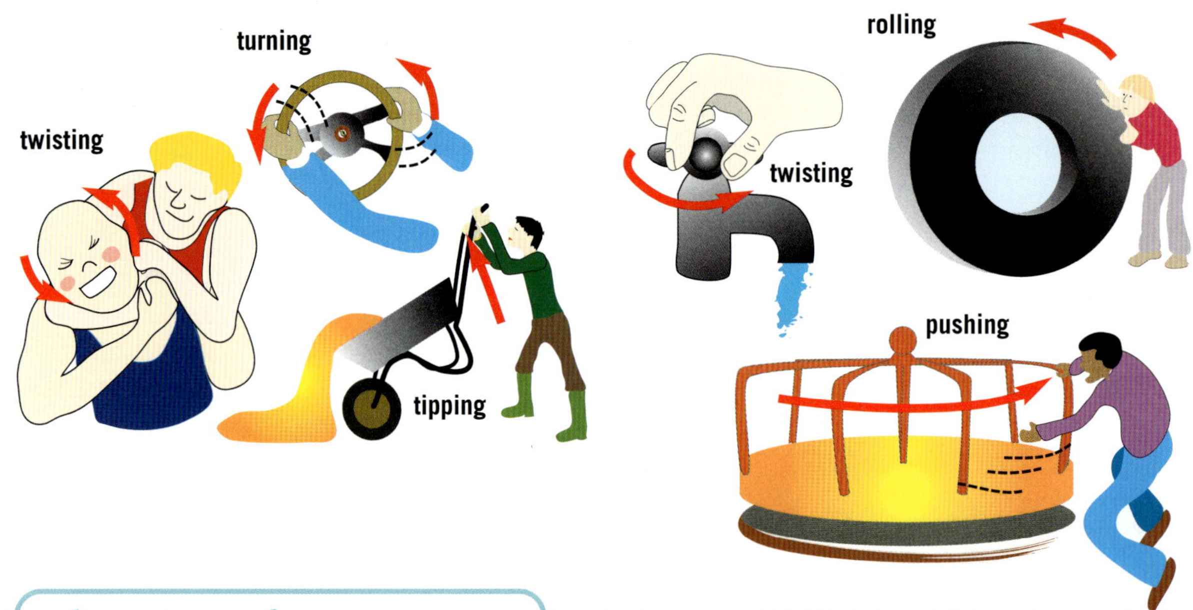

The size of a moment

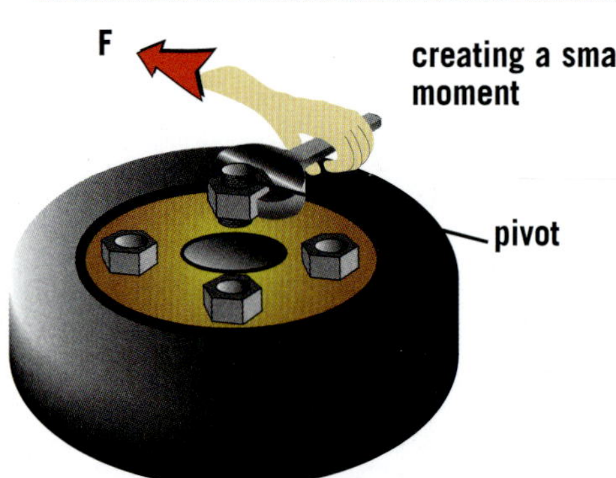

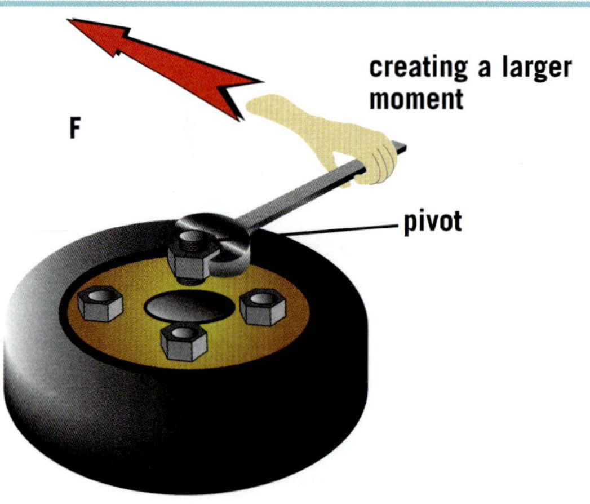

- This **moment** is trying to undo a nut. The point the spanner will turn around is called the **pivot**.
- We measure moments in Nm.
- If the nut is too stiff we can increase the size of the moment by:

a) using a longer spanner or
b) applying a bigger force to the spanner.

100 N
pivot
0.5 m

- The size of a moment can be calculated using the equation:

moment of a force = force × perpendicular distance of force from pivot

- The moment being applied to this spanner is $100\ \text{N} \times 0.5\ \text{m} = 50\ \text{Nm}$

When calculating the size of a moment remember it must be the perpendicular distance of the force from the pivot you use in the equation.

Balancing moments

- If the moments trying to turn an object **clockwise** are equal to the moments trying to turn it **anticlockwise**, the moments will **balance** and there will be no turning.

Example

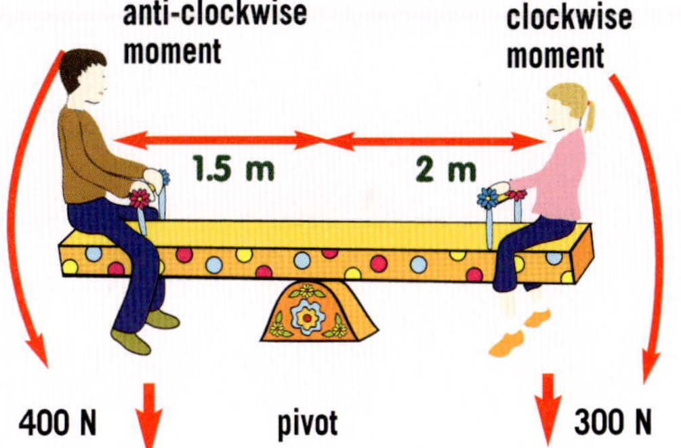

clockwise moment = 2 × 300 = 600 Nm
anticlockwise = 1.5 × 400 = 600 Nm

Result: The see-saw is balanced and does not turn.

Example

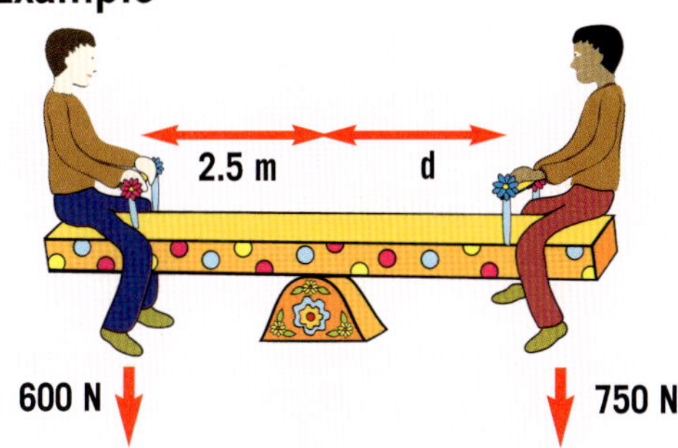

clockwise moment = 2 × 400 = 800 Nm
anticlockwise = 1.5 × 300 = 450 Nm

Result: The see-saw is not balanced and turns clockwise.

KEY TERMS

Make sure you understand these terms before moving on!

- moment
- pivot
- balance
- clockwise
- anticlockwise

QUICK TEST

1. What is a moment?
2. A force of 200 N is applied perpendicular to and at the end of a spanner 0.4 m long. Calculate the moment created by the force.
3. Suggest two ways in which you could increase the moment applied by the spanner.
4. Under what conditions will two moments applied to the same object balance?
5. A man weighing 1200 N sits 1.5 m to the left of the centre of a see-saw. His friend weighs 1100 N and sits on the opposite side, 1.8 m from the centre. Why does the see-saw not balance?
6. Which way does the see-saw in question 5 turn?

Pressure

Working under pressure is never easy. But if you understand how pressure is created you will deal with it much better.

What is pressure?

Pressure is a measure of how concentrated or spread out a force is.

- If a force is applied over a small area it creates a large pressure.
- If the force is applied over a **large area** it creates a small pressure.

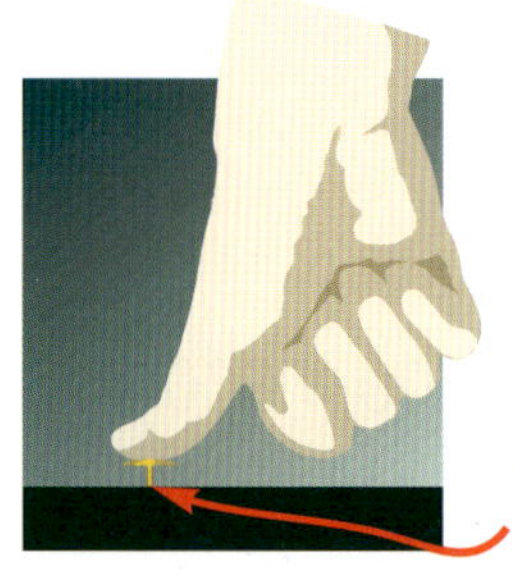

If a knife is sharp the pressure under its blade is high and cutting the cheese is easy. If the blade is blunt the pressure is lower and cutting the cheese is much more difficult.

If the handles of a carrier bag are thin they can create an uncomfortably high pressure on your hands.

Camels have large feet to prevent them from sinking into the sand.

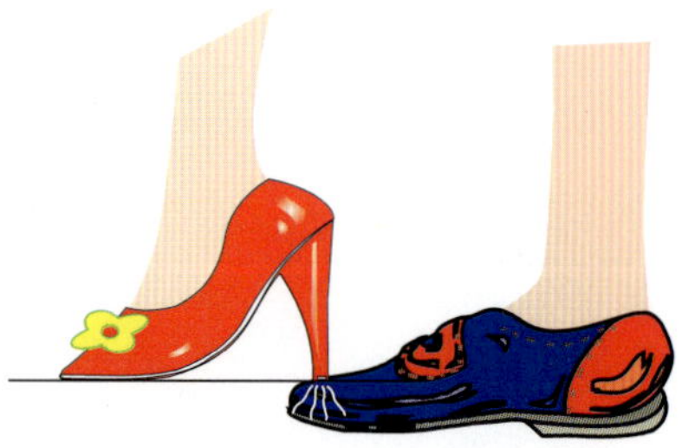

If all your weight is concentrated on a small area the pressure created can be very painful.

Calculating pressure

We can calculate the pressure created by a force using the equation:

$$\text{pressure} = \frac{\text{force}}{\text{area}} \text{ or } P = \frac{F}{A}$$

Force 1 N

Area 1 m²

- We measure pressure in **pascals (Pa)**. 1 Pa = 1 N/m^2

Example

A crate weighing 1000 N is standing upright on one of its sides which measures 2 m × 2 m. Calculate the pressure created on the ground by the crate.

$$P = \frac{F}{A} = \frac{1000}{4} = 250\,N/m^2 = 250\,Pa$$

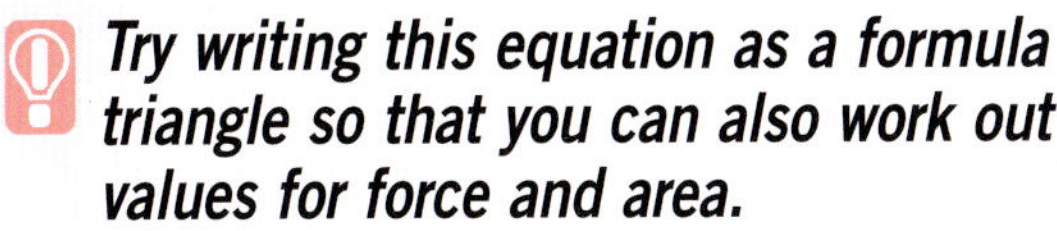

Try writing this equation as a formula triangle so that you can also work out values for force and area.

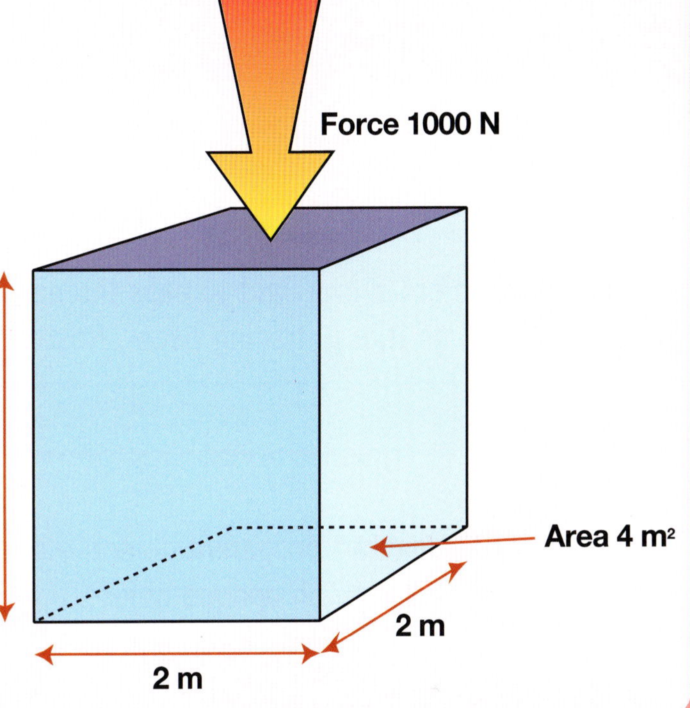

KEY TERMS

Make sure you understand these terms before moving on!

- pressure
- pascals (Pa)

QUICK TEST

1. How do we create a high pressure?
2. How can we avoid or reduce a high pressure?
3. Why are full carrier bags sometimes painful to carry?
4. In what units do we measure pressure?
5. Why does a sharp knife cut through a piece of cheese easier than a blunt knife?
6. Calculate the pressure created when a force of 50 N is over an area of 2.5 m^2.
7. Calculate the pressure created when a crate weighing 4000 N is standing on the side of the crate measuring 4 m × 2 m.
8. What force when applied to an area of 2 m^2 will create a pressure of 40 Pa?

Light rays and reflection

Light travels in straight lines.

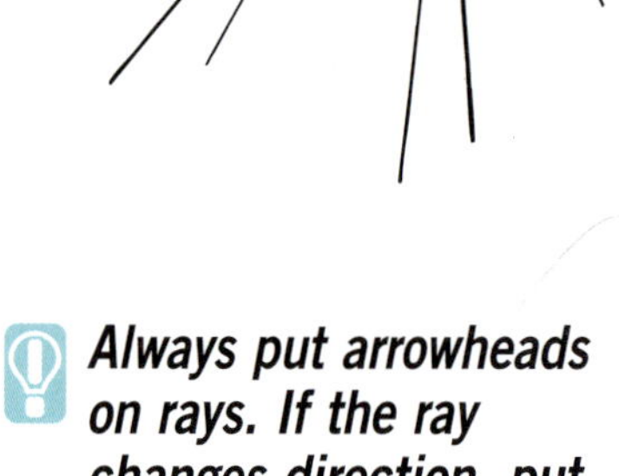

Seeing objects

- We see **luminous objects** such as fires, light bulbs and stars because some of the light they **emit** enters our eyes.
- We see non-luminous objects because some of the light they **reflect** enters our eyes.

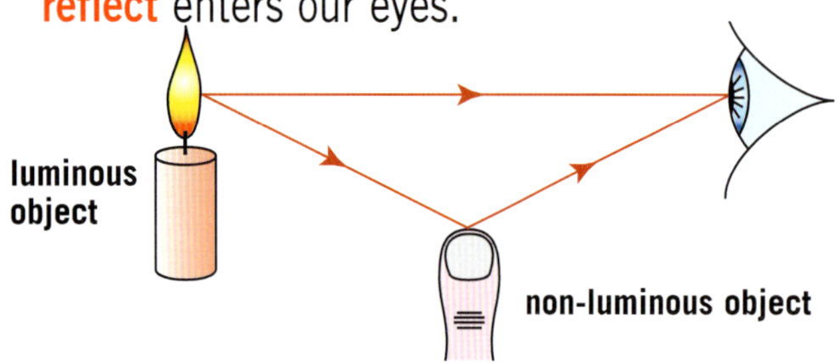

A **translucent** object allows light to pass through it but we cannot see through it, e.g. tracing paper, frosted glass.

Always put arrowheads on rays. If the ray changes direction, put one arrowhead on the ray before the change and one after.

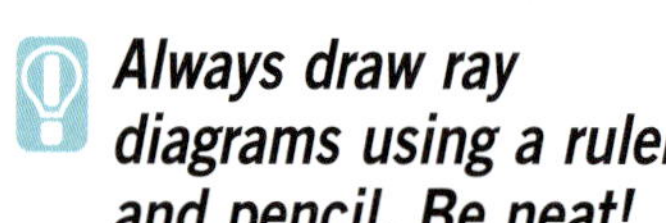

Always draw ray diagrams using a ruler and pencil. Be neat!

Shadows

- We can see through a **transparent** object, e.g. a pane of plane glass.
- We cannot see through an **opaque** object, e.g. a piece of wood, because the light cannot pass through it.
- An opaque object placed in front of a source of light will create a **shadow**.
- A shadow is a dark area where there is little or no light.
- The shadow will have the same shape as the object creating it.
- This is because **light travels in straight lines**.

The speed of light

- Light travels very quickly.
- Over short distances it seems to be there **almost instantaneously**.
- It takes light just eight minutes to travel from the Sun to the Earth.
- It travels at a speed of 300 million metres a second.
- Sound travels at a speed of just 340 metres a second.
- Because light travels much more quickly there is sometimes a delay between seeing and hearing.
- The fireworks in the diagram are seen to explode but then there is a delay of several seconds before we hear the explosion.

Reflection from a plane mirror

- When a ray of light strikes a plane mirror it is reflected so that the **angle of incidence** is equal to the **angle of reflection**. The angles are always measured from the normal.

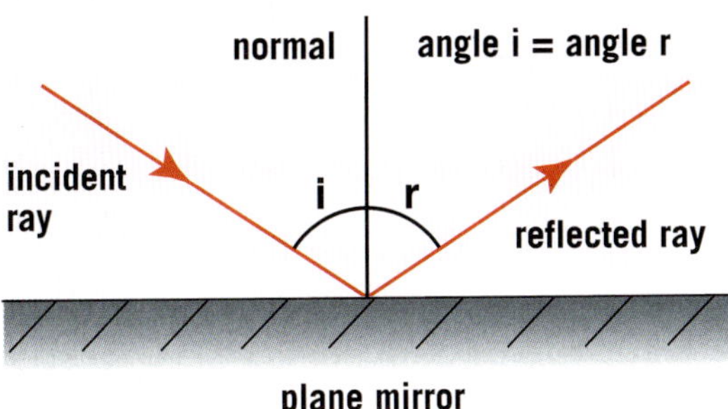

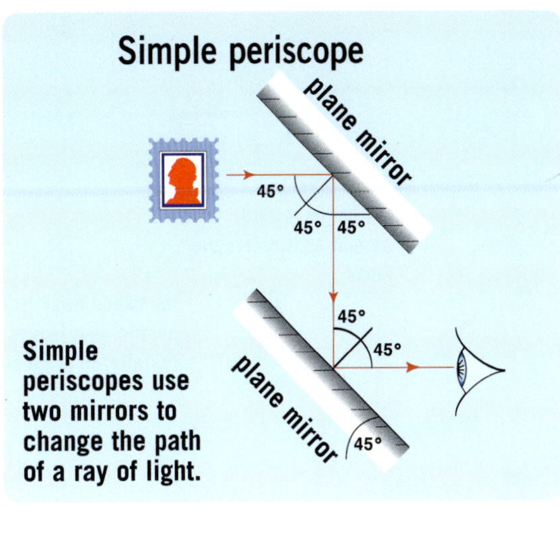

Plane and diffusion reflection

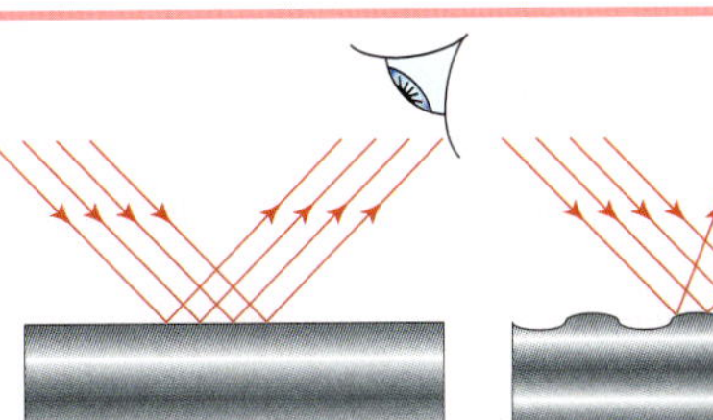
shiny surface

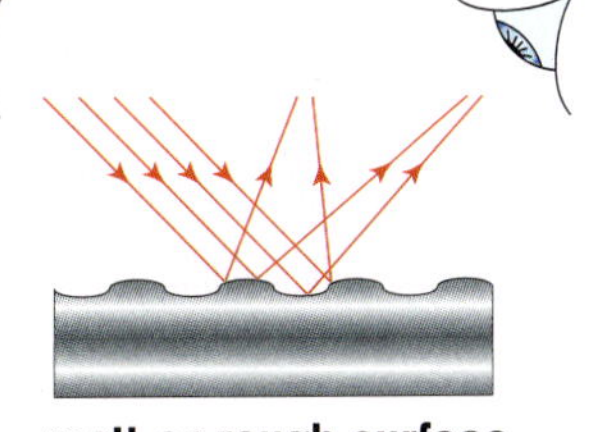
matt or rough surface

- All the rays are reflected in the **same direction**. Lots of light enters our eyes so the surface looks **shiny or glossy**.

- Because the light is **scattered**, only a little of it enters our eyes so the surface appears dull or matt.

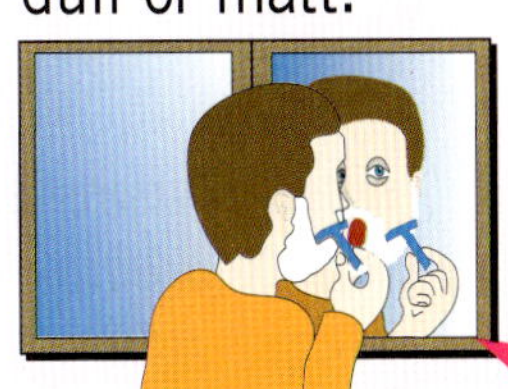

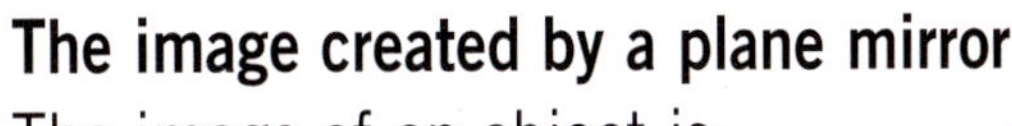

The image created by a plane mirror

The image of an object is:

- upright
- the same size as the object
- the same distance behind the mirror as the object is in front
- **laterally inverted**, i.e. the left is on the right and the right is on the left
- a **virtual image**, i.e. it cannot be formed on a screen placed behind the mirror.

KEY TERMS

- translucent
- emit
- reflect
- luminous object
- transparent
- opaque
- shadow
- angle of incidence
- angle of reflection
- laterally inverted
- virtual image

QUICK TEST

1. How do we know light travels in straight lines?
2. What is an opaque object?
3. What is a transparent object?
4. What is a luminous object?
5. How do we see a non-luminous object?
6. The angle of incidence is equal to ....
7. Describe the image that is created by a plane mirror.

Refraction and colour

Refraction

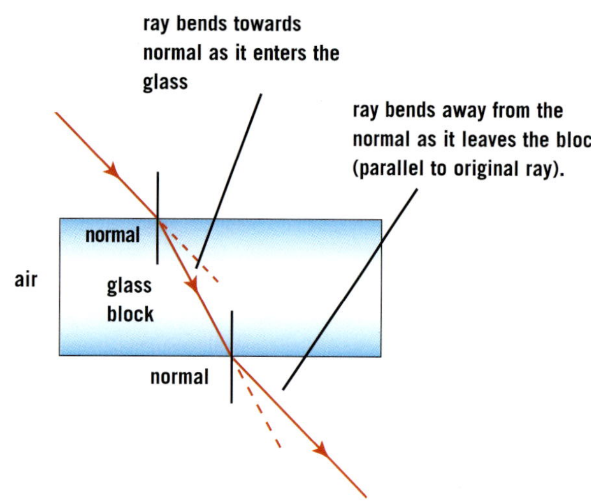

- When a ray of light enters a glass block, it slows down and bends towards the normal.
- This **change of direction** is called **refraction**.
- When the ray emerges from the block, it **speeds up** and bends **away from the normal**.
- But if the ray meets the surface at 90° it continues in a straight line.

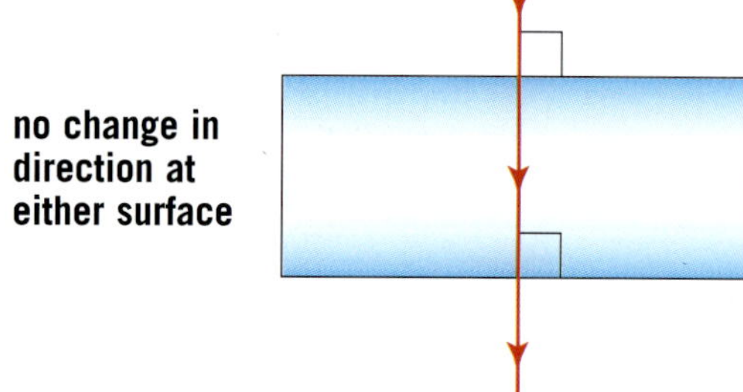

Strange effects of refraction

This pencil looks bent because the rays of light are refracted as they emerge from the water.

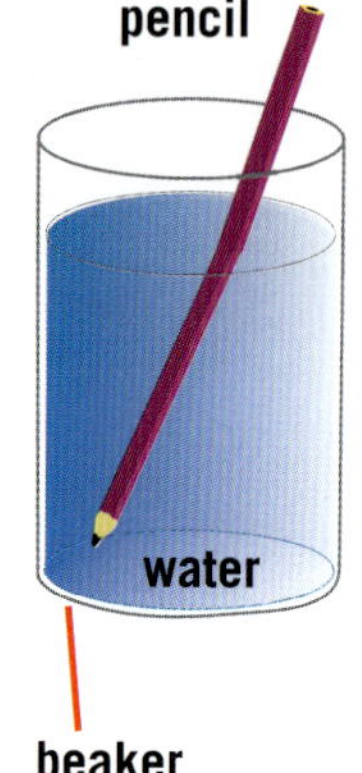

This swimming pool is deeper than it appears. This is also caused by refraction.

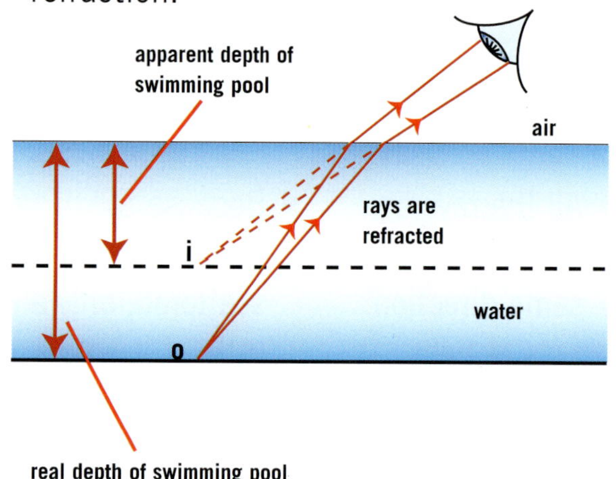

When revising any topic about light be sure to practise drawing ray diagrams using a ruler and pencil.

Dispersion

- White light is a **mixture of coloured lights**.
- When white light travels through a **prism**, the different colours are refracted by different amounts. This is called **dispersion**.
- A **band of colours** called a **spectrum** is produced.
- The colours of the spectrum are always in the same order: red, orange, yellow, green, blue, indigo and violet.

source of white light
prism
spectrum
red
orange
yellow
green
blue
indigo
violet

Easy to remember: Richard Of York Gave Battle In Vain.

Coloured objects

- Coloured objects contain chemicals called **dyes**.
- When white light hits a coloured object all the colours of the spectrum are **absorbed** by the dye **except for its own colour**. This is reflected into the eye of the observer.
- White objects reflect all colours.
- Black objects reflect no light.

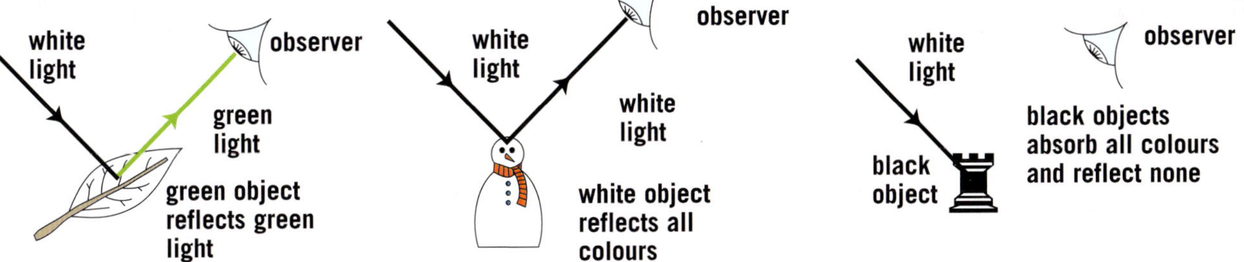

Coloured filters

Filters are coloured pieces of transparent plastic or glass which **only allow light of the same colour to pass through.** For example, green light can pass through a green filter but red or blue light will be absorbed.

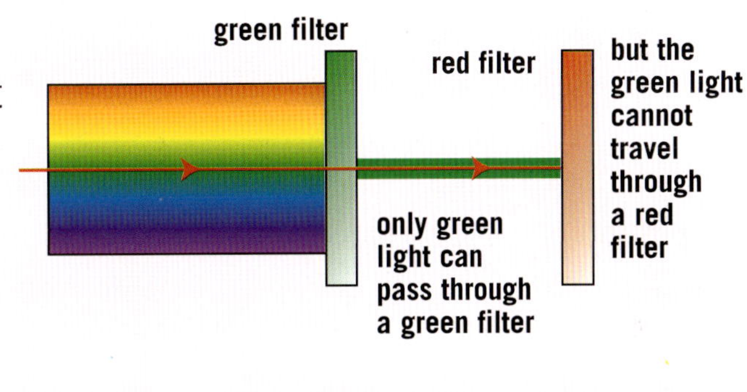

KEY TERMS

Make sure you understand these terms before moving on!

- refraction
- prism
- dispersion
- spectrum
- dyes
- absorbed
- filters

QUICK TEST

1. What is the bending of a ray of light as it enters a glass block called?
2. Which way does a ray bend as it travels from air into glass?
3. Explain how an observer sees a green object in white light.
4. What is a spectrum?
5. How is a spectrum produced?
6. What is a green filter?

Sounds

All sounds begin with an object that is vibrating. These vibrations travel outwards from the source. If they strike someone's eardrum, they may be heard.

Pitch and frequency

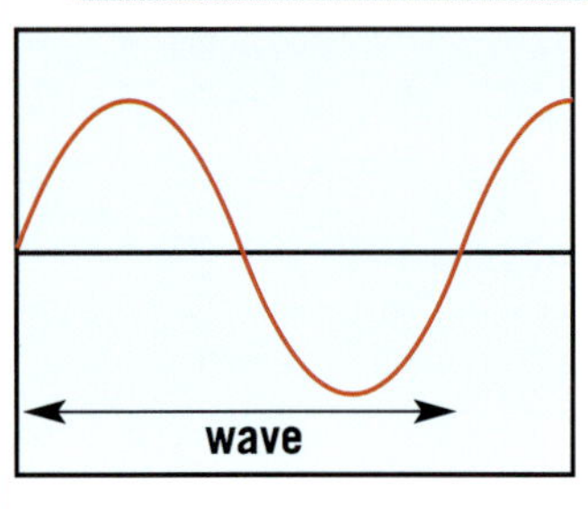

low pitched sound

- Large objects vibrate slowly and produce just a few waves each second. These waves have a low frequency and produce low **pitched** sounds.

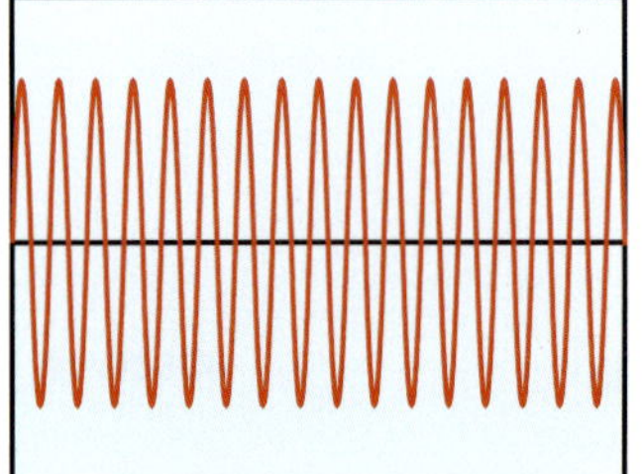

high pitched sound

- Small objects vibrate quickly and produce lots of waves each second. These waves have a high frequency and produce high pitched sounds.
- We measure the **frequency** of a wave or its source in **hertz (Hz)**. An object which vibrates once every second and produces one complete wave every second has a frequency of 1 Hz.

Loudness

- Objects that vibrate with large **amplitudes** produce loud sounds.
- Objects that have small vibrations produce quiet sounds.

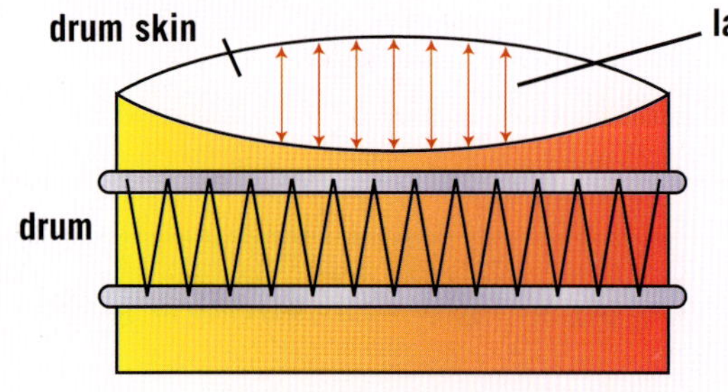

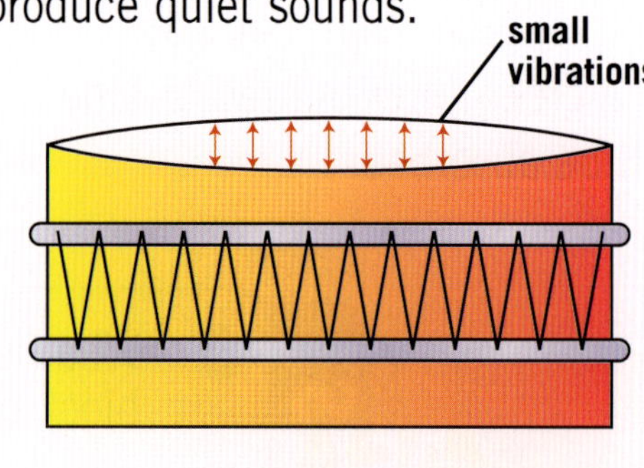

loud sound

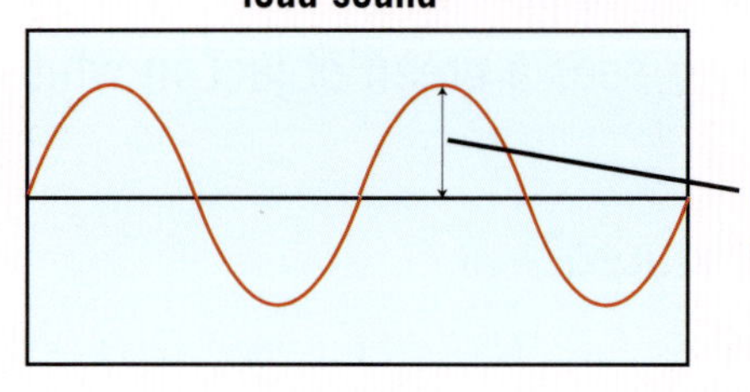

quiet sound

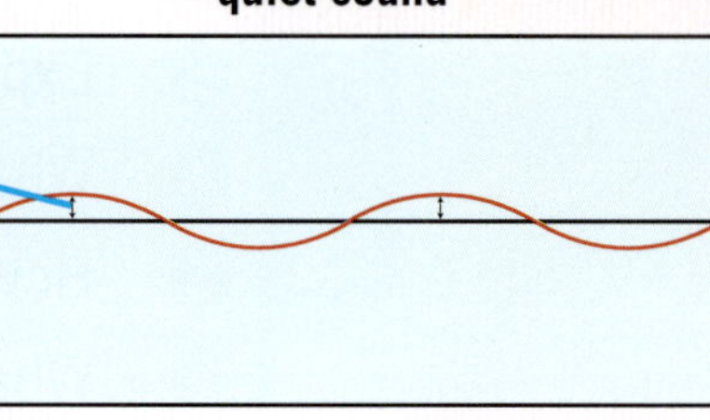

Travelling sound waves

- Although we normally think of sound waves as travelling through air they can travel through solids, liquids and gases. Sound waves travel by making particles vibrate.
- There are no particles in a vacuum therefore **sound waves cannot travel through a vacuum.**
- When the bell is turned on we can see and hear it ring.
- When all the air has been sucked out of the jar by the vacuum pump we can see that the bell is still ringing but we cannot hear it.
- Conclusion: Light waves can travel through a vacuum but sound waves cannot.

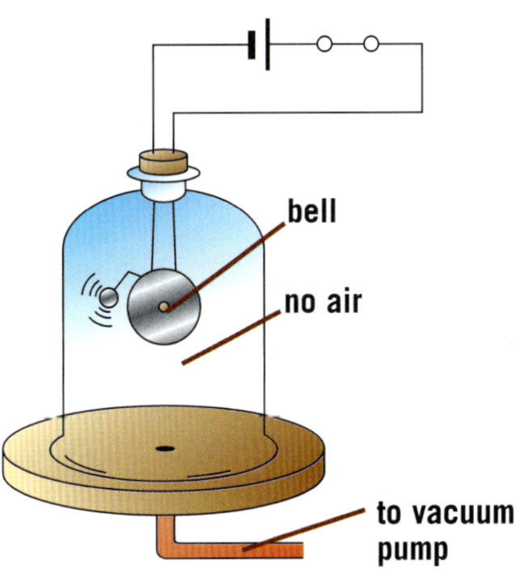

- Sound waves travel much more slowly than light waves. This is why we often see an event before we hear it, e.g. thunder and lightning.

Be sure to remember at least one example which demonstrates that sound travels much more slowly than light waves.

QUICK TEST

1. All sounds begin with an object which is ....
2. A large object will produce a .... sound.
3. A small object will produce a .... sound.
4. Loud sounds are produced by objects with large .... of vibration.
5. What are soundwaves unable to travel through? Explain your answer.
6. Why do we see lightning before we hear the thunder?

KEY TERMS

Make sure you understand these terms before moving on!

- pitch
- frequency
- hertz (Hz)
- amplitudes

Echoes and hearing

Echoes

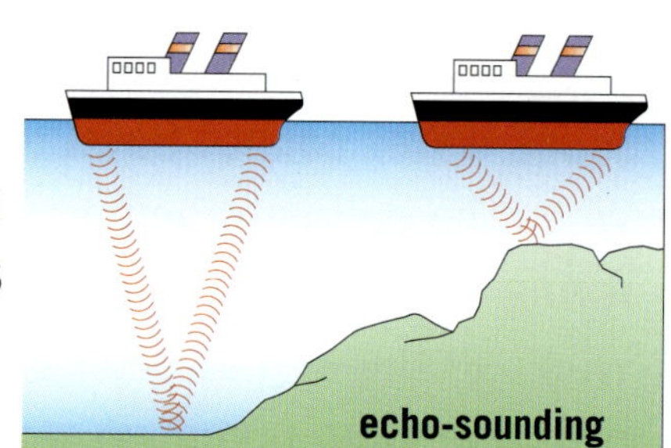

- When sound waves strike a hard surface they are reflected. This reflected sound is called an **echo**.
- Ships use echoes to find the depth of the ocean beneath them. An echo-sounder emits sound waves down towards the seabed. When the waves strike the seabed, they are reflected back up to the surface. A sound detector 'listens' for the echo.
- The deeper the ocean the longer it is before the echo is heard. Sound waves used in this way are called **SONAR**. This stands for SOund Navigation And Ranging.
- Fishing boats often use sonar to detect shoals of fish. If an echo is heard sooner than expected it is likely that the wave has been reflected from a shoal of fish swimming beneath the boat.

Hearing range (sometimes called audible range)

- An average person can only hear sounds that have a frequency above **20 Hz but below 20 000 Hz**. This band of frequencies is called our **hearing range**.
- Hearing ranges vary slightly from person to person but in general as we get older our hearing range becomes narrower.
- Sounds that have a frequency which is too high for the human ear to detect are called **ultrasounds**.
- Ultrasounds can be heard by some animals.
- Dog whistles produce notes we cannot detect but they can be heard by a dog.

Don't try to memorise any of the figures from this section but do try to understand that different people have different hearing ranges and that loud sounds can cause permanent hearing problems.

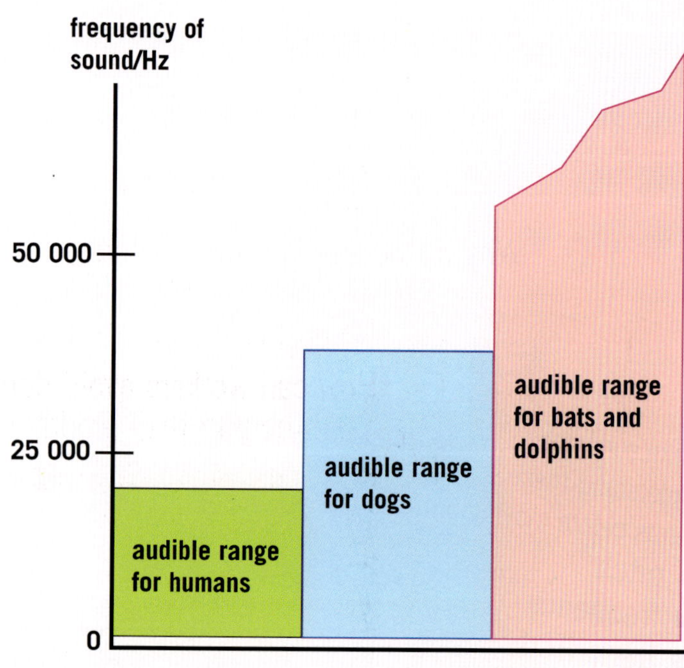

Loudness and the decibel scale

- Constant exposure to loud sounds can damage your hearing.
- People who work with noisy machinery should wear **ear defenders** to protect their hearing.
- People listening to music through earphones should be careful not to have the volume turned up too high. The **damage** caused to their hearing by persistent exposure to loud sounds could be permanent.

- We measure **loudness** on the **decibel scale**.

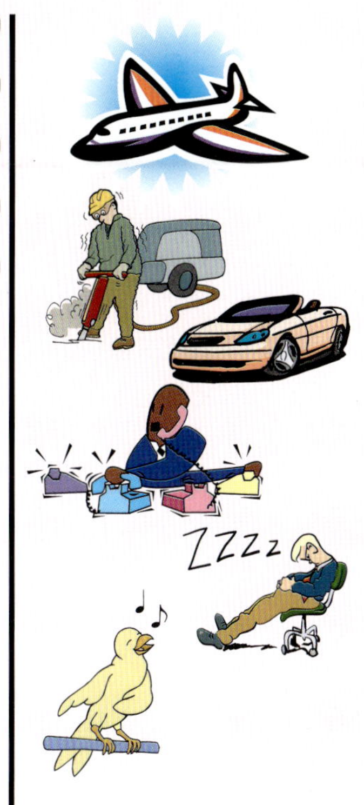

KEY TERMS

Make sure you understand the following terms before moving on:

- echo
- SONAR
- hearing range
- ultrasounds
- ear defenders
- loudness
- decibel scale

QUICK TEST

1. What is an echo?
2. What is the hearing range of an average person?
3. What is an ultrasound?
4. Name two animals that can hear ultrasounds.
5. How can workers avoid damage to their hearing if they use noisy machinery in their work?
6. How can you avoid damaging your hearing when listening to your personal stereo?

Energy

We all need energy in order to be able to do things. As human beings we get this energy from the food we eat. Food is a form of chemical energy. But there are other forms of energy.

Different forms of energy

Heat or thermal energy

Hot objects are sources of **heat energy**.

Light energy

The Sun, light bulbs and lamps are luminous objects. They give off **light energy**.

Sound energy

Vibrating objects give off **sound energy**.

Electrical energy

Electrical energy is available every time a current flows. The electrical energy from this battery is being used to make the bulb glow.

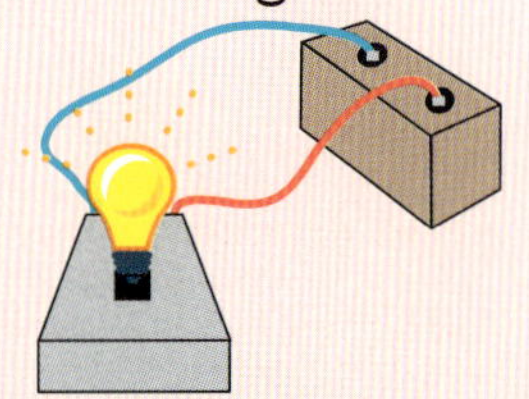

Chemical energy

Food, fuels and batteries all contain **chemical energy**.

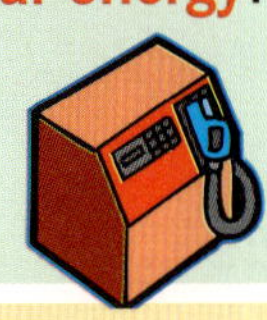

Kinetic energy

This is the energy an object has because it is moving. Wind (moving air) and flowing water have **kinetic energy**.

Elastic potential energy

Objects such as springs and rubber bands that are stretched or twisted or bent contain **elastic potential energy**.

Gravitational potential energy

Objects that have a high position and are able to fall have **gravitational potential** energy.

Nuclear energy

Reactions in the centre or nucleus of an atom are the source of **nuclear energy**.

Stored energy

- Chemical energy, elastic potential energy and gravitational potential energy are often referred to as forms of **stored energy**.
- They are forms of energy that are waiting to be used.

chemical energy in the wax

Energy transfers

When energy is used **it does not disappear**.
It is **transferred into different forms** of energy.

A light bulb changes electrical energy into heat and light energy.

A log fire changes chemical energy into heat and light energy.

A loudspeaker changes electrical energy into sound.

Other examples of energy changes:

Energy in	Energy changer	Energy out
Chemical (food)	Animal	Heat, kinetic, chemical
Light	Solar cell	Electrical
Kinetic	Wind turbine	Electrical
Elastic potential energy	Bow and arrow	Kinetic
Chemical	Battery	Electrical
Electrical	Battery charger	Chemical
Sound	Microphone	Electrical
Electrical	Electric motor	Kinetic
Kinetic energy	Generator	Electrical
Gravitational potential energy	Falling object	Kinetic
Elastic potential energy	Clockwork car	Kinetic

This is another topic that crops up nearly every year in all the exams. Make sure you know lots of examples of energy changes. Write down the names of some machines and devices, then try to describe the energy transfers that take place when they are used.

KEY TERMS

Make sure you understand the following terms before moving on!

- heat energy
- electrical energy
- gravitational potential
- light energy
- chemical energy
- nuclear energy
- sound energy
- kinetic energy
- stored energy
- elastic potential energy

QUICK TEST

1. Name five different types of energy.
2. Name three types of stored energy.
3. What kind of energy does a crate gain as it is lifted by a crane?
4. What kind of energy does water gain as it travels down a waterfall?
5. Write down the energy transfer that takes place when using a hair drier.
6. Write down the energy transfer that takes place when you speak into a microphone.

Using energy resources

Electrical energy is one of the most convenient forms of energy. It is easily converted into other forms of energy.

Fossil fuels

Coal, oil and gas are called **fossil fuels**. They are **concentrated sources** of energy.

- Fossil fuels are formed from plants and animals that died over 100 million years ago.
- When they died they became covered with many layers of mud and earth.
- The resulting large pressures and high temperatures changed them into fossil fuels.

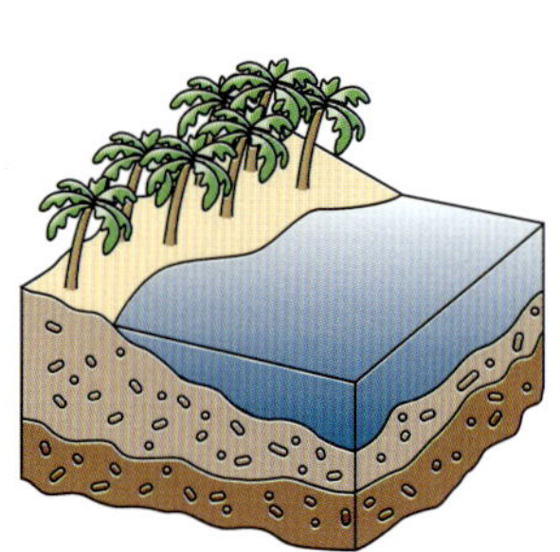

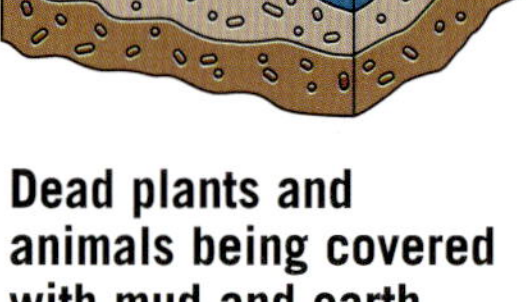

Dead plants and animals being covered with mud and earth.

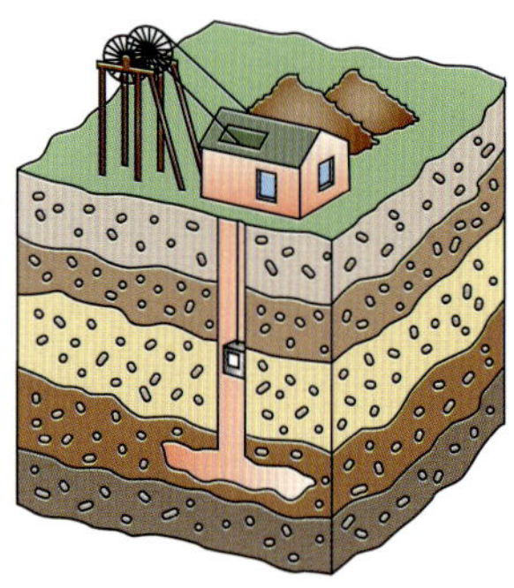

After hundreds of millions of years they have changed into fossil fuels such as coal.

- Because they take millions of years to form these fuels are called **non-renewable fuels**.
- Once they have been used up they cannot be replaced.

The problems with fossil fuels

- When any of the fossil fuels are burned they produce carbon dioxide. Increasing the amount of carbon dioxide in the atmosphere will cause the temperature of the Earth and its atmosphere to rise. This is called the **greenhouse effect**.
- When coal and oil are burned they also produce gases that cause **acid rain**.
- Environmental problems are created by mining and spillage of oil during transport.
- We are using fossil fuels up very quickly and will soon have to find other sources of energy but we need to start looking now.

The solutions

- We need to slow down the rate at which we are using fossil fuels so that they will last longer. There are several ways in which we can do this.
- **Reduce petrol consumption** by driving smaller cars, using public transport or walking or cycling. More efficient car engines would also use less petrol.
- **Improve the insulation** to our homes and factories so less energy is wasted heating them.
- **Increase public awareness** of how people are wasting energy so that they turn off lights and turn down heating where possible.
- **Renewable sources of energy** such as wind, waves, tidal, solar, geothermal, biomass and hydroelectric need to be developed. Each of these sources have some advantages and disadvantages. These are described in more detail on pages 110–11.
- In the UK some of our electricity is generated by nuclear power stations.

Power stations

Most of the electrical energy we use at home is generated at **power stations**. There are several different types of power station but most in the UK use coal or gas as their source of energy (fuel).

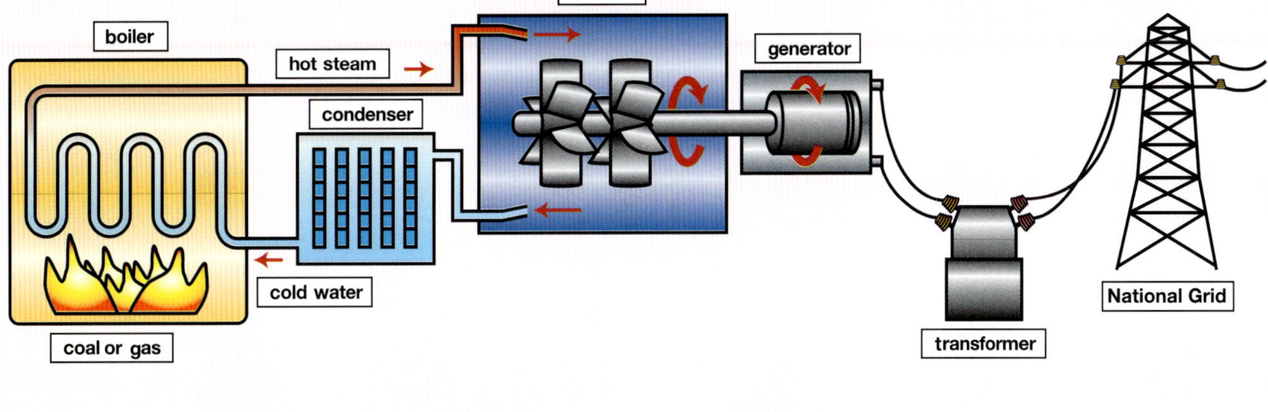

The fuel is burned to release its **chemical energy.**	The **heat energy released** is used to heat water and turn it into **steam**.	The steam **turns turbines**.	The turbines **turn large generators**.	The **generators produce electrical energy**.	The electrical energy is carried to our homes through the **National Grid**.

This is a very popular topic and appears regularly on exam papers. Make sure that you understand the energy changes that take place when electricity is generated at the power station. Also learn the problems that burning fossil fuels creates for the atmosphere and the environment.

KEY TERMS

Make sure you understand the following terms before moving on!

- fossil fuel
- non-renewable fuels
- greenhouse effect
- acid rain
- renewable sources of energy
- power stations
- National Grid

QUICK TEST

1. Name three fossil fuels.
2. What is the main gas causing the greenhouse effect?
3. Which fossil fuels when burned cause acid rain?
4. Name one type of environmental damage that might be caused as a result of using fossil fuels in our power stations.
5. Why are fossil fuels called non-renewable sources of energy?
6. Suggest three ways in which we could make fossil fuels last longer.

Alternative energy sources

Geothermal

Geothermal energy is harnesed from hot rocks underground.

- Cold water is pumped below the ground.
- Hot rocks warm the water changing it into steam.
- This steam is then used to generate electricity.

+ Renewable source of energy.
+ No pollution and no environmental problems.

– Very few suitable sites.
– High cost of drilling deep into the ground.

water is pumped several kilometres below the ground to hot rocks

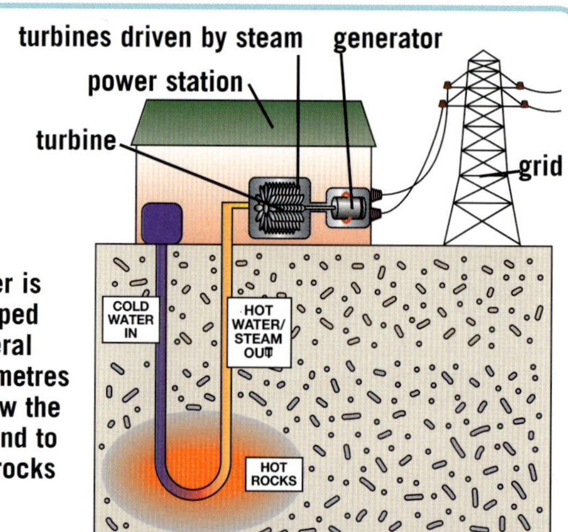

radioactive decay produces heat to warm the rocks close to the surface

Tidal power

Tidal power can be managed by building dams. At high tide, water is trapped behind a dam. When it is released at low tide it drives turbines which generate electricity.

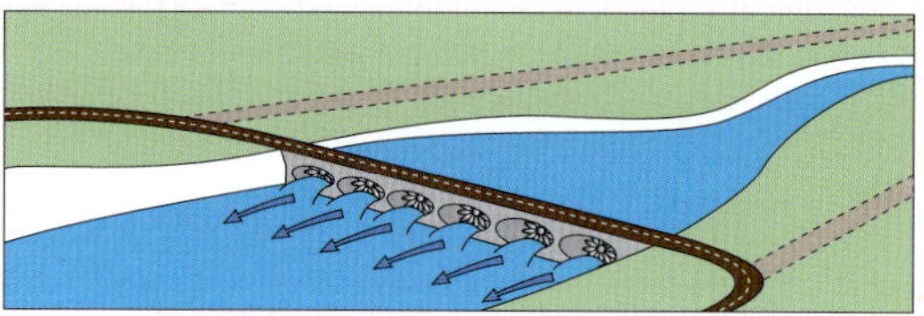

+ Renewable source.
+ Reliable: two tides per day.
+ No atmospheric pollution.
+ Low running costs.
– High initial cost.
– Possible damage to environment, e.g. flooding.
– Obstacle to water transport.

Don't waste time memorising the diagrams. Do look at them and remember the advantages and disadvantages of each resource.

Solar energy

Solar energy comes directly from the sun. The energy carried in the Sun's rays can be converted directly into electricity using **solar cells**.

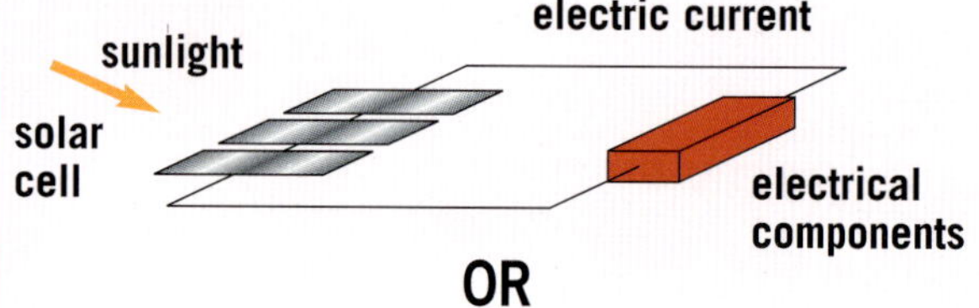

OR

The energy carried in the Sun's rays can be absorbed by dark coloured panels and used to heat water.

matt black solar panels on roof

+ No pollution.

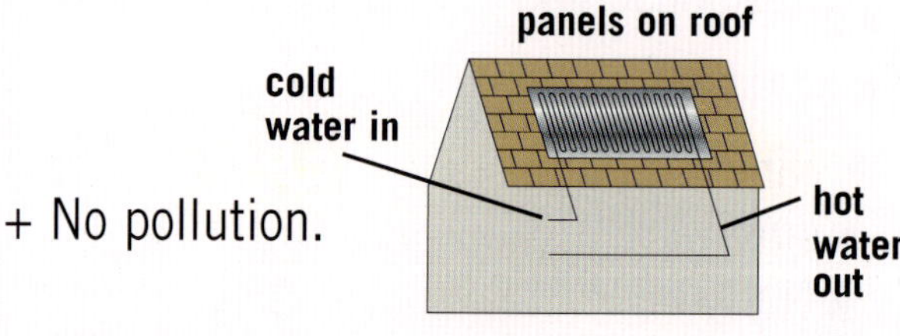

– Initially quite expensive.
– May not be so useful in regions where there is limited sunshine.

Biomass

The chemical energy stored in **things that were once alive**, e.g. wood, can be released by burning to create **biomass**.

+ Renewable source of energy.
+ Low-level technology, therefore useful in developing countries.
+ Does not add to the greenhouse effect as the carbon dioxide plants and trees release when burned was taken from the atmosphere as they grew.
– Large areas of land needed to grow sufficient numbers of trees.

Hydroelectricity

Flowing water is used to drive turbines and generate **hydroelectricity**.

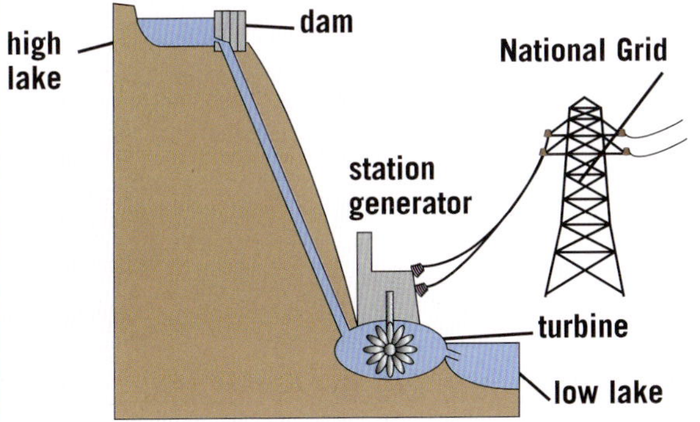

+ **Renewable** source.
+ Energy can be **stored** until required.
+ No atmospheric pollution.
– **High** initial cost.
– **High** cost to environment, e.g. flooding, loss of habitat.

KEY TERMS

Make sure you understand the following terms before moving on:

- geothermal
- solar energy
- biomass
- hydroelectricity
- tidal power
- solar cells
- wind energy
- wave power

Wind energy

Wind energy is used to drive turbines and generate electricity.

+ It is a renewable source of energy and therefore will not be exhausted.
+ Has low-level technology and therefore can be used in developing countries.
+ No atmospheric pollution.
– Visual and noise pollution.
– Limited to windy sites.
– No wind, no energy.

Wave power

The rocking motion of the **waves** is used to generate electricity.

simple wave machine
the energy in the water waves makes this machine rock
this motion is then used to generate electricity

+ Renewable source.
+ No atmospheric pollution.
+ Useful for isolated islands.
– High initial cost.
– Visual pollution.
– Poor energy capture. Large area of machines for small energy return.
– Can be damaged by storms.

QUICK TEST

1. Name three ways in which water could be used as an energy resource.
2. Name two energy resources whose use may pollute the environment visually.
3. Name two energy resources which could be easily used, and maintained, in developing countries.
4. Name one energy resource that must be burned to release energy.
5. Name one energy resource whose capture might cause noise pollution.

Heat transfer

Heat will flow when there is a temperature difference between two places. It will flow from the hotter to the cooler place. There are three methods by which it can do this. These are conduction, convection and radiation.

Conduction

Heat is being transferred along this rod by **conduction**.

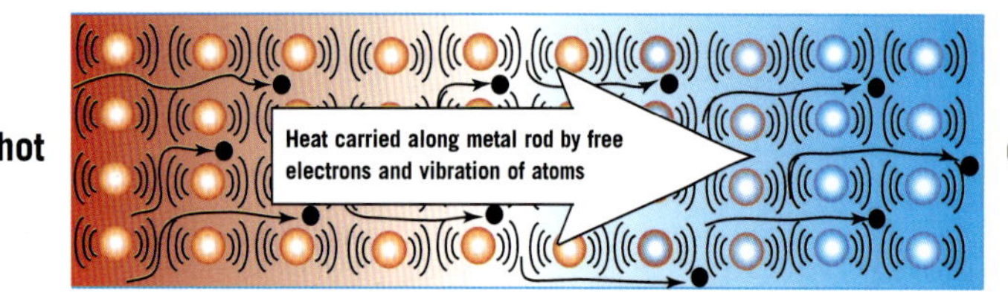

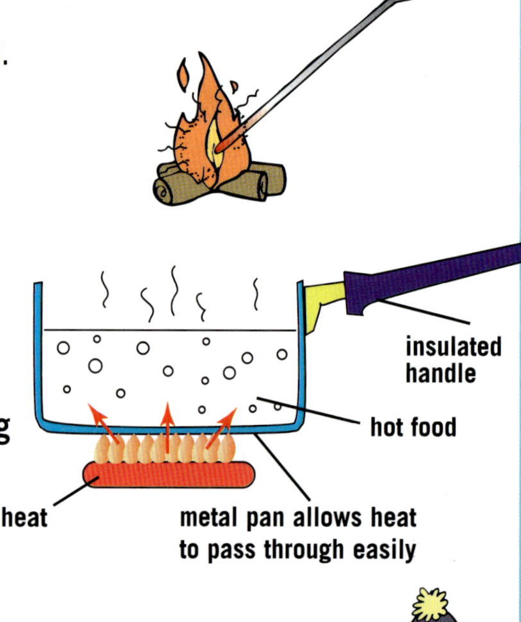

- Particles at the hot end **vibrate** and move around **more vigorously**.
- These **extra vibrations** are **passed on to neighbouring particles** causing them to move more vigorously.
- As a result the cold end of the rod gradually becomes warmer.
- All **metals** are **good conductors** of heat.
- Most **non-metals** are **poor conductors** of heat.
- Most liquids are poor conductors.
- **Gases** (air) are **excellent insulators** because they do no allow heat to pass through them easily by conduction.
- Woven materials, e.g. wool and cotton, contain trapped air and are excellent insulators.

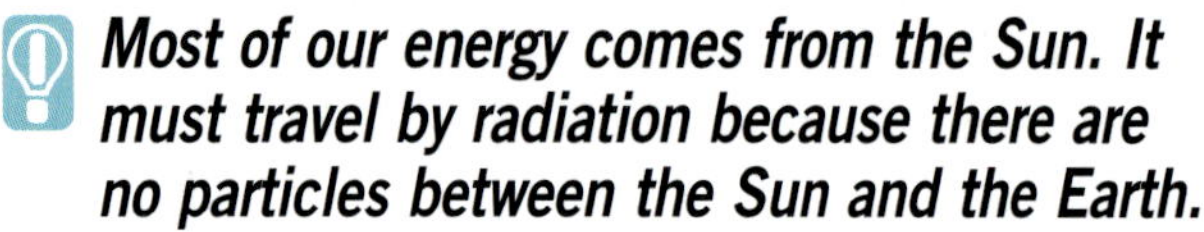

Most of our energy comes from the Sun. It must travel by radiation because there are no particles between the Sun and the Earth.

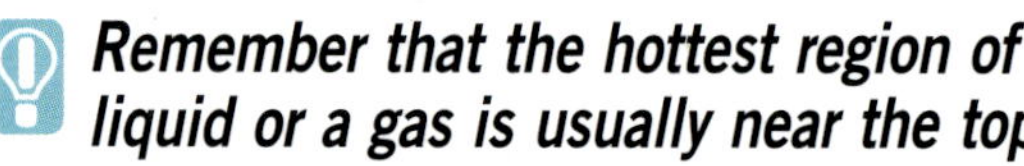

Remember that the hottest region of a liquid or a gas is usually near the top.

Convection

Convention takes place in liquids and gases.

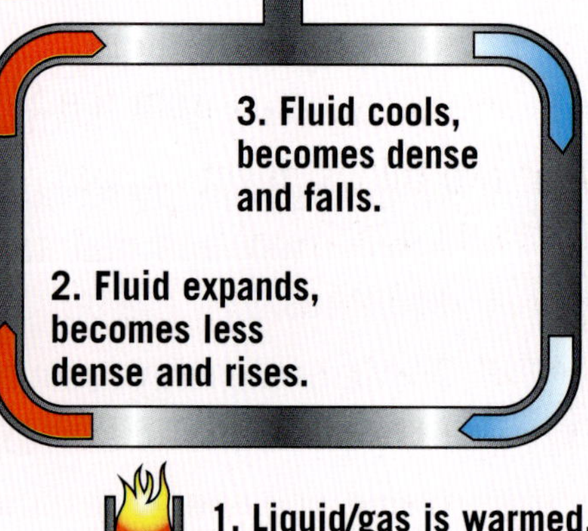

Heat is carried to all parts of the tube by convection current.

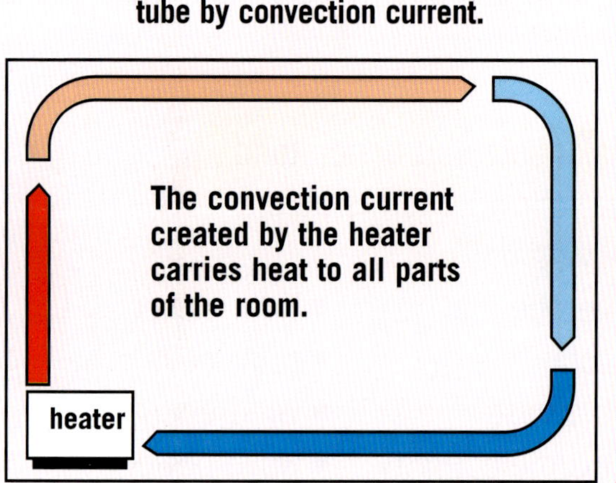

Radiation

Radiation is heat travelling as rays.

- Objects with **dark, rough surfaces absorb most of the radiation** and become warm/hot.

- Objects with light **coloured, shiny surfaces reflect most of the radiation** and will remain cooler.

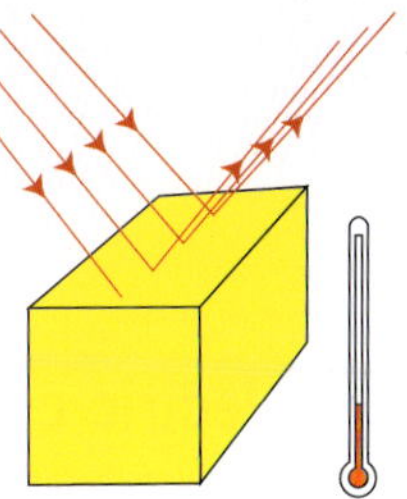

- Houses in hot countries are often painted white so they reflect the radiation and stay cool.

Insulating the home

This diagram shows how heat may escape from a house that has not been insulated.

KEY TERMS

Make sure you understand the following terms before moving on!

- conduction
- convection
- radiation
- double glazing
- draught excluders
- insulation into loft
- carpets and underlay

QUICK TEST

1. Name three methods by which heat can travel.
2. Give one example and one use of a good conductor.
3. Give one example and one use of an insulator.
4. Why do metals feel colder than wood?
5. What is double glazing?
6. Suggest five methods by which you could reduce the heat escaping from your house.
7. How does heat travel from the Sun to the Earth?
8. What two things might happen when heat radiation strikes an object?
9. How is the heat from a radiator transferred to all parts of a room?

Circuits and components

Electric current

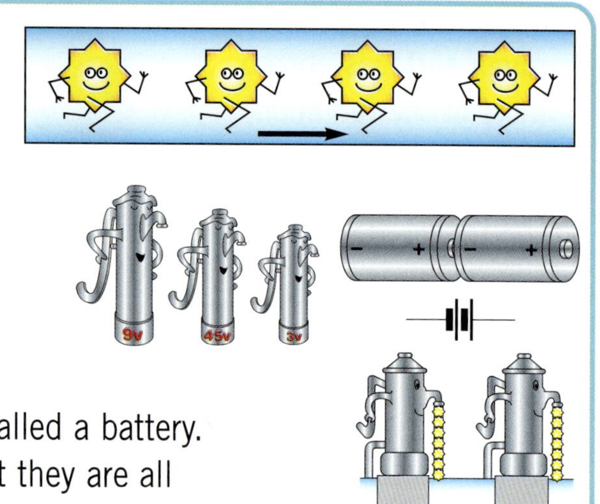

- An **electric current** is a **flow of charge**.
- Charges can be made to flow using a **cell** or a **battery**.
- Cells and batteries act as **charge pumps**.
- They give charges **energy**.
- Several cells connected together can produce a **larger current**.
- Several cells connected together like this are called a battery.
- Care must be taken to connect the cells so that they are all pumping in **the same direction**.

Simple circuits

- Charges can flow through wires in the same way that pumped water flows through pipes.
- The wires, cells, bulbs, etc. must be connected to form a **complete loop** (or circuit).
- If there are gaps the circuit will be **incomplete** and no current will flow.

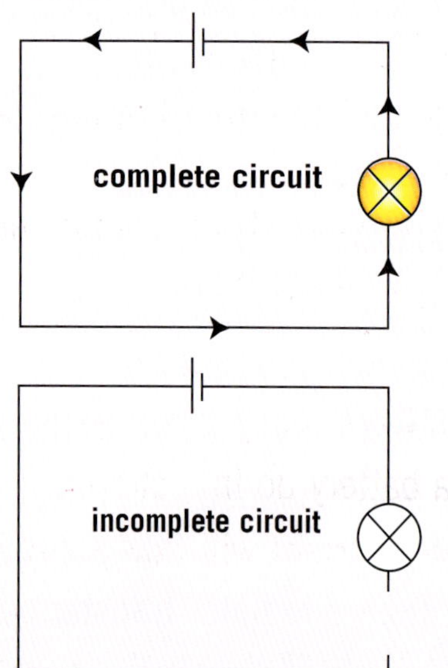

Circuit diagrams

Instead of trying to draw diagrams of the actual components in a circuit we use **circuit diagrams** containing easy-to-draw symbols for the components, as shown in the diagram below.

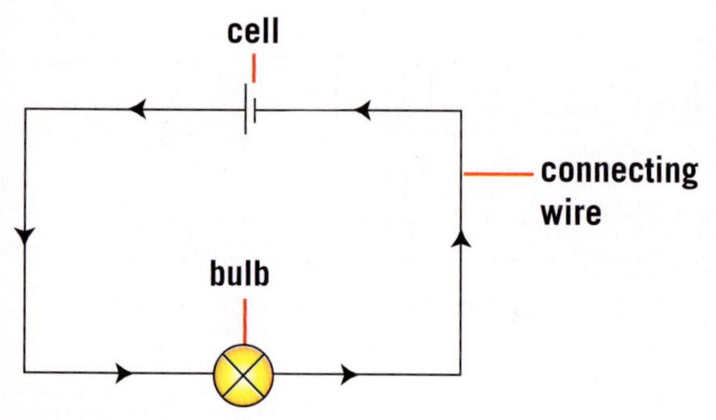

Make sure you know most of the basic electrical symbols.

Circuit symbols

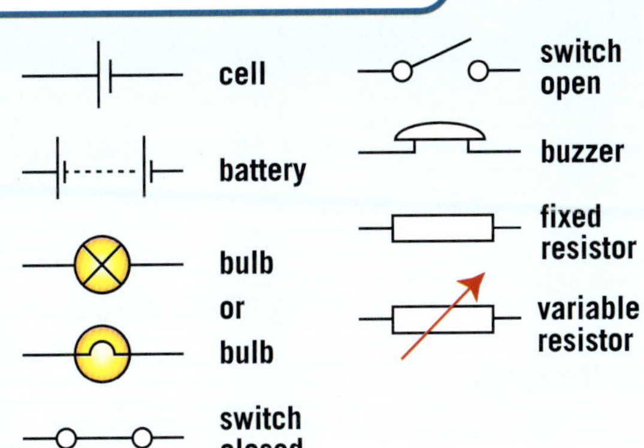

Conductors and insulators

- Metals are good conductors of electricity.
- They allow charges to move through them easily.
- Non-metals are mainly poor conductors (or insulators).
- They do not allow charges to move through them easily.

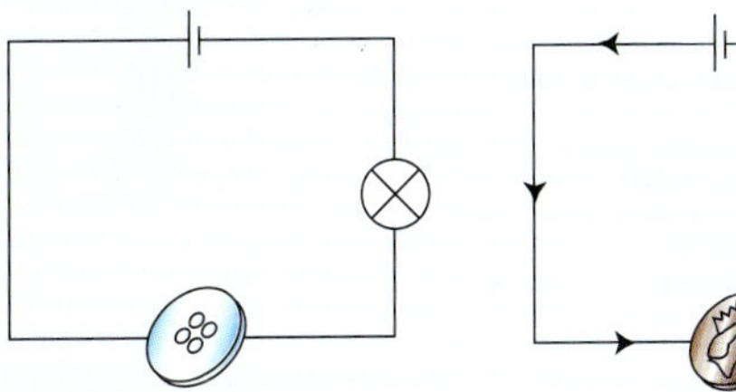
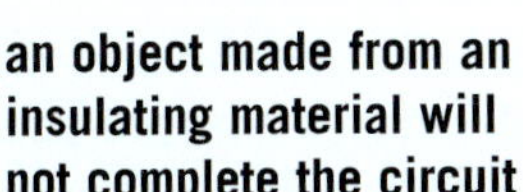
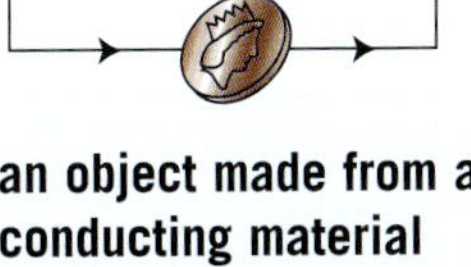

an object made from an insulating material will not complete the circuit

an object made from a conducting material completes the circuit

Switches

- **Switches** behave like drawbridges, making a circuit complete when they are closed and incomplete when they are open.

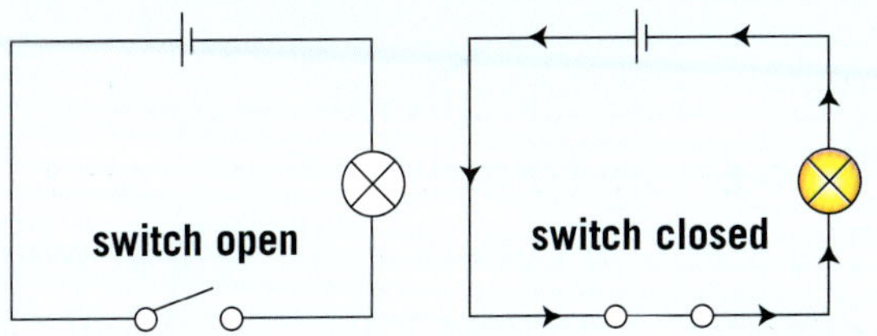

- When the switch is **open** the circuit is **incomplete**, current will not flow and the bulb is turned **off**.
- When the switch is **closed** the circuit is **complete**, current will flow and the bulb is turned **on**.

Resistors

- **Resistors** are used to **control the size of current** flowing through a circuit.
- With no resistor in this circuit the current is large and the bulb glows brightly.

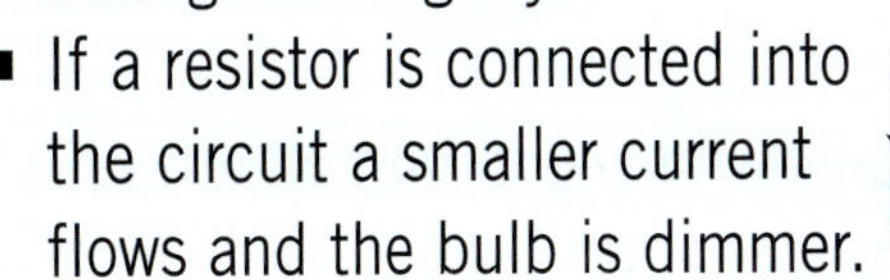

- If a resistor is connected into the circuit a smaller current flows and the bulb is dimmer.

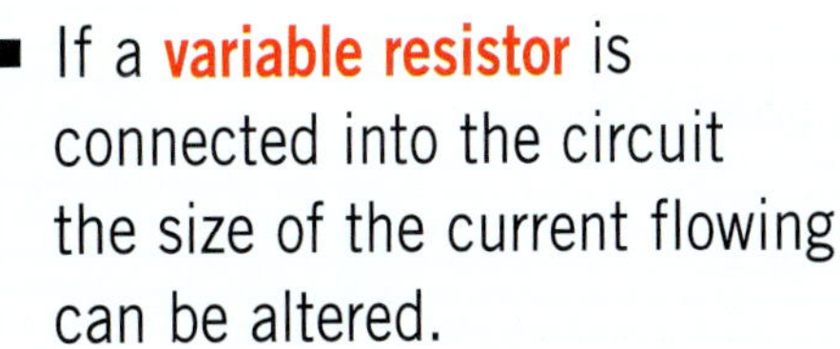

- If a **variable resistor** is connected into the circuit the size of the current flowing can be altered.

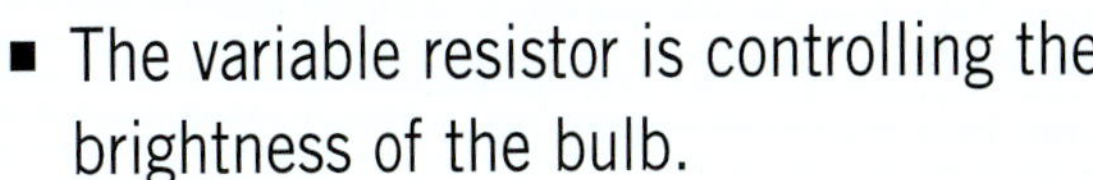

- The variable resistor is controlling the brightness of the bulb.

KEY TERMS

Make sure you understand the following terms before moving on!

- electric current
- flow of charge
- cell
- battery
- switches
- resistors
- variable resistor

QUICK TEST

1. What is a battery?
2. What does a battery do in a circuit?
3. In order that a current will flow a circuit must be ....
4. Name one material that is a) a conductor and b) an insulator.
5. What does a resistor do in a circuit?
6. What is a variable resistor?

Circuits – current & voltage

Measuring current

- We measure current with an **ammeter**.
- We measure current in **amperes** or **amps (A)**.
- The size of a current is the **rate at which charge is flowing**.
- Ammeter 1 is measuring the current flowing through AB
- Ammeter 2 is measuring the current flowing through BC
- Ammeter 3 is measuring the current flowing through CD
- All three ammeters show that the same current is flowing in all parts of the circuit.
- This proves that **current is not used up as it flows around a circuit**.

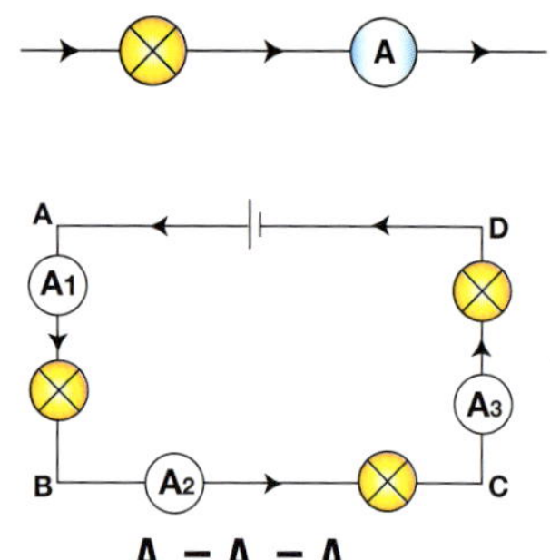

$A_1 = A_2 = A_3$

Energy and circuits

- Charges are given energy as they pass through a cell or battery.
- The higher the **voltage** of a cell or battery the greater the amount of **energy** given to the **charges**.
- We can measure the energy given to the charges by the cell or battery using a **voltmeter**.
- The voltmeter is connected across the cell.
- As charges flow around a circuit they give away the energy they were given by the cell/battery.
- This **energy is changed into other forms** by the **components** in the circuit.

V_{cell}
This voltmeter is measuring the energy given to charges by the cell.

V_1
This voltmeter is measuring the electrical energy changed into heat and light energy by the bulb.

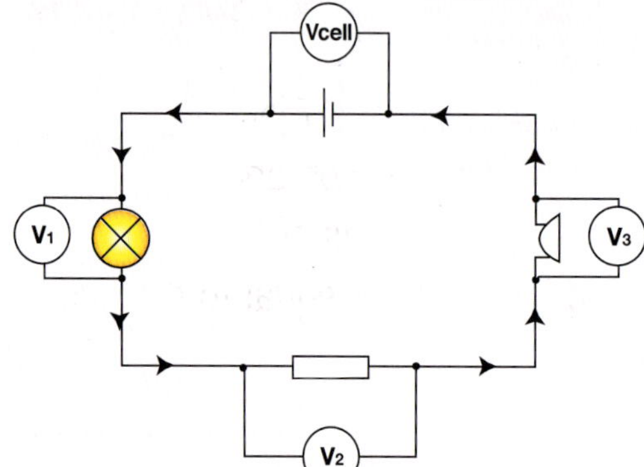

V_3
This voltmeter is measuring the electrical energy changed into sound energy by the buzzer.

V_2
This voltmeter is measuring the electrical energy changed into heat energy by the resistor.

$V_{cell} = V_1 + V_2 + V_3$

- A **bulb changes** electrical energy into **heat** and **light** energy.
- A **resistor changes** electrical energy into **heat** energy.
- A **buzzer changes** electrical energy into **sound** energy.

Ammeters are connected in series. Voltmeters are connected in parallel.

Series and parallel circuits

There are two types of circuit: **series circuits** and **parallel circuits**.

Series circuits

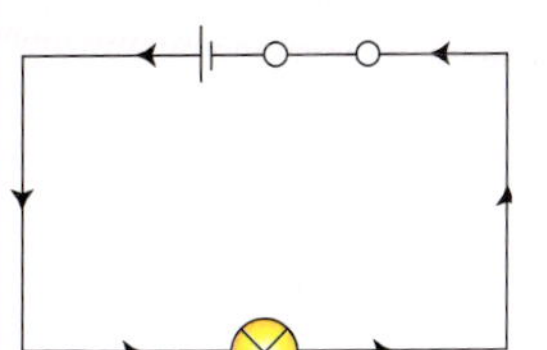

No branches only one path to follow.

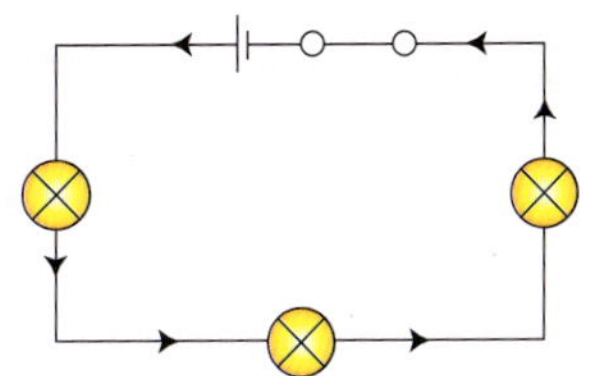

Same current in all parts.

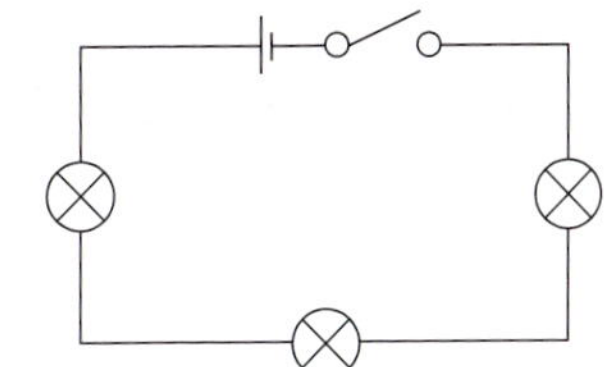

Switch open — no current anywhere in the circuit.

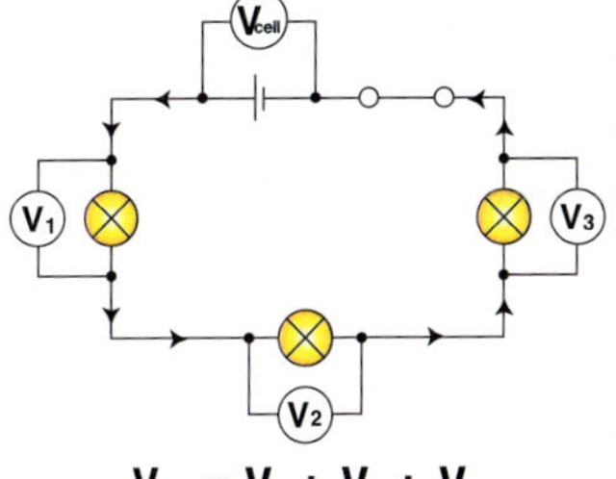

$V_{cell} = V_1 + V_2 + V_3$

- These have no branches or junctions.
- They only have one path for the current to follow.
- Can be turned on and off by a single switch anywhere in the circuit: 'one out, all out'.
- They have the same current flowing in all parts of the circuit.
- The sum of the voltages across all the components is equal to the voltage across the cell or battery.

Parallel circuits

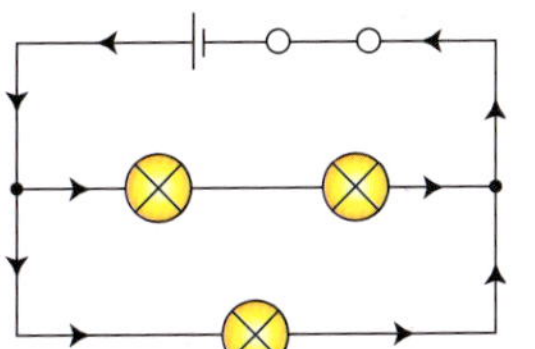

Parallel circuits have branches and more than one path to follow. Current may be different in different parts of the circuit.

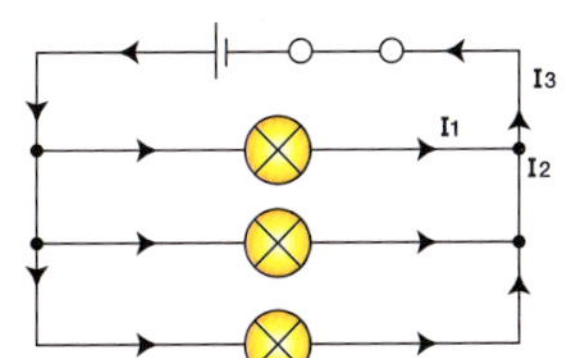

Currents flowing into junction = currents flowing out i.e. $I_1 + I_2 = I_3$

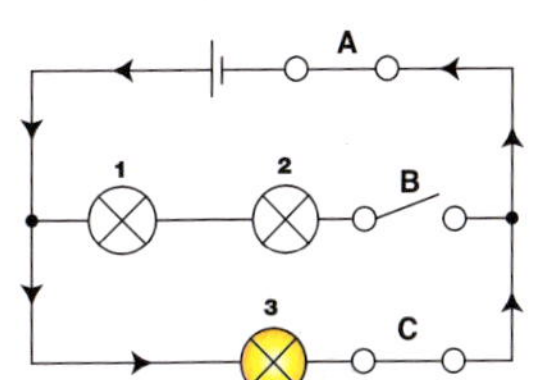

Opening switch B turns off bulbs 1 and 2 but current can still flow through bulb 3. Bulb 3 can be turned on and off with switch C. Switch A can turn all three bulbs on and off.

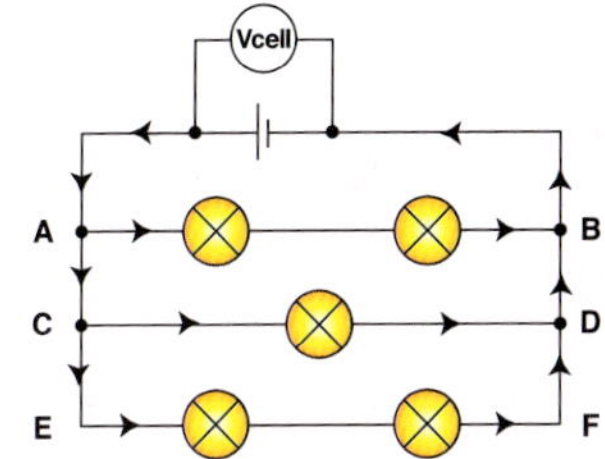

$V_{cell} = V_{AB} = V_{CD} = V_{EF}$

- These have **branches and junctions**.
- There is more than one path for the current to follow.
- Switches can be put into the circuit to turn on and off all or just part of the circuit.
- The size of currents flowing in different parts of the circuit may be different.
- The current flowing into a junction must be equal to the current flowing out of the junction.

Make sure you understand the following terms before moving on!

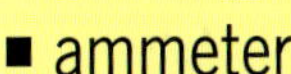

- ammeter
- amperes
- amps (A)
- voltage
- voltmeter
- seies circuits
- parallel circuits

QUICK TEST

1. What is an electric current?
2. How do we measure the size of an electric current?
3. In what units do we measure electric current?
4. What is not used up in an electrical circuit?
5. What is carried around a circuit by the charges?

Magnets & electromagnets

Magnets

- **Magnets** attract **magnetic materials**, e.g. iron, steel, nickel and cobalt.
- Magnets do not attract **non-magnetic materials**, e.g. wood, plastic, copper, aluminium.

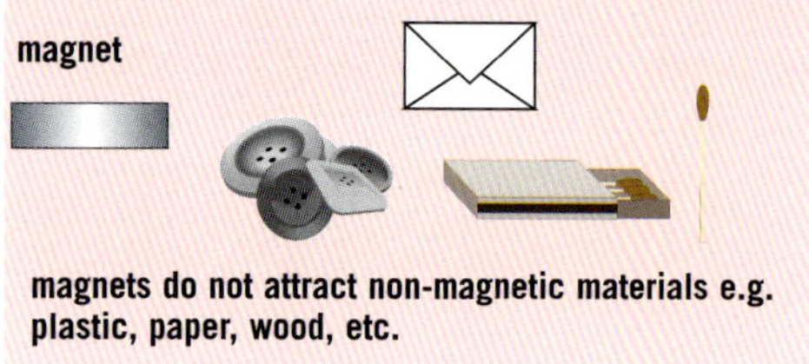

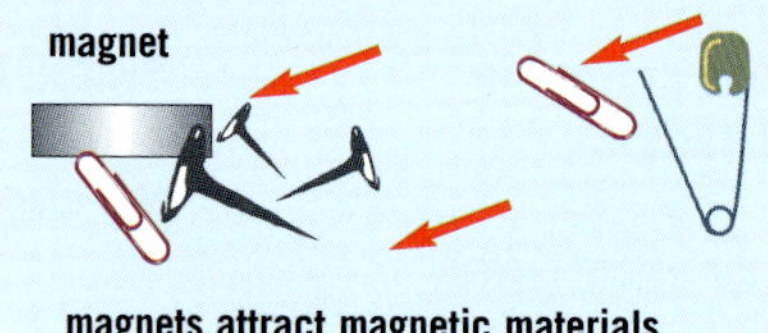

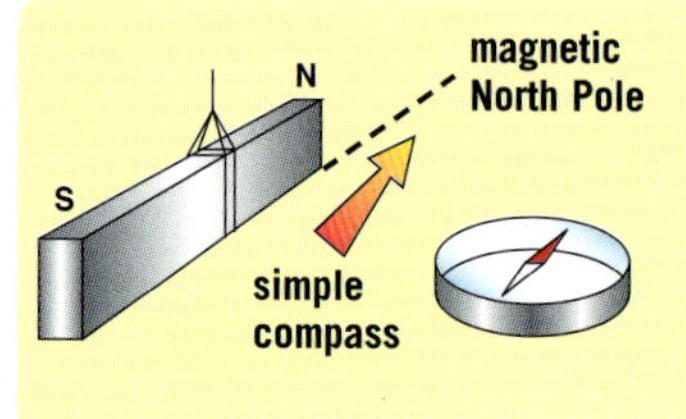

- The strongest parts of a magnet are its **poles**.
- Most magnets have two poles: a North pole and a South pole.
- A bar magnet suspended horizontally will align itself with the Earth's magnetic field so that its North pole points north and its South pole points south. The magnet behaves like a **compass**.

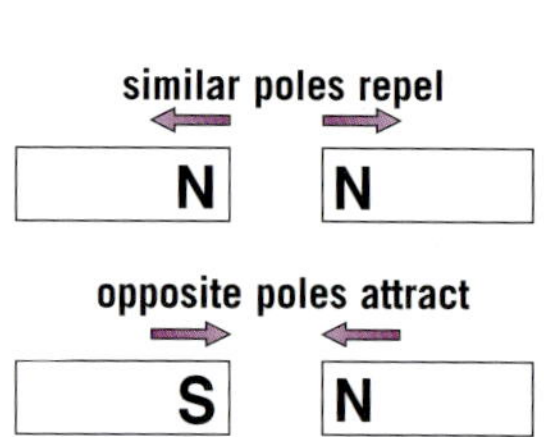

Electromagnets

- If a current is passed through a wire which is wrapped around a piece of iron a strong **magnetic field** is created.
- This combination of **coil and core** is called an **electromagnet**.
- The magnetic field around this electromagnet is the same shape as that of a bar magnet.

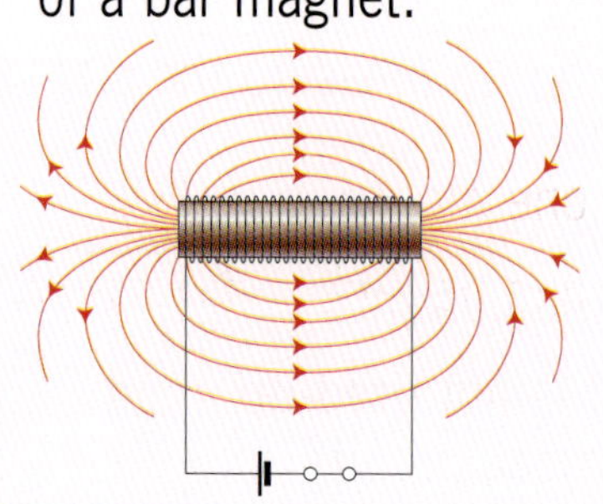

To make the magnetic **field stronger** we can:

- **increase the current**

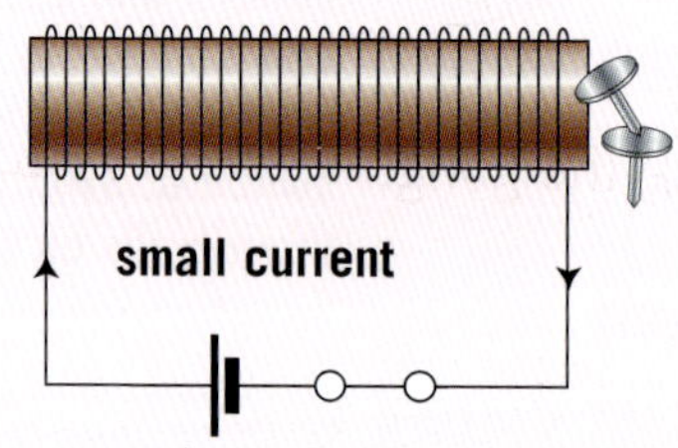

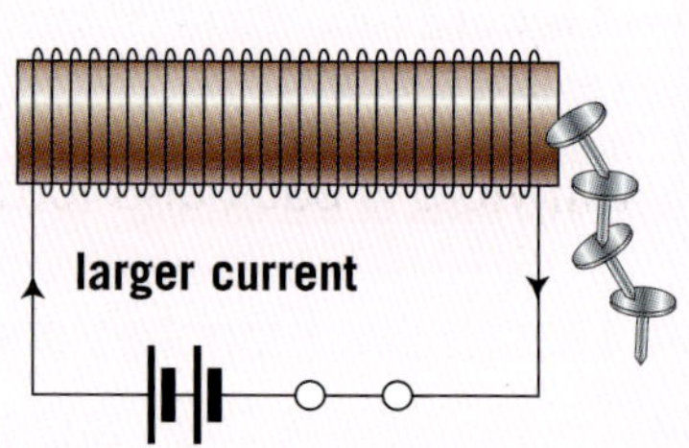

- **increase the number of turns** on the coil.

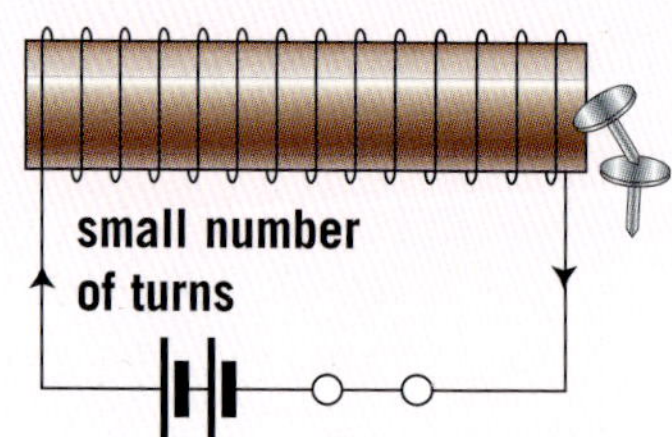

- One of the main advantages of an electromagnet over a permanent magnet is that **it can be turned on and off**.

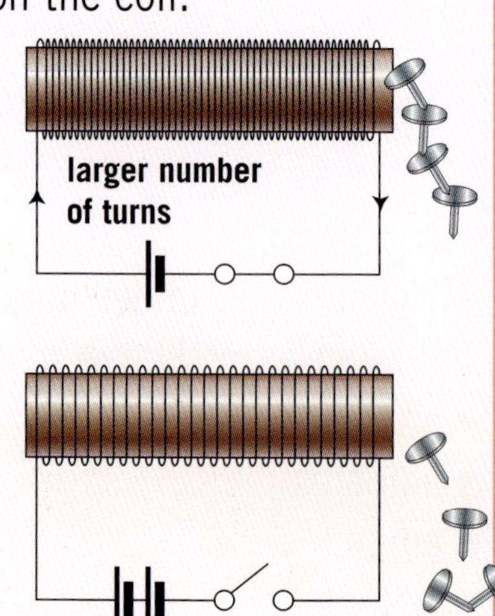

Magnetic fields

- A magnetic field is a volume of space where magnetic effects, e.g. attraction and repulsion, can be detected.
- The shape of the magnetic field around a bar magnet can be seen using **iron filings** or plotting compasses.

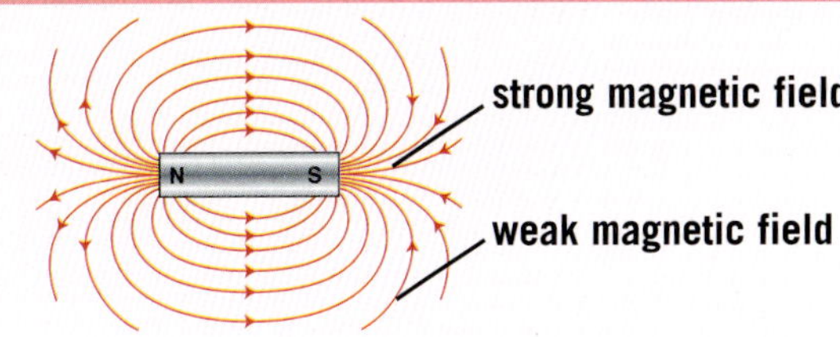

- The **shape**, strength and direction of magnetic fields is shown using **magnetic lines of force**.
- The lines are **close together** where the field is **strong**.
- The lines are **far apart** where the field is **weak**.
- The lines travel from **north to south**.

Uses of electromagnets

Electric bell

- When the bell push is pressed the circuit is complete and the electromagnet is turned on.
- The **soft iron armature** is pulled towards the electromagnet and the **hammer** hits the **gong**.
- At the same time a gap is created at **C** and the electromagnet is turned off.
- The armature now springs back to its original position and the whole process starts again.
- As long as the bell push is pressed, the armature will vibrate back and forth striking the gong.

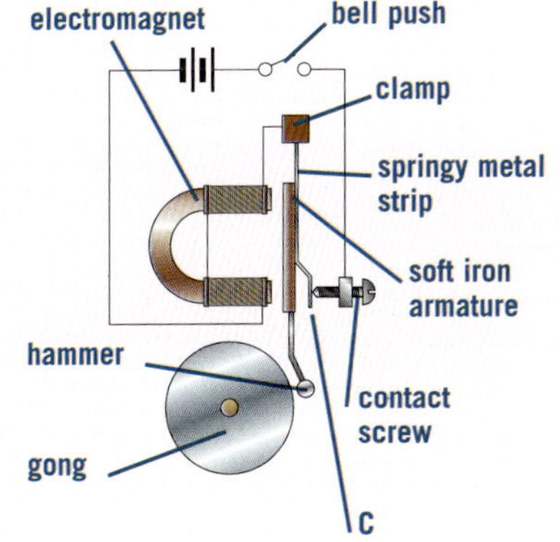

Scrap-yard electromagnet

- When current flows through the coil, a very strong electromagnet is created which is able to pick up cars.
- When the magnet is turned off the magnetic field collapses and the car is released.

Don't try to remember how to draw circuits for the electric bell. Just try to understand how they work.

KEY TERMS

Make sure you understand the following terms before moving on!

- magnet
- pole
- compass
- electromagnet
- magnetic material
- non-magnetic material
- magnetic field

1. Name one magnetic material.
2. Name one non-magnetic material.
3. .... poles repel
4. .... poles attract

5. What is an electromagnet?
6. Give two uses for electromagnets.

The Earth in space

We live on a planet called the Earth. Although we cannot feel it, the Earth is spinning. The Earth completes one turn every 24 hours (one day).

The seasons

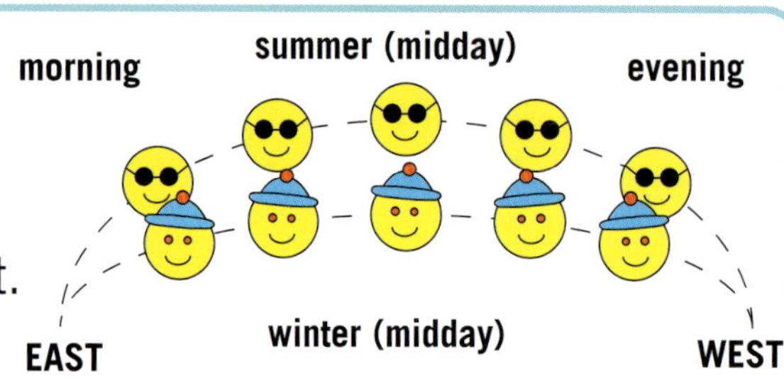

The highs and lows of the Sun

- Because the Earth is turning, the Sun appears to travel across the sky from the East to the West.
- In the summer the Sun's path is high in the sky.
- In the winter its path is much lower.

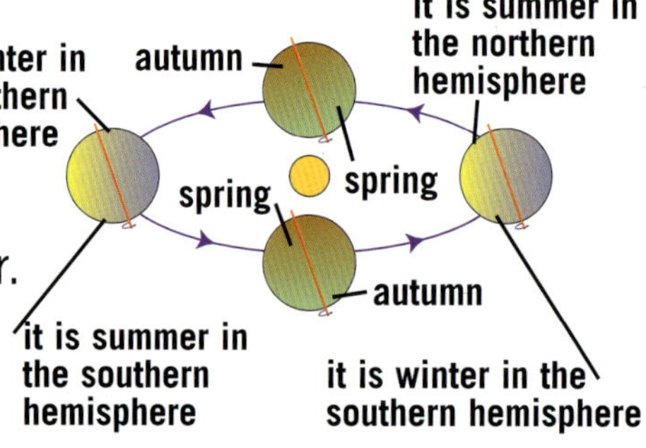

The seasonal tilt

- The Earth **orbits** the Sun once every year.
- Because the Earth is tilted we experience **the different seasons** – spring, summer, autumn and winter.
- When the northern part of the Earth is tilted towards the Sun it is **summer** in the northern hemisphere and winter in the southern hemisphere.
- When the northern part of the Earth is **tilted away** from the Sun it is **winter** in the northern hemisphere and summer in the southern hemisphere.

The solar system

Our **solar system** consists of a **star**, a number of **planets**, **moons**, **asteroids** and **comets**. We call our star **the Sun**. It contains over 99% of all the mass in our solar system. The planets, their moons, the asteroids and the comets all orbit the Sun.

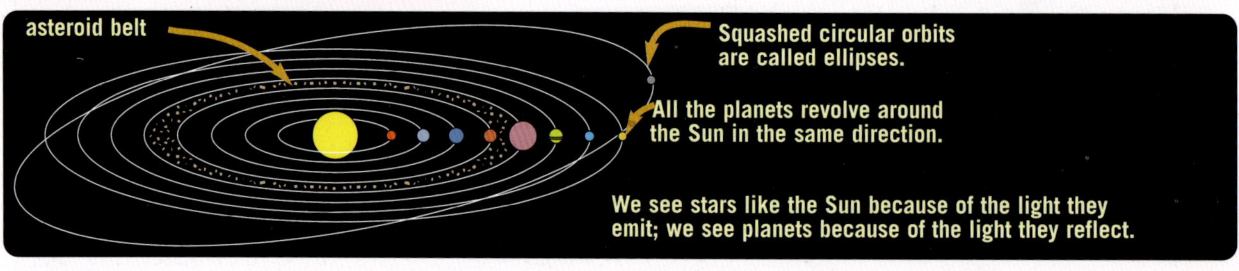

- The Earth is one of **nine** planets. In order from the planet nearest the Sun they are: Mercury, Venus, Earth, Mars, Jupiter, Saturn, Uranus, Neptune and Pluto.
- We can remember the order using the sentence: **Many Very Energetic Men Jog Slowly Upto Newport Pagnell**.
- We see stars like the Sun because of the light they **emit**. Stars are **luminous** objects.
- We see planets and moons because of the light they **reflect**. They are **non-luminous** objects.

Gravitational forces

The planets

- The planets move in orbits because they are being **'pulled' by the gravity of the Sun**.

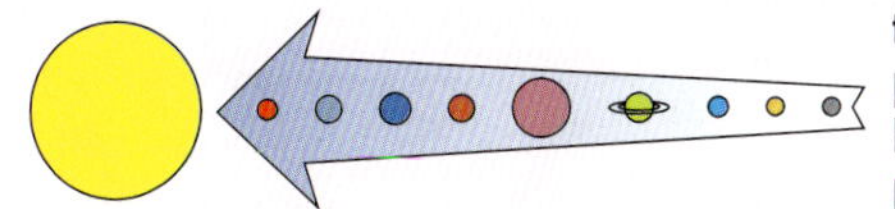

- Objects which are **close** to the Sun feel **strong pulls** and follow **very curved paths**.
- Objects that are **further** from the Sun feel **weaker pulls** and follow **less curved orbits**.

Comets

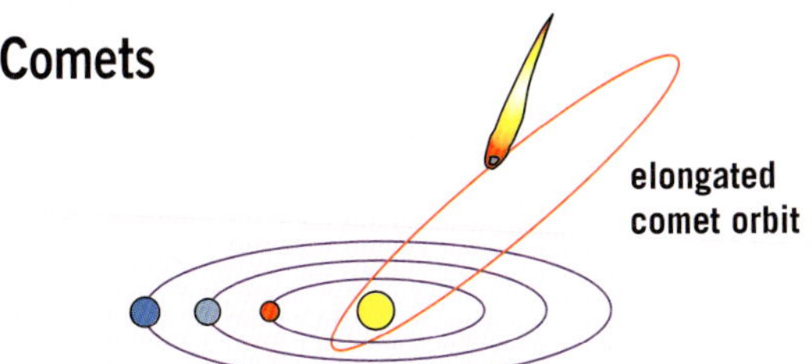

- Comets are large, rock-like pieces of ice that orbit the Sun.
- They have very **elliptical** orbits.
- They **travel fastest** when they are **close to the Sun** because the gravitational forces here are large.
- Close to the Sun some of a comet's ice vaporises, creating a long tail.

Asteroids

- Asteroids are lumps of rock orbiting the Sun.
- They vary in size from several metres to about 1000 km.
- Most asteroids are found in a belt between Mars and Jupiter.

Satellites

- Moons are large natural satellites that orbit a planet.
- An object will weigh less on our Moon than it does on the Earth.

Artificial satellites launched by man can be put into orbit around the Earth. They have three main uses:

- To **look away from the Earth** into deep space, e.g. the Hubble telescope.
- To **monitor conditions on the surface of the Earth**, e.g. weather satellites. Satellites that monitor the Earth's surface are often put into low polar orbits.
- **Geostationary satellites** that stay above the same place on the Earth's surface the whole time, e.g. **communications satellites**.

KEY TERMS

Make sure you understand the following terms before moving on!

- planets
- orbits
- seasons
- solar system
- star
- moons
- asteroids
- comets
- The Sun
- elliptical
- Geostationary satellites

QUICK TEST

1. How long does it take for the Earth to complete one rotation about its axis?
2. How long does it take the Earth to make one complete orbit of the Sun?
3. What season is it in the southern hemisphere when the northern hemisphere is tilted towards the Sun?
4. Name one body in the sky which is a) luminous and b) non-luminous.
5. What forces keep all the planets in orbit around the Sun?
6. Where during their orbit of the Sun do comets travel fastest?
7. What is a natural satellite?
8. Give three uses for artificial satellites.

Practice questions

Use the questions to test your progress. Check your answers on page 125.

1. The diagram opposite shows two tug of war teams pulling on a rope. At the moment neither of the teams is moving. 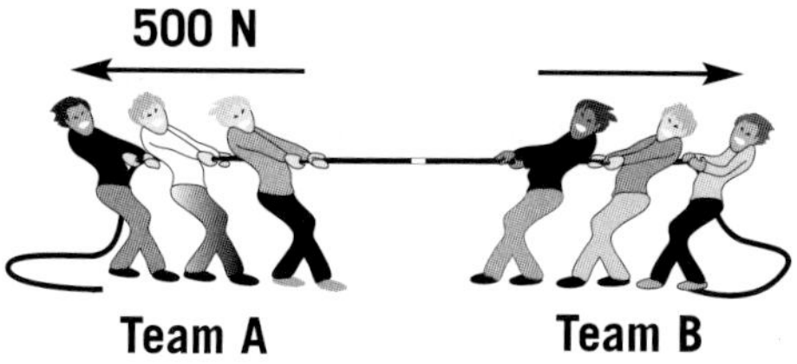
   (i) What is the size of the force being applied to the rope by team B?
   ....
   (ii) Explain your answer.
   ....

500 N

Team A Team B

2. The diagram opposite shows a diagram of a periscope. Complete the diagram of the periscope by drawing in the path of a ray of light from the object to the eye of the observer.

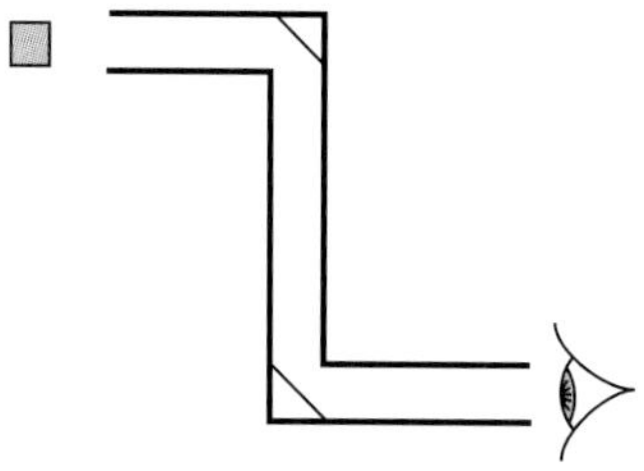

3. The graph below shows the journey of a cyclist.
   (i) During which part of the journey is the cyclist not moving? 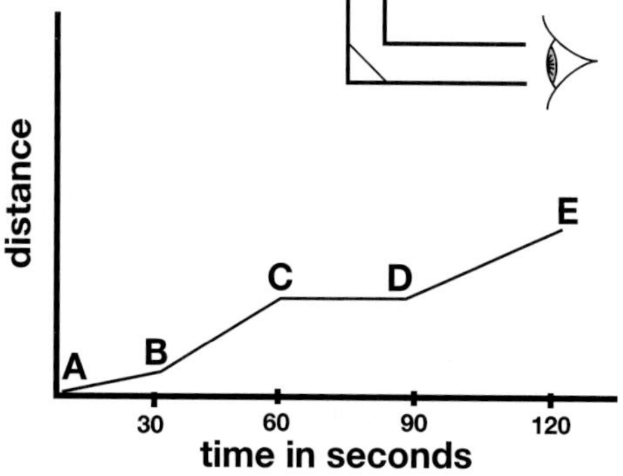
   ....
   (ii) During which part of the journey is the cyclist travelling fastest?
   ....
   (iii) How long did the whole journey take?
   ....

distance

A B C D E

30 60 90 120

time in seconds

4. The diagram opposite shows a piece of wood labelled A being spun quickly whilst in contact with another piece of wood labelled B.
   There is a large amount of friction between the two pieces of wood. 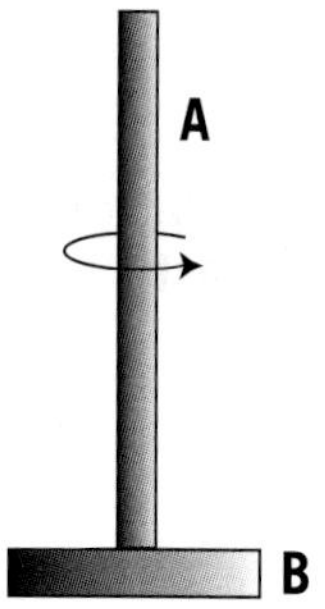
   (i) Name two possible effects of this friction.
   ....
   (ii) Suggest one way in which this friction could be reduced.
   ....
   (iii) Suggest two ways in which the friction between a car tyre and a road may be reduced.
   ....

A

B

5. The diagram opposite shows a crowd of people watching a firework display. 
   (i) Name one object in the diagram which is luminous.
   ....
   (ii) Name one object in the diagram which is non-luminous.
   ....
   (iii) Explain why during the display there is a delay between seeing and then hearing the fireworks explode.
   ....

6. If a bee flies close by we can hear its buzzing.
   (i) Which part of the bee creates these sounds? ....
   (ii) Explain in your own words how these sounds travel to our ears ....

7. (i) Name three fossil fuels ....
(ii) Name two environmental problems caused by burning fossil fuels ....
(iii) Name three alternative sources of energy ....
....

8. (i) Explain why double glazing is far more efficient at keeping your house warm than single glazing with a thick piece of glass.
....
(ii) Explain why on a sunny day a black car becomes hotter than a white car parked at the side of it.
....

9. In which of the circuits drawn below will the bulb glow the brightest?

A B C D

10. The diagram opposite shows a magnet being used to try to pick up objects made from different materials
(i) Name 3 objects the magnet can not pick up ....
(ii) Why can the magnet not pick these objects up? ....
(iii) What are the strongest parts of a magnet called? ....

N S

11. (i) Describe two ways in which the strength of an electromagnet can be increased.
....
(ii) Give two uses of an electromagnet.
....

12. Complete the table shown below

Energy in	Energy changer	Energy out
Electrical	Light bulb	Heat and a) ....
Elastic	Catapult	b) ....
c)	Radio	Sound
d)	Candle	e) .... and f) ....

13. A skier travels 200m in 5s.
(i) Calculate her speed ....
(ii) If she continues to travel at the same speed how far will she travel in the next 10s?
....

14. The diagram opposite shows a spanner being used to undo a nut.
(i) Calculate the moment created by the force.........................
(ii) Suggest two ways in which the size of the moment could be increased.
....

50 N
0.3 m

15. The illustration opposite shows a fakir sitting on a bed of nails.
Explain why the fakir feels less pain if more nails are added to his bed ....
Calculate the pressure created when a force of 200N is applied over an area of $5m^2$.
....

How well did you do? 1-4 Try again 5-8 Getting there 9-11 Good work 12-15 Excellent!

Answers

Biology

Quick test answers

Page 5 Cells
1. Plant cell has chloroplasts, cell wall and a vacuole.
2. It controls what passes in and out of the cell.
3. Gives a plant cell extra strength and support.
4. A cell that has changed its shape to do a particular job.
5. Tissue.

Page 7 Organ systems
1. Photosynthesis.
2. Endocrine system.
3. Kidney.
4. Chloroplasts/chlorophyll.
5. Xylem.

Page 9 Nutrition and food tests
1. Energy.
2. Iodine solution; a blue/black colour means starch is present.
3. Benedict's solution and heat; an orange precipitate means glucose is present.
4. Store energy, make cell membranes and insulation.
5. Repair and replace cells, and make new cells for growth.
6. Biuret test; if solution turns purple, protein is present.
7. It helps food move through your system and prevents constipation.

Page 11 The digestive system
1. Incisors, canines, premolars and molars.
2. Glucose.
3. Amino acids.
4. Fatty acids and glycerol.
5. Small intestine.

Page 13 The heart
1. Arteries.
2. Veins.
3. Lerft side.
4. Pulmonary artery and aorta.
5. To prevent back flowof blood in the heart and the veins.

Page 15 Blood and circulation
1. Plasma, red blood cells, white blood cells and platelets.
2. Red blood cells.
3. To collect oxygen/to release CO_2.
4. Blood passes through the heart twice.

Page 17 Movement
1. Support, protection and movement.
2. When bones meet.
3. To reduce friction.
4. Muscles that work opposite each other to produce movement.
5. They join muscle to bone.
6. They join bone to bone.

Page 19 The lungs and breathing
1. In the alveoli of the lungs.
2. They have a large surface area, moist thin walls and are close to blood capillaries.
3. Breaking down glucose with oxygen.
4. In the cell cytoplasm.
5. Water and carbon dioxide.

Page 21 The menstrual cycle
1. Testes.
2. Ovaries.
3. Every 28 days.
4. The release of an egg on approximately day 14 of the cycle.
5. Four to seven days.
6. Testosterone and oestrogen.

Page 23 Reproduction
1. An embryo.
2. The embryo embedding itself into the uterus lining.
3. In the Fallopian tube.
4. The fusing together of the sperm nucleus with the egg nucleus.
5. By the umbilical cord.
6. Nine months/40 weeks.

Page 25 Drugs
1. Brain, liver and nervous system.
2. Drugs that speed up the nervous system.
3. Tar, nicotene and carbon monoxide.
4. Emphysema, bronchitis, lung cancer, heart disease.
5. Cirrhosis.

Page 27 Fighting disease
1. Bacteria, viruses and fungi.
2. Antibodies.
3. Dead or weak forms of a disease that give you artificial immunity.
4. HIV, colds, flu, chicken pox, measles (any two).
5. Food poisoning, tuberculosis, whooping cough (any two).

Page 29 Photosynthesis
1. Carbon dioxide, water, chlorophyll, light and suitable temperature.
2. Oxygen and glucose.
3. The leaf.
4. They release energy in respiration, generate other useful substances and store it as starch.
5. Nitrates, phosphates and potassium.

Page 31 Plant reproduction
1. Carpel.
2. Stamen.
3. By animals, popping out of pods and the wind.
4. The joining of a male pollen nucleus with a female ovule nucleus.

Page 33 The carbon and nitrogen cycles
1. Photosynthesis.
2. Respiration and burning/combustion.
3. Turned into fossil fuels.
4. For making proteins.
5. Nitrates.

Page 35 Classification
1. Sorting living organisms into groups according to their similarities.
2. Animal without a backbone.
3. Animal with a backbone.
4. Birds, mammals, fish, amphibians and reptiles.

Page 37 Variation
1. Inherited.
2. Height and weight.
3. Eye colour, blood group, hair colour, tongue rolling (any two).
4. Breeding animals and plants together to produce the best offspring.

Page 39 Food chains and webs
1. A plant that produces food from the Sun's energy.
2. An animal that eats other plants and animals.
3. The Sun.
4. The numbers of organisms involved in a food chain.
5. The mass of organisms involved in a food chain.

Page 41 Adaptation and competition
1. Where an organism lives.
2. Food, water, and space.
3. Light, space, water and nutrients.
4. Because of the predator–prey cycle.
5. Only the best-adapted organism will survive.

Pages 43–44 Practice questions
1. a) Nucleus b) Cytoplasm c) Cell membrane.
2. The Chloroplasts.
3. A red blood cell, transports oxygen around the body.
4. 1b, 2c, 3a.
5. Flower, root, root hair, leaf, stem.
6. The circulatory system.
7. (i) anther (ii) ovary.
8. a) Water b) Chlorophyll c) Oxygen.
9. Reptiles.
10. Gets churned up and mixed with gastric juices containing protease enzymes and hydrochloric acid.
11. In the nucleus of cells.
12. It passes into the large intestine, water and salts are removed and it is turned into faeces.
13. The small intestine.
14. Oak tree leaves ➡ Snail ➡ Blackbird.
15. Emphysema, bronchitis and lung cancer.
16. a) Oxygen b) Water c) Energy.
17. Plasma, platelets, red blood cells, white blood cells.
18. An artery carries blood away from the heart at high pressure and has much thicker walls; a vein carries blood back to the heart at low pressure and has thinner walls.
19. 1. Produce antibodies. 2. Engulf bacteria and viruses.
20. The thick lining of the womb, the placenta and the amniotic fluid surrounding the baby.
21. Support, protection and movement.
22. a) Trachea b) Bronchus c) Bronchiole d) Alveoli e) Diaphragm f) Intercostal muscles.
23. Where the immune system has a memory for a particular microbe and can produce antibodies much quicker to destroy the disease.
24. Nitrates, phosphates and potassium.
25. The female part of a flowering plant, made up of a stigma, style and an ovary containing ovules.
26. Selective breeding.
27. The air we breathe out is cleaner, warmer, contains more water vapour, more carbon dioxide, less oxygen.
28. 46
29. The transfer of pollen from an anther to a stigma.
30. Carbohyrates, proteins, fats, vitamins, minerals, fibre and water.

Chemistry

Quick test answers

Page 45 Rocks
1. Igneous.
2. Igneous.
3. Extrusive e.g. basalt.
4. Intrusive e.g. granite.
5. Heat, pressure.
6. Sedimentary.
7. Millions of years.
8. Sandstone, limestone.
9. Basalt and granite.
10. Schist, gneiss.

Page 47 The Rock cycle
1. The breaking down of larger rocks to smaller pieces.
2. Changes in temperature.
3. Water.
4. Water freezes and expands in existing cracks, breaking rocks apart.
5. Other gases, including sulphur dioxide, dissolve in the rain water.
6. The movement of eroded rock pieces.
7. Water/wind/glaciers.
8. Deposition.

Page 49 Pollution
1. Sulphur dioxide.
2. Acid rain.
3. It can damage statues and buildings, trees, animals and plants.
4. Limestone/chalk/marble.
5. Carbon dioxide.
6. Because fossil fuels are being burnt.
7. It dissolves in oceans.
8. Extensive flooding.
9. We need land to live and grow food on.

Page 51 States of matter
1. Solid, liquid and gas.
2. Yes.
3. Liquid.
4. No.
5. Yes.
6. boiling.
7. Melting.
8. See below.

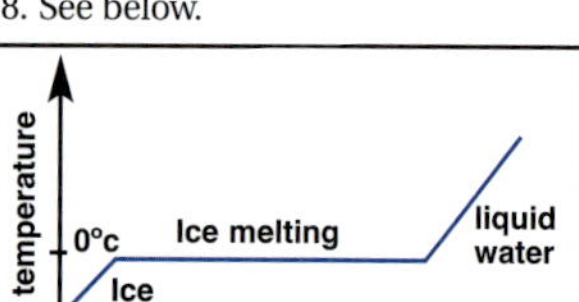

Page 53 Dissolving
1. 102 g.
2. The solute.
3. The solvent.
4. A solution.
5. Soluble.
6. Normally the substance becomes more soluble.
7. No more will dissolve at that temperature.
8. 400 g per 100 g of water.
9. 900 g per 100 g of water.
10. It becomes more soluble.

Page 55 Particle theory
1. Scent molecules from the flower diffuse through the air to your nose.
2. Gas particles move quickly in all directions.
3. Yes, but more slowly than gases.
4. When gas particles crash into the walls of a container.
5. Because the gas particles crash into the walls of the container harder and more often.
6. They move around more.
7. A liquid.
8. No.
9. To allow for expansion in hot weather.

Page 57 Atoms and elements
1. It only contains one type of atom.
2. About 100.
3. Periodic table.
4. Increasing atomic number.
5. Nucleus.
6. Neutrons and protons.
7. Electrons.
8. Negative.

Page 59
1. See table.

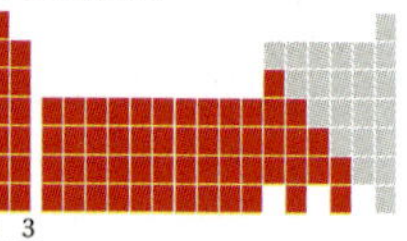

2. $\frac{3}{4}$

3. Mercury.
4. It pings when hit.
5. Good conductors, high m.p. and b.p., strong/dense, malleable and ductile, shiny, sonorous, forms alloys.
6. $\frac{1}{4}$
7. Bromine.
8. Low density.
9. No.
10. Carbon.

Page 61 Unusual elements
1. Solid.
2. Mercury.
3. They expand.
4. Thermometers.
5. It is less dense than water.
6. It is very vigorous and hydrogen and sodium hydroxide are produced.
7. Diamond and graphite.
8. It is hard and has a very high melting point.
9. It conducts electricity.
10. Bromine.

Page 63 Chemical reactions
1. It removes water.
2. It removes air dissolved in water.
3. To stop air reaching the water.
4. Oxygen and water.
5. By alloying iron with chromium (Cr), which does not rust.
6. When magnesium (Mg) or zinc (Zn) is in contact with iron (Fe), Fe is protected as Mg/Zn reacts first.

Page 65 Reactivity series
1. Electrolysis.
2. Heat with carbon.
3. Observing reactions with air, water, acid.

Page 67 Displacement
1. A more reactive metal will displace a less reactive metal from a compound.
2. Iron.
3. Iron + copper sulphate ⇨ iron sulphate + copper.
4. Zinc.
5. Zinc + iron sulphate ⇨ zinc sulphate + iron.
6. Magnesium.
7. Magnesium + copper sulphate ⇨ magnesium sulphate + copper.
8. No reaction.

Page 69 Acids and alkalis
1. Green.
2. Blue.
3. Red.
4. 7
5. 14
6. 6
7. Green.
8. Red.
9. Alkalis are soluble bases.
10. Hydrochloric acid, sulphuric acid, nitric acid.

Page 71 Making salts
1. Potassium chloride + water.
2. Sodium sulphate + water.
3. Carbon dioxide.
4. Zinc chloride + water + carbon dioxide.
5. Magnesium sulphate + water + carbon dioxide.
6. Remove unreacted solid by filtering, then evaporate off the water.
7. Magnesium chloride + hydrogen.
8. Zinc sulphate + hydrogen.
9. Zinc chloride + water.
10. Copper sulphate + water.

Page 73
1. See top p.73.
2. Gas is bubbled through limewater which turns milky.
3. Lighted splint gives 'squeaky pop'.
4. A measuring cylinder.
5. Filter funnel and filter paper.

Page 75 Mixtures
1. Yes.
2. The individual substances are not joined together.
3. Yes.
4. Yes.
5. No.
6. Yes.
7. Water, salts and gases.
8. Nitrogen, oxygen, water vapour, carbon dioxide, argon and neon.
9. 80%.
10. Different minerals.

Page 77 Separation techniques
1. No.
2. Yes.
3. Filtration.
4. Through crystallisation which will evaporate the water.
5. Chromatography.
6. They have different solubilities.
7. By distillation.

Page 79 Compounds
1. Atoms of two elements.
2. Molecules of an element.
3. Molecules of a compound.
4. Gas.
5. Thermometer.
6. Reactants.
7. Products.
8. Iron is no longer magnetic, there is change in colour, etc.
9. Yes.
10. No.

Page 81 Naming compounds
1. When atoms of two or more elements are joined together.
2. Magnesium oxide.
3. Magnesium bromide.
4. 1 Mg and 2 Cl.
5. 1 C and 1 O.
6. Sodium + chlorine ⇨ sodium chloride.
7. Hydrogen + oxygen ⇨ water.
8. Magnesium + oxygen ⇨ magnesium oxide.

Page 83 Symbols
1. S.
2. Sodium.
3. The c must be a capital letter.
4. The second letter must be lower case.
5. One.
6. One.
7. Three.
8. Two.
9. One.
10. Four.

Pages 85–86 Practice questions
1. a) B or C b) D c) A
2. a) solid to liquid b) gas to liquid
3. D
4.

Object tested	Attracted to magnet
plastic knife	✗
steel pin	✓
iron nail	✓
wooden ruler	✗
aluminium foil	✗

5. a) solution
   b) 105.5 g
6. c)
7. a) green
   b) blue and yellow
8. a) iodine
   b) bromine
   c) fluorine/chlorine
9. a) magnesium + oxygen ➡ magnesium oxide
   b) The magnesium combines with oxygen.
10. a) iron oxide, carbon monoxide, carbon dioxide
    b) iron or carbon
11. calcium carbonate ➡ calcium oxide + carbon dioxide
12. a) magnesium, zinc, iron, copper
    b) magnesium + zinc sulphate ➡ zinc + magnesium sulphate
13. methane + oxygen ➡ water vapour + carbon dioxide
14. a) magma cooled faster at T
    b) V is made from sandstone, U is made from limestone

Physics

Quick test answers

Page 87 Speed
1. Distance travelled and time taken.
2. m/s and km/h.
3. 5 m/s.
4. 20 s.
5. 300 km.

Page 89 Graphs of motion
1. a) A stationary object.
   b) Greater constant speed.
   c) Lower constant speed.
2. See graph.
3. a) Constant speed.
   b) Large constant acceleration.
   c) Small constant deceleration.
4. See graph.

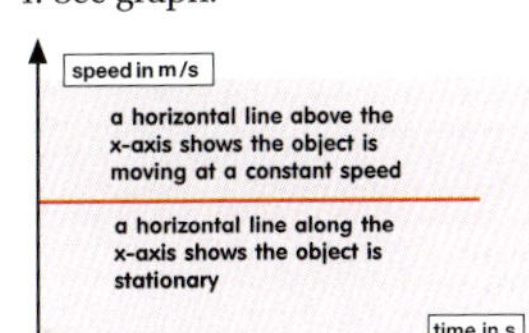

Page 91 Forces
1. It may speed up, slow down, change direction or change shape.
2. Magnetic and gravitational forces.
3. The size of a force.
4. No effect.
5. Change direction, change speed.
6. The pull of gravity on the object is 12 N.

Page 93 Friction and terminal velocity
1. A force that opposes motion.
2. The opposite direction to motion.
3. Shaping to reduce resistance.
4. It has a constant velocity, or zero acceleration.
5. Heat and wearing away of the surface.

Page 95 Moments
1. Turning effect of a force defined as force x perpendicular distance.
2. 80 Nm.
3. Apply a larger force and apply same force at point further from pivot.
4. Clockwise moments = anticlockwise moments.
5. Clockwise moments do not equal anticlockwise moments.
6. Clockwise.

Page 97 Pressure
1. Large force over a small area.
2. Spread the force over a large area.
3. Weight of contents concentrated over very small area.
4. Pascal (Pa).
5. Greater pressure under blade.
6. 20 Pa.
7. 500 Pa.
8. 80 N.

Page 99 Light rays and reflection
1. Shadows are the same shape as the object.
2. One which light cannot pass through.
3. One which is see-through.
4. One which gives off its own light.
5. By the light it reflects.
6. The angle of reflection.
7. Upright, same size, same distance behind mirror and laterally inverted, virtual.

Page 101 Reflaction and colour
1. Refraction.
2. Towards the normal.
3. Only green light is reflected.
4. Band of colours.
5. Dispersion.
6. Transparent plastic or glass that only allows green light through.

Page 103 Sounds
1. Vibrating.
2. Low-pitched.
3. High-pitched.
4. Amplitudes.
5. A vacuum. It contains no particles to vibrate.
6. Light waves travel much faster than sound waves.

Page 105 Echoes and hearing
1. Reflection of a sound wave.
2. 20 Hz to 20 000 Hz.
3. Frequency too high for humans to hear.
4. Dogs, bats.
5. Wear ear defenders.
6. Turn down the volume.

Page 107 Energy
1. Heat, light, sound, electricity, chemical.
2. Chemical, elastic and gravitational potential energy.
3. Gravitational potential energy.
4. Kinetic energy.
5. Electrical to heat, kinetic and sound.
6. Sound to electrical energy.

Page 109 Using energy resources
1. Coal, oil and gas.
2. Carbon dioxide.
3. Coal and oil.
4. Oil spillage.
5. Cannot be replaced.
6. More efficient insulation and engines. Make more use of alternative sources of energy.

Page 111 Alternative energy resources
1. Hydroelectricity, tidal, wave.
2. Wind, waves.
3. Wind, biomass.
4. Biomass.
5. Wind.

Page 113 Heat transfer
1. Conduction, convection and radiation.
2. Metal, saucepan.
3. Plastic, tablemat.
4. Conduct heat from body quickly.
5. Two panes of glass with air in between.
6. Fibreglass in loft, double glazing, draught excluders, cavity wall insulation, carpets and underlay.
7. Radiation.
8. Absorbed or reflected.
9. Convection current.

Page 115 Circuits and components
1. Several cells connected together.
2. Push charge around.
3. Complete.
4. a) Any metal, b) plastic.
5. Controls the size of current that flows.
6. A resistor whose resistance can be changed.

Page 117 Circuits – current & voltage
1. Flow of charge.
2. Ammeter.
3. Amperes or amps.
4. Current.
5. Energy.

Page 119 Magnets & electromagnets
1. Iron.
2. Plastic.
3. Like.
4. Opposite.
5. A combination of coil and core.
6. Scrap-yard, electric bell.

Page 121 The Earth in space
1. 1 day.
2. 1 year.
3. Winter.
4. a) The Sun. b) All planets and moons.
5. Gravitational forces.
6. When they are closest to the Sun.
7. A moon.

Answers

8. Looking into space, weather and communications.

Pages 122–123 Practice questions

1. (i) 500N. (ii) The forces must be balanced.
2. Path of light
3. (i) CD. (ii) BC. (iii) 120s
4. (i) Wearing away of surfaces and heat. (ii) Use a lubricant, e.g. oil or water. (iii) Worn tyre (lack of tread), smooth road surface or wet/greasy road surface.
5. (i) Exploding firework. (ii) People in crowd.
   (iii) Light travels much faster than sound.
6. (i) Its vibrating wings. (ii) The vibrating wings create sound waves some of which enter our ears.
7. (i) Coal, oil and gas. (ii) Global warming (greenhouse effect) and acid rain. (iii) Geothermal, tidal, solar, biomass, hydroelectric, wind and wave.
8. (i) It is the air trapped between the two panes of glass which is the real barrier to heat escaping from the house, not the glass. (ii) The dark car absorbs most of the radiation from the Sun and so becomes hot. The white car will reflect most of the radiation and so will be cooler.
9. C.
10. (i) The matchstick, the piece of paper, the piece of cloth. (ii) None of these objects are made from a magnetic material. (iii) The poles of the magnet.
11. (i) Increase the current flowing through the coil and increase the number of turns on the coil.
    (ii) Electric bell, relay switch, scrapyard.
12. A. Light, B. Kinetic energy,
    C. Electrical energy, D. Chemical energy,
    E. Heat. F. Light.
13. (i) 40m/s (ii) 400m
14. (i) 15Nm. (ii) Increase the size of the force applied to the spanner, use a longer spanner.
15. (i) The more nails there are in his bed the larger the area his weight is spread over and therefore the less pressure (pain) there is on each nail.
    (ii) 40Pa

Index